Heritage as an action word

Uses beyond communal memory

Edited by

Susan Shay

Heritage Research Centre, University of Cambridge, United Kingdom

Kelly M. Britt

*Brooklyn College and The Graduate Center,
City University of New York, United States*

Series in Heritage Studies

VERNON PRESS

In the Americas:	*In the rest of the world:*
Vernon Press	Vernon Press
1000 N West Street, Suite 1200,	C/Sancti Espiritu 17,
Wilmington, Delaware 19801	Malaga, 29006
United States	Spain

Series in Heritage Studies

Library of Congress Control Number: 2023952286

ISBN: 979-8-8819-0175-2

Also available: 978-1-64889-844-0 [Hardback]; 978-1-64889-882-2 [PDF, E-Book]

Product and company names mentioned in this work are the trademarks of their respective owners. While every care has been taken in preparing this work, neither the authors nor Vernon Art and Science Inc. may be held responsible for any loss or damage caused or alleged to be caused directly or indirectly by the information contained in it.

Every effort has been made to trace all copyright holders, but if any have been inadvertently overlooked the publisher will be pleased to include any necessary credits in any subsequent reprint or edition.

Cover design by Vernon Press. Images from Unsplash, Pexels and Freepik.

Table of contents

List of figures

Introduction

Susan Shay

Heritage Research Centre, University of Cambridge, United Kingdom

Abstract

The introduction clarifies the broad nature of heritage studies and explores how heritage can be an exceptionally valuable and significant tool for political, economic, environmental and social change. Importantly, it introduces examples of how heritage can be of value in responding to contemporary challenges.

The chapter presents the organization of the volume's three sections, *Fostering Collective Memory, Activating Indigenous Heritage,* and *Repurposing Heritage,* and introduces the case study chapters. It discusses how heritage researchers, archaeologists, environmentalists, organizational leaders, and others around the world are involved in social change and have moved beyond seeing heritage as only social memory, a mere interpretation of static past events, people, places, and practices, and instead have been inspired to adopt innovative interdisciplinary approaches to explore critically the variety of ways heritage is engaged in the present, and can be employed strategically for a better, more sustainable and socially just future.

Keywords: archaeology, heritage, heritage studies, critical heritage studies, climate change, community engagement, futures-thinking, empowerment, preservation, resilience, sustainability, transformation

***

The idea for this volume emerged in an unusual way. It was the result of a panel proposal for the 2020 World Archaeological Conference (WAC), and the focus of the session was to highlight and explore innovative ways heritage is being utilized throughout the world. Specifically, we wanted to investigate the reflexive and responsive nature of heritage, and how it is or can be actively used by and within communities to address a social, economic, or political problem. In response to our call for papers, we received submissions from around the world, each elaborating on an innovative heritage study. Significantly, each paper came from a different part of the world, and each presented a completely distinctive perspective on the active use of heritage, opening new avenues for examination in the field of heritage studies.

It is not surprising that this volume emerged from planning for a World Archaeological Conference. The World Archaeological Congress (WAC) came about as a result of discriminatory limitations imposed on previous archaeological conferences.[1] The first WAC organizers recognized the historical and social role of archaeology and the political nature of site and object recognition, interpretation, and control, and were committed toward moving the field toward equal representation and inclusion. Importantly, they noted that archaeological science had been based on a value system that was linked to dominant social concerns, nationalist identities, and territorial claims. Rejecting these notions, they stressed the need to make archaeological research accessible and relevant to a wide range of interests and communities, and to make debates and discussions open and responsive to everyone. To that end, WAC "values diversity against institutionalized mechanisms that marginalize the cultural heritage of indigenous peoples, minorities, and the poor".[2]

One of the most important contributions WAC makes to the academic and professional world is to draw attention to research being done in less developed parts of the world and in remote, overlooked, or marginalized communities trying to preserve and protect important local sites and resources. Highlighting this type of research gives voice to these peoples and their issues and thereby has the potential to protect sacred and/or valuable historic and cultural sites from development, particularly those belonging to minority, Indigenous and non-Western groups. This volume builds on that mission. We are optimistic that the attention gained for the projects described in the following chapters will inspire the development of further innovative explorations, inform heritage professionals of new perspectives for research and analysis, encourage local involvement, support community growth and sustainability, and motivate heritage studies professionals, government authorities, and community members toward more effective and responsible programs and projects.

Collaborating during a pandemic

Life is unpredictable, and due to the worldwide COVID-19 emergency, the WAC 2020 conference was repeatedly postponed. Yet we found the papers so interesting, the subject so compelling, and the findings so relevant and valuable, that we forwarded a request to the conference organizers for their approval to turn the as yet undelivered papers into an academic volume. This book is the result of that effort. In the years that we have been putting it together, the incredible need for this type of research has become more apparent. As we approach fall 2023, the world is still reeling from the dual nightmare of COVID-19 and the global onslaught of climate-related emergencies. Added to these tensions and disasters is the ongoing war between Russia and Ukraine, and rapidly increasing global human migrations. More than ever research studies such as the ones provided here are needed to understand how heritage can support programs that build resilience and support community well-being.

Producing this book became a broad, international, interdisciplinary project. As the editors, Kelly M. Britt and I engaged with a worldwide group of scholars[3] on the use of heritage for positive action. Unbeknownst to us in 2020, the COVID-19 pandemic would continue for years; each of our authors would have to address the impacts and stresses of maintaining life, home, and community through a very trying time. Some of our authors also had to simultaneously deal with vaccine shortages in their countries; the onslaught of severe environmental challenges; escalating campus academic uncertainty; the discovery of physical evidence of systemic, government-authorized, cultural elimination and human genocide at Indigenous residential schools; as well as other forms of social, economic, and political unrest (personal communications). And finally, when it seemed as if the world was beginning to emerge from lockdown and we began to re-introduce ourselves, war broke out between Ukraine and Russia, unsettling political and economic spheres worldwide, and rattling accepted contemporary concepts of national sovereignty, economic security, cultural determination, and democracy (Abrams 2023; Cordesman 2022; Kammer et al. 2022; Masters 2023). At present, the world is fraught with tension over what will emerge from this clash. It has been a thought-provoking and challenging project working on this volume and bringing it to completion.

We sincerely thank all of our contributors in the US, Canada, Nigeria, India, and Russia for their efforts and cooperation. This has truly been a remarkable collaboration between people from different parts of the world and diverse cultures. The last two years have highlighted the need for academic research that investigates, identifies, and proposes effective ways to promote mutual respect between cultures, to foster considerate interactions between communities, and to inspire individual and communal obligation for mitigating against future disasters and conflicts. Our hope is that a wide variety of individuals, from academics to government officials, and from community leaders to organizational managers, find this information interesting, motivating, and beneficial, and that they will utilize these case studies viewing heritage, in all its many forms and interpretations, as a valuable and essential element toward building a better world.

Heritage and its uses

What is 'heritage' in a world of blended cultures and rapidly changing societies? The word appears everywhere. 'Heritage' is used today to describe everything from constructed (World Monuments Fund)[4], reconstructed (Cameron 2008), and preserved sites, places, objects (Mohn 2019; Hartley 2004), and projects of the past (Montgomery 2004; Gabriel 2016), to traditional foods (Logan 2020; Claus 2017; Asakura 2016.), clothing (Maskiell 1999), fabrics (Indonesian Batik, Inscribed as World Heritage, UNESCO 2009), customs (Young 2004), and hairstyles (Walker 2000; Doty 1976). As early as 2010, the renowned heritage scholars Laurajane Smith and Emma Waterton noted that there were certain words that had come into the common lexicon that were "used, abused and reused" within the social sciences, such as 'identity', 'culture' and 'community' (Waterton and Smith 2010, 4). They argued that the expressions of 'community' within academia and political arenas narrowly focused on homogeneity and nostalgia, and that this limited interpretation served to facilitate the continuation of systemic issues. To this list, I now wish to add the word 'heritage'. At present there are international (UNESCO World Heritage, World Monuments Fund, International Center for the Study and Preservation of Cultural Property (ICCROM), International Council on Monuments and Sites (ICOMOS), etc.), national (for example, Historic England, US National Landmarks, Society for American Archaeology (SAA), Society for the Protection of Afghan Archaeology, Indian National Trust for Art and Cultural Heritage), and local authorized protective designations of 'heritage' material and culture (i.e. New York City Landmarks Preservation Commission; Parlament de Catalunya5), for everything from buildings, sites, monuments, landscapes, to foods, clothing, and cultural and traditional practices. There are heritage myths for national unity (US 'One Nation Under God; 'Mother' Russia; the German 'Fatherland'), and heritage cultural practices, narratives and values used to distinguish and control one community over another (Cusack 2000, 2001, 2004). Additionally, the word is employed to commodify traditional practices, as in hula from Hawai'i, freeze site usage for tourism, as was evident in the development plan for Jambudwip, India (Jalais 2007), or sell items such as toys, clothes, songs, trinkets, and even hairstyles, all for financial gain.

The question remains, therefore, of what heritage actually *is*, how it is employed actively by contemporary populations and peoples, and in which ways it can be used to address current needs for a better future. The answer is difficult to define. Within academia, heritage studies are a relatively new field (Sorensøn and Carman 2009). As a result, there is no one fixed and accepted definition of what constitutes heritage (Lowenthal 1985, 1996; Carman 2002), and appropriately, there is much debate on the word's definition. In actuality, the scope and range of the word heritage has been intentionally widely expanded by both scholars and governments over the last fifty years (Ahmad 2006).

Heritage, notes historian David Lowenthal, concerns memorializing the past for present purposes (Lowenthal 1996, xi). Through analyses of the myriad heritage items, narratives, sites, concepts, practices, and perspectives discussed within the following chapters, it is clear that the scope of what is and can be considered heritage is enormous. Heritage can be both intangible, including narratives, songs, practices, dances, art, music, food, and traditional knowledge, and tangible, comprising sites, landscapes, memorials, buildings, and material culture. Both forms of heritage, tangible and intangible, support and reinforce the communal memorialization of events, narratives, and practices that are important to the collective fabric of community (Smith 2004, 2006; Sørensen and Carman 2009). Intangible heritage values, imbued within sites and objects, underpin social cohesiveness throughout the world (Smith 2006; Smith and Akagawa 2009). These shared communal memories provide a vital role in linking individuals together socially, and through the resulting complex networks of relationships, provide a sense of belonging. From this awareness of belonging emerges a sense of identity. Knowing who we are provides a framework to define what we are a part of and what we are not, who is inside our network and who is not, and who is part of the community and who is outside. Furthermore, these shared memories and networks, ideas, and values that underpin identity are continually reinforced through contact with tangible culture, such as objects and buildings, through reminders such as memorials and protected landscapes, as well as through intangible heritage, such as traditional food, language, music, clothing, and traditional practices. As Rodney Harrison notes, heritage can be envisioned as "something passed down from one generation to the next, something that can be conserved or inherited, and something that has historic or cultural value" (Harrison 2010, 9). In other words, heritage is knowledge learned, absorbed, and experienced, and then passed down from generation to generation. The shared memories and knowledge, the sense of belonging, all provide complex information on who are, where we belong, and who we understand ourselves to be.

According to Smith, heritage is furthermore "a cultural and social process which engages with acts of remembering that work to create ways to understand and engage with the present" (Smith 2006, 3). It is not fixed, she continues, "but instead may equally be about cultural change. It may, for instance, be about reworking the meanings of the past as the cultural, social, and political needs of the present change and develop" (Smith 2006, 4). This is but one definition among many, but it is useful in that it conveys that heritage is a cultural communicative process, critical for meaning making, that serves as the basis for identity, and is constantly evolving to serve present needs. Heritage supports and sustains individuals, families, and communities through transmitted generational knowledge, encourages community cohesion with collective history and common experience (Smith 2006; Smith and Akagawa 2009; Sørensen and Carman 2009), and can unify nations with common goals, values, and identity (Anderson 2006). What should not be overlooked is that heritage can also be a useful tool for economic, political, social, and environmental change (Fairclough 1992).

Heritage is therefore a vital element of contemporary social relationships, forming the basis for individual, familial, communal, ethnic, tribal, and national identity, and it has cultural, as well as political and economic, usefulness. It contains knowledge, morals, and values that help individuals evaluate and make sense of the world in which they live, determine right from wrong, ascertain whom to trust and where to feel safe, and guide them in navigating to whom they can turn in times of tragedy, distress, or disaster. Importantly, heritage contains an abundance of knowledge from the past that, when used strategically and sensitively, can positively impact individuals and communities. In this way, heritage is, and should be, a vital, critical, and essential part of our lives. Heritage impacts our views of the past, informs our present understanding of who we are and what we believe, provides critical knowledge to face current challenges, and allows us to plan and adjudicate our responses for the future.

Heritage also has political and economic value, and it can be an important and significant tool for legal, economic, or social change. Local and national authorities and governments employ heritage through manipulation of memory in performances of power (Schneck 1987; Foucault 1980, 1983) by building and maintaining national narratives to unify a diverse population in support of civil, administrative, and legal objectives (Anderson 2006). While national narratives and heritage policies can be used to empower some groups, they can also be used to control, dominate, and subordinate others. In this manner, governments protect and preserve some forms of heritage over others through legislation and legal policies in what is known as an Authorized Heritage Discourse or AHD (Smith 2006). The AHD serves to legitimize or de-legitimize forms of heritage. It is the basis for debates over the nature and significance of forms of heritage, including various sites, narratives, memorials, and objects. Legally, the word heritage has very specific and clearly defined meanings (Garner 2019), and the legal frameworks of most nations do not consider alternative epistemologies or ways of knowing (Foster 2014; Mazel 2009, 149). Instead, the word heritage is used to narrowly categorize what is officially valued, and through formal processes of identification and designation such as the AHD, apply a series of definitions and obligations to things and places that are legally protected. In this way, power is demonstrated through the authorized designation of selected sites as worthy of government protection over others deemed less significant. For example, in Beijing, two physical and cultural landmarks, the Bell and Drum Towers, are the centrepieces to a historical and cultural protection zone located near the Forbidden City. However, in 2010 an ambitious government plan revealed the local authorities planned to demolish many historic structures in the protection zone in order to expand the commercial core for tourism. The result was public protest over the loss of historic homes to increase municipal revenue (Bideau and Yan 2018, 97-99). Another example involves the preservation of the Medieval City of Ani in Turkey, which is caught in the middle of a dispute over memory, history, and politics. Nominated for World Heritage status by Turkey, the site is a symbol of nationalism to both the Turkish people, whose government now controls the site, and the Armenian people, who long for management of the medieval ruins (Watenpaugh 2014; Apaydin 2017, 354-355; 2020, 21-23). The result is social tension between communities; between the government and ethnic, cultural, and racial groups; and between people in competition for resources and political recognition. This cross-comparative, interdisciplinary volume can provide innovative and important sources of information on the use of heritage toward planning, creating, developing, and building a more inclusive, understanding, equitable, peaceful, and sustainable world.

As noted above, not all heritage narratives are positive, nor are they all pleasant. Dark heritage is the memorialization and preservation of sites, stories and objects associated with death, atrocity, human depravity, tragedy, war, hardship, slavery, genocide, and disease (Convey, Corsane and Davis 2014). It includes concentration camps, crime scenes, and battlefields, as well as sites associated with slavery, barbarism, and other forms of human suffering. Along with the preservation of the sites of dark heritage, a form of tourism has emerged involving travel to places historically associated with death and destruction. This is known as 'dark tourism' (Cochrane 2015; Price and Shores 2017). In both dark heritage and dark tourism, details take on great significance as the historical narrative presented tries to engage with the viewer by stirring powerful emotions. Focusing on tourists' experiences, knowledge, and bodily perceptions, visits to dark heritage sites may educate and attract or, alternatively, horrify and repel. Depending on their historical perspective and political allegiances, to some visitors, a site may be the source of great pride, while to others, the site may highlight dynamics of shame, avoidance, or ambivalence (Casella and Fennelly 2016, 519). Memories of horrors strategically forgotten are unearthed, interpreted, and appropriated for new tourism experiences (De Antoni 2019), as often determined by the politically dominant narrative (Cochrane 2015). The Culloden Battlefield, protected by the National Trust of Scotland, exemplifies one such dark heritage site. Culloden was the site of the 1745 Jacobite Rising, a battle when the supporters of the Scottish Stuart king tried to reclaim Scotland from the English. Of those fighting, 1,250 Scottish Jacobites were slaughtered by the British forces. The National Trust of Scotland uses language that tries to describe the intense feelings the Scottish people associate with this site, such as "powerful", "harrowing", "tragic", and "a bloody [battle] that changed life in the Highlands forever". [6] Many items sold in the site's gift shop commemorate the battle, and are an example of the commodification of dark tourism, in this instance of the Scottish losses in the Culloden conflict.[7] Another powerful dark heritage memorial is the statue of a 'comfort woman' in front of the Japanese Embassy in Seoul. The statue commemorates Korean women who were forced to become prostitutes for Japanese soldiers during World War II. The statue highlights an ongoing controversy over Japan's limited apologies for the forced military victimization of women (Shim 2023)[8], and was intentionally placed facing the embassy in order to both publicize the controversy to the general public and garner social and political capital for greater forms of restitution (Shim 2023). Each of these examples highlights controversies on the representation and interpretation of the past and demonstrates the power and impact of heritage preservation and narrative presentation.

Contemporary uses of heritage: the future of the past

Learning from the past has become more important than ever in the twenty-first century. Faced with a rapidly changing world, individuals, communities, governments, and other organizational bodies are striving to deal with the onslaught of change and the pressures of our post-modern condition. Among these are quickly accelerating technological advancements, a seemingly endless global pandemic, ongoing dramatic climate changes, increased globalization, rising economic class stratification, extensive waves of global human migration, and growing Indigenous and minority struggles for recognition. Additionally, heritage is impacted by the constant onslaught of globalizing media and the popular actors, institutions, and traditions presented in schools and through public demonstrations, rites, and commemorations. This bombardment of information reinforces some ideas, fosters others, renews political hegemonies, and challenges notions of identity and belonging. It has resulted, according to Garcia Canclini, in an ongoing dramatic loss of relationships between cultures and the geographic social territories from which they emerge and continue (1995). Importantly, this volume responds to Tim Winter's call "for heritage studies to account for its relationship to today's regional and global transformations by developing post-western understandings of culture, heritage and the socio-political forces that actualize them" (Winter 2012, 532).

In the search for ways to facilitate a more comfortable, secure, and sustainable existence in the face of so much ongoing turmoil and disaster, much research has turned toward exploring knowledge that can be gained from the past and applied in the present to plan for a better future. We feel that two current areas of heritage investigation are relevant and valuable to our research agenda: heritage activism and heritage futures. Heritage activism is a term used to describe the use of cultural heritage in movements to directly address social issues. It is a field of study within Critical Heritage Studies that has gained considerable scholarly attention in the past few years (Mozaffari and Jones 2020). 'Critical heritage studies' is distinguished from 'heritage studies' in that the former emphasizes and explores the *critical* political, social, economic, and social complexities in which cultural heritage is enmeshed. Whereas heritage activism typically describes involvement in the use of heritage for organized social movements for recognition, for human rights, to control development, to promote sustainability, to overcome injustice, and to alleviate many other injustices including poverty, abuse and war, our focus is instead on local actions to improve or alter local conditions. However, we adopt heritage activist authors Mozaffari and Jones's call for a bottom-up approach to activism to promote and elevate heritage, and their emphasis that communities be actively engaged in local movements to be heard. They note that engagement will strengthen both local heritage and build a greater sense of community (2020).

Heritage Futures is an area of study focusing on exploring and advocating ways heritage researchers can consider and build awareness of the legacy of their efforts. This forward-thinking approach to heritage research has been popularized by Cornelius Holtorf, one of the editors of *Cultural Heritage and the Future*. He is the UNESCO Chair on Heritage Futures and has written extensively on the need for heritage professionals to reconsider heritage as both process-oriented and constantly changing to suit contemporary needs (Holtorf and Hogberg 2014; Holtorf 2016, 2018a, 2018b, 2020). The fact that a Chair exists within UNESCO is one indication of the importance of shifting current perceptions of heritage and conservation, and that heritage can "help future generations solve important challenges".

Although neither of these two areas of study fully covers the exact direction of our discussion, together they contribute essential elements. When combined, these two areas of inquiry significantly contribute to our area of interest, but do not define it. This volume adds to the body of knowledge by highlighting case studies from around the world on the use of heritage for addressing and solving contemporary concerns, in recognition of, and as part of, ongoing processes of social change and adaptation. Building on these two areas of heritage research, this volume presents case studies where heritage has been effectively utilized as an actionable tool.

It is important to note at this point that in alignment with Emma Waterton and Steve Watson in *Heritage as a Focus of Research* (2015, 10), we did not give the contributors to this volume a 'working' definition of heritage. Instead, we told them that in general heritage is the use of the past in the present, and that we were focusing this volume on the active use of heritage. We understood that chapter authors would provide widely different interpretations of heritage, and we, like Waterton and Watson, relish the rich diversity of responses. They are representative of the limitless possibilities of what heritage is and can be.

Uses of this collection

This volume is an ardent call for academics, researchers, and governments to broaden their definitions of heritage. Further, we call on scholars, community members, organizational leaders, and local and national authorities to be critically informed on the myriad ways heritage can be actively and intentionally employed in a positive and respectful way to improve lives throughout the world. Thankfully, heritage researchers, archaeologists, environmentalists, academics, organizational leaders, and others involved in social change have begun to move beyond seeing heritage as only social memory—a mere interpretation of static past events, people, places, and practices. Instead, they have been inspired to adopt innovative, interdisciplinary approaches to explore critically the variety of ways heritage is engaged in the present, and can be employed strategically for a better, more sustainable, and socially just future.

Significantly, the chapters in this book present a broad, global perspective from diverse scholars, each exploring the uses of heritage from different contexts. They use a variety of cultural lenses, scholarly perspectives, and professional outlooks and experiences to present heritage as a forward-looking, dynamic, creative, and imaginative tool when utilized in a wide variety of situations and environments, and by different people and cultures. It is our hope that presenting this collection of investigations and case studies, with their thought-provoking ideas and innovative proposals, will inspire reconsideration of the role of heritage in our lives, and for that reassessment to foster the development of new applications of heritage to improve the present and inspire and plan for a better future.

The goal of this volume

This innovative collection of studies aims to broaden, expand, and refocus our understanding of what heritage is to different communities. We seek to challenge current understandings and perceptions of the uses of the past and explore how contemporary communities are employing elements of their tangible and intangible heritage to achieve positive, modern goals. In pursuing this project, we have come to concur with Winter (2013) that critical heritage studies can positively contribute to programs addressing the critical issues facing communities throughout the world today, including environmental sustainability, economic inequality, and social and political conflict. Winter, who investigates how the past is used for nationalistic and geopolitical goals, suggests researchers should seek new perspectives on approaching socio-political conflicts and complexities concerning heritage. He advises researchers to look at the broader issues facing communities, and to explore how heritage issues are and can be involved. We need to recognize that there are benefits related to safeguarding and preserving tangible and intangible heritage, but also understand the implications of what we are doing, why we are doing it, and the repercussions of our actions. Particularly, we need to be more inclusive, involving a wider range of stakeholders, and pursuing and adopting multiple perspectives beyond those that are Western (Winter 2013). And we should always be mindful that the present needs force reconsideration and reshaping in the use of what remains from the past.

Archaeological research adds to our historical and scholarly understanding of the past through discovery, interpretation, and presentation of tangible heritage. As will be very apparent in the following chapters, heritage can also be exceptionally valuable for developing a communal understanding of the past, recognizing shared and dark histories, strengthening interpersonal bonds, and building respect and mutual understanding. We acknowledge that the past is unknowable (Lowenthal 1985) and narratives can be debated, but we also accept that the 'past' does not exist independently of the present, but rather in relation to the present. Heritage researchers should always be cognizant that new interpretations of place are essential in this increasingly multicultural world, as the identities, beliefs, and practices of each community are constantly under threat (Apaydin 2020; Assman 2008; Assman and Czaplica 1995). Broader issues of conservation and preservation should be explored, and heritage professionals and authorities should fully consider how heritage issues are or can be involved. In our work we recognize that heritage can be a positive enabler for change.

Our ultimate interests in creating this volume as editors, researchers, parents, and concerned citizens, are not only to change the scope and direction of heritage studies, but to inspire heritage professionals to make a difference in the world. We want to change the way heritage professionals think, plan, and work, and to inspire them to present innovative and creative examples of the positive use of heritage. We sincerely believe that heritage is and should be utilized for citizen empowerment and social transformation. Towards this goal, in the following chapters heritage is presented as flexible, responsive, reconsidered, and repurposed.

The volume's structure

The goal of this book is to highlight and illustrate the numerous and valuable ways in which heritage is, has been, and can be intentionally and creatively employed throughout the world in bettering lives of contemporary communities and societies. This is done through three particular themes. The three themes clarify the broad nature of heritage, demonstrate the positive use of heritage to respond to contemporary social, political, and environmental needs and challenges, and offer suggestions on how heritage can be utilized to build toward a more positive, equitable, secure, and sustainable future.

The first theme, *Fostering Collective Memory,* examines how communities can cultivate collective memory for present and future societal needs, such as for the promotion of peace, mitigating against environmental destruction due to climate change, or for addressing social power imbalances. In many ways, this is the beginning phase of putting heritage into action.

Within the first chapter of this theme, Vladimir I. Ionesov of Samara, Russia, takes an in-depth, theoretical look at the foundational principles and objectives of museums of peace. His research investigates peace museums, and he delves into the very political nature of heritage and memory as he explores the current presentation of images of war to promote peace. He suggests that effective displays can redirect efforts toward overcoming ethnic and national conflicts, promote peaceful interactions, and help in the avoidance of future catastrophic altercations. In his insightful, timely, and important analysis, he further investigates the philosophical theory behind peace-making as a museum strategy and proposes alternative approaches for museums in building interpersonal relationships through new, modern, novel displays, viewer dialogue, and alternative museum spatial re-organizations to create venues for greater intercultural understandings and interaction.

Addressing social conflict from another perspective and country, in Chapter 2 Kelly M. Britt looks at the role of the senses in experiencing heritage and how this experience galvanizes community members to work together to preserve tangible and intangible heritage. She explores this innovative approach through the work she is doing with the United Order of Tents Eastern District #3, the oldest Black women's fraternal order in the United States, and their headquarters, a historical nineteenth-century house in Brooklyn, NY. Working with local community members, she exposes through visitor sensory experiences the significant, previously undocumented meanings of this site and what the history of the order holds for and within the local predominantly Black community. Rebuilding membership of the oldest Black women's fraternal organization and their physical home restores a historical legacy through outreach, communal interaction, and historic preservation. It also gives agency to the larger community in the making of their built environment, which, being historically Black, has been systematically discriminated against in the urban planning process. While these actions cannot stop the gentrification of this urban community, the United Order of Tents building has provided a place of unity, pride, and belonging. Using alternative methods of historic preservation assessment, like the intangible sensory experience of place, Britt opens up new avenues of interacting with heritage sites, particularly ones not included in the Authorized Heritage Discourse, that can be used as tools for organizing and empowering local communities. Her findings also have the potential to provide new focal points for the fight for preservation of not only the tangible components of a rich and significant past, but of the intangible ones as well.

The past can also teach us a great deal in other ways toward resolving differences, facing disasters, and mitigating against future losses. Catastrophic disasters have occurred worldwide throughout the historical past and are documented in both archival and archaeological records, as well as noted in myth and traditional narratives. Now, in our world of drastic climate change, social unrest, and rapid technological development, we should learn from the archaeological record how people in the past coped with and adapted to these impactful occasions and apply that knowledge today. We should redirect our efforts toward greater community involvement to ensure that the information gained and presented has relevance to current populations and is accessible to those in the future. Collectively working toward common goals of building a more sustainable future also has the potential for building stronger relationships between communities.

Insightfully, in Chapter 3, Uzi Baram asks the existential question of what our collective responsibility is to the environment and to each other. In his research, he explores this question through the lens of rapid environmental change as he presents case studies from Florida's coastal region. He examines the impact ecological transformation from sea level rise is having on archaeological sites and their associated heritage and values. He carefully notes the transformative impact of engaging local residents in archaeological excavations, site interpretation, and public presentations, and demonstrates how such involvement has the potential to instil pride in the community, inspire greater communal participation, overcome racial tensions, empower local minority and marginalized groups, and build better communication between diverse communities toward a more equitable society.

Notably, Baram argues we are all personally accountable as members of society to make a difference in the world. He discusses how transformational thinking about responsibility can spark greater engagement with communities to address historic inequalities and other social problems, while effectively responding to threats from climate change. Baram ultimately appeals for a new perspective on knowledge from the past and proposes that the field of archaeology undergo a radical shift in perspective so that archaeologists take greater social responsibility in using their education and skills to engage with local communities in projects. His findings indicate that while not all places of heritage can and will be saved for future generations due to climate changes, residents, scholars, and others can work together to strive to preserve or memorialize these places.

The second theme, *Activating Indigenous Heritage*, investigates the impact of colonialism and the use of intangible and tangible heritage for restoring Indigenous land control and developing greater understandings between disparate communities, or between communities, governments, and local authorities, over nature-culture epistemological divides and ethnic-cultural differences. The chapters in this section investigate and discuss programs of restorative justice, environmental restoration, political and legal action, and community negotiation for overcoming generational trauma, toward building modern, empowered Indigenous and ethnic identities for greater sovereignty efforts. This section highlights heritage in action—essentially heritage actively working in the present with direct impacts to the future. Such efforts have the unintentional impact of building and supporting communal bonds between residents, thereby strengthening identities and senses of belonging, and in doing so, unifying communities for more sustainable futures.

In Chapter 4, the authors, two informed and experienced academics, who are also regional experts, and a traditional knowledge holder from British Columbia, Canada, present a complex program for environmental restoration through Native land control. The program would be instituted cooperatively between the Katzie First Nation in British Columbia and the Canadian government, and the land would be protected through an authorized designation. The management plan would be developed in recognition of the longstanding contentious relationship between Canada's First Nations peoples and the Canadian government, and would focus, in particular, on returning land to Indigenous management and applying traditional resource management techniques. This important program focuses on restorative justice for the Katzie, one of Canada's many Native communities that historically have been adversely impacted by the policies and programs of the Canadian government. The program was designed to achieve several objectives: to protect the ancestral land and resources of the Katzie People; to restore Indigenous land control that had been lost through colonization; to create a program of respectful communication between the government and an Indigenous community; to develop an understanding and acceptance of epistemological differences; and to construct a framework for acknowledgement and protection of culturally significant Indigenous sites.

The authors note that through a cooperative program such as this, there is a potential for creating a more meaningful and equitable society. This program demonstrates the immense potential of heritage to restore and rebuild relationships critical for future community survival, growth, and security. Additionally, such programs may also achieve many strategic and significant goals, including helping communities overcome trauma from centuries of political oppression, building respect for difference, and reconciling ontological conflicts in the nature/culture divide.

Susan Shay in Chapter 5 discusses how Indigenous epistemology is intricately tied to ancestral land and natural resources, and how the loss of land threatens the continued existence of distinctive communities. She demonstrates that Indigenous empowerment and the fight for greater forms of sovereignty can come about through many different programs and pathways. Through her case study of the US Pacific island state of Hawai'i, she shows how Native Hawaiian heritage was adversely impacted in the nineteenth and twentieth centuries due to a loss of Indigenous control over land and the outlawing of language and traditional practices. Taking their land battles into state and national courts, Native Hawaiians have used their heritage as a useful tool to affect significant change for their community. They have employed heritage in court narratives that delve into the conflict between Hawai'i's two sets of legal statutes, one from the nineteenth century that protects Native Hawaiian culture and the other that prioritizes land development in the modern state. Through their efforts, they have taken back the legal narrative of Native Hawaiian history based on cultural claims supported by retrieved archival evidence. Interestingly, the unintentional and unexpected outcome of archival research for legal narrative construction has been the discovery of lost archival material about both intangible and tangible Native Hawaiian culture and tradition. Furthermore, she demonstrates that by taking land claim cases into the courts, Native Hawaiians have learned how to overcome cultural, political, and economic obstacles to achieve greater levels of sovereignty, and in the process, strengthened their own community and built a new modern empowered identity for the future. The increased number of Native Hawaiian professionals in court has served to instil pride among community members, inspired greater communal efforts, encouraged new leadership and involvement, encouraged cultural participation, and fostered a new, empowered identity needed for future contemporary sovereignty efforts.

The third theme, *Repurposing Heritage,* continues the investigation of social change through the use and *reuse* of heritage and explores the intentional and direct application of intangible heritage in cultural and religious festivals to strengthen communal ties and resolve social and political conflict.

Turning to the African continent, Ifeyinwa Emejulu examines the long-lasting impact that colonialization and the arrival of Christian values in the nineteenth century have had on society and social order and the role of traditional ceremonies in Nigeria in Chapter 6. She discusses how throughout history, globalization and other expansionist programs have resulted in cultural, social, economic, and political shifts and changes worldwide. On a local level, with the arrival of new residents, whether they are colonists, reformers, occupiers, or conquerors, transient or permanent, each person brought with them new practices, viewpoints, social structures, and values. New ideas and concepts, routines and traditions have been introduced, some of which were incorporated into the daily lives of the local population. While in some instances a change came about through authorized, destructive programs and policies, other transformations occurred as cultures blended together through organic processes of incorporation and adaptation. She focuses on the rebirth of a traditional festival of the people of Umuchu, Nigeria, to understand how and why a heritage festival was revived, and how the intentional restoration of selected elements of intangible culture has had the power to restore cultural pride, unify diasporic communities, and rebuild respectful relationships lost through decades of political, religious, and social transformation. Emejulu's work expands our understanding of the dynamic nature of heritage, and how memories of the past are re-interpreted in new and useful ways in response to the needs of the community.

In Chapter 7 Bishnupriya Basak focuses on archaeological remains in India, and how over time, impacted by social, economic, and political forces, the memories and the meanings associated with archaeological heritage can evolve through personal social exchanges between different constituent groups. She notes how through such social interactions, new meanings and values are introduced and incorporated into traditional practices.

This is particularly evident through her case study of the people of a small village located in the Sundarbans in West Bengal, India, which provides insight into the impact of the interaction between groups of different social status. Of significance is her emphasis on how marginalized groups incorporate elements of culture from cohort groups of differing religious and ethnic status, and how such multicultural interactions reformulate our interpretations of the world and ourselves and help to support and encourage more modern forms of identity. Her findings reveal how such actions can be exceptionally transformative for lower caste groups, as they have the potential to not only reinforce and reinvigorate culture, but also promote positive and social change. Her research calls for further consideration of the importance of the ongoing process of transformation of heritage and memory.

Conclusion

These seven chapters offer a range of case studies and associated insights on the uses of heritage, and in doing so, they broaden our understanding of the ways in which heritage has been, is currently, and can be used in the future to enrich and improve the lives of different communities. Presented through different cultural lenses from scholars and cultural leaders around the world, the chapters in this book explore how contemporary communities are facing a variety of modern challenges, and how they have, in response, re-considered and re-interpreted knowledge of the past in innovative and useful ways. They demonstrate how knowledge of the past can redefine our understandings of the past and can be used to strengthen community, to restore and rebuild collective memory, to address contemporary social problems, and to build imaginative and sustainable responses to environmental, social, environmental, and political change.

Notes

[1] See https://worldarch.org/history-wac/ for the history of the World Archaeological Congress.

[2] https://worldarch.org/history-wac/ Accessed 11 July, 2023.

[3] The chapter authors include an architect, archaeologists, anthropologists, culture and heritage experts, and a tribal knowledge holder.

[4] See World Monuments Fund, 2022 World Monuments Fund Watch, https://www.wmf.org/2022watch?gclid=Cj0KCQjw6KunBhDxARIsAKFUGs8uC 4tiEgLx-8cI5OkfMShdQqOXRDIoLLjXp01_3yioUMQPfZFyAAoaAlYzEALw_wcB.

[5] See Law 9/1993, On Catalon Cultural Heritage.

[6] See The National Trust of Scotland website, https://www.nts.org.uk/visit/places/culloden/the-battle-of-culloden.

[7] See the National Trust of Scotland Culloden gift shop website, https://www.nts.org.uk/shop/collections/gifts-inspired-by-our-places/inspired-by-culloden.

[8] See Sites of Contested Memory: Comfort Women Statue (Seoul) https://bordersofmemory.com/dispute-map-locations/comfort-women-statue#:~:text=The%20Statue%20of%20Peace%20serves,a%20full%20and%20formal%20apology.

Bibliography

Abrams, Elliott. 2023. "*Implications of the Russia-Ukraine War*". Council on Foreign Relations Blog. February 26, 2023. Accessed 30 August, 2023. https://www.cfr.org/blog/implications-russia-ukraine-war.

Ahmad, Yahaya. 2006. "The Scope and Definitions of Heritage: From Tangible to Intangible". *International Journal of Heritage Studies* 12 (3): 292-300.

Anderson, Benedict. 2006. *Imagined Communities*. London: Verso.

Apaydin, Veysel. 2017. "Heritage Values and Communities: Examining Heritage Perceptions and Public Engagements". *Journal of Eastern Mediterranean Archaeology & Heritage Studies* 5 (3-4): 349-64.

Apaydin, Veysel. 2020. "The interlinkage of cultural memory, heritage and discourses of construction, transformation and destruction". In *Critical Perspectives on Cultural Memory and Heritage: Construction, Transformation and Destruction*, edited by Veysel Apaydin, 13-30. London: UCL Press.

Asakura, Toshio. 2016. "Cultural Heritage in Korea – from a Japanese perspective". In *Reconsidering Cultural Heritage in East Asia*, edited by Akira Matsuda and Luisa Elena Mengoni, 103-120. London: Ubiquity Press.

Assman, Aleida. 2008. "Transformations between History and Memory". *Social Research* 75 (1): 49-72.

Assman, Jan and John Czaplicka. 1995. "Collective Memory and Cultural Identity". *New German Critique* 65: 125-133.

Bideau, Florence Graezer, and Haiming Yan. 2018. "4 Historic Urban Landscape in Beijing: The Gulou Project and Its Contested Memories". In *Chinese Heritage in the Making: Experiences, Negotiations and Contestations*, edited by Christina Maags and Marina Svensson, 93-118. Amsterdam: Amsterdam University Press.

Cameron, Christina. 2008. "From Warsaw to Mostar: The World Heritage Committee and Authenticity". *APT Bulletin: The Journal of Preservation Technology* 39 (2/3): 19–24.

Carman, John. 2002. *Archaeology and Heritage: An Introduction*. London: Continuum.

Casella, Eleanor Conlin, and Katherine Fennelly. 2016. "Ghosts of Sorrow, Sin and Crime: Dark Tourism and Convict Heritage in Van Diemen's Land, Australia". *International Journal of Historical Archaeology* 20 (3): 506-520.

Claus, C. Anne. 2017. "Beyond Merroir: The Okinawan Taste for Clams". *Gastronomica* 17 (3): 49-57.

Cochrane, Feargal. 2015. "The Paradox of Conflict Tourism: The Commodification of War or Conflict Transformation in Practice?" *The Brown Journal of World Affairs* 22 (1): 51-69.

Convey, Ian, Gerard Corsane, and Peter Davis, eds. 2014. *Displaced Heritage: Responses to Disaster, Trauma, and Loss*. Rochester, NY: Boydell & Brewer.

Cordesman, Anthony H. 2022. "The Longer-Term Impact of the Ukraine Conflict and the Growing Importance of the Civil Side of War". Center for Strategic and International Studies. June 6. Accessed 30 August, 2023. https://www.csis.org/analysis/longer-term-impact-ukraine-conflict-and-growing-importance-civil-side-war.

De Antoni, Andrea. 2019. "Down in a Hole: Dark Tourism, Haunted Places as Affective Meshworks, and the Obliteration of Korean Laborers in Contemporary Kyoto". *Japan Review* 33: 271–297.

Doty, Peggy. 1976. "Constitutional Law: The Right to Wear a Traditional Indian Hair Style: Recognition of a Heritage". *American Indian Law Review* 4 (1): 105–20.

Fairclough, Norman. 1992. *Discourse and Social Change*. Cambridge, UK: Polity Press.

Foster, Laura A. 2014. "Critical Cultural Translation: A Socio-Legal Framework for Regulatory Orders". *Indiana Journal of Global Legal Studies* 21 (1): 79-105.

Foucault, Michel. 1980. "Truth and Power". In *Power/Knowledge: Selected Interviews and Other Writings, 1972-1977*, edited by Colin Gordon and translated by Colin Gordon, Leo Marshal, John Mepham, and Kate Sober, 109-133. New York: Pantheon.

———. 1983. "The Subject and Power". In *Michel Foucault: Beyond Structuralism and Hermeneutics*, 2nd ed., edited by Hubert Dreyfus and Paul Rabinow, 208-228. Chicago: University of Chicago Press.

Gabriel, Festo W. 2016. "Defining Cultural Heritage among the Makonde of Tanzania". In *African Archaeology Without Frontiers: Papers from the 2014 PanAfrican Archaeological Association Congress*, edited by Karim Sadr, Amanda Esterhusyen, and Chrissie Sievers, 32–47. Johannesburg, SA: Wits University Press.

Garcia Canclini, N. 1995. *Hybrid Cultures: Strategies for Entering and Leaving Modernity*. Translated by Christopher L. Chaiappari and Silvinia L. Lopez. Minneapolis: University of Minnesota Press.

Garner, Bryan A., 2019. *Black's Law Dictionary*. London: Sweet & Maxwell.

Harrison, Rodney. 2010. "Introduction". In *Understanding the Politics of Heritage*, edited by Rodney Harrison, 1-42. Manchester, UK: Manchester University Press.

Harrison, Rodney, Caitlin Desilvey, Cornelius Holtorf, MacDonald Sharon, Nadia Bartolini, Esther Breithoff, Harald Fredheim, Antony Lyons, Sarah May, Jennie Morgan, and Sefryn Penrose. 2020. *Heritage Futures: Comparative Approaches to Natural and Cultural Heritage Practices*. London: UCL Press.

Hartley, Julie. 2004. "Cultural Tourism in Utah". In *Folklore in Utah: A History and Guide to Resources*, edited by David Stanley, 240-245. Denver: University Press of Colorado.

Holtorf, Cornelius. 2016. "The Contemporary Archaeology of Nuclear Waste: Communicating with the Future". *Arkæologisk Forum* 35: 31-37.

———. 2018a. "Conservation and Heritage as Future-Making". *ICOMOS University Forum* 1: 1-13.

———. 2018b. "How Cultural Resilience is increased through Cultural Heritage". *World Archaeology* 50 (4): 639-650.

———. 2020. "Conservation and Heritage as Creative Processes of Future Making". *International Journal of Cultural Property* 27 (2): 277-290.

Holtorf, Cornelius, and Anders Hogberg. 2014. "Communicating with Future Generations: What are the Benefits of Preserving for Future Generations? Nuclear Power and Beyond". *The European Journal of Post-Classical Archaeologies* 4: 315-330.

Holtorf, Cornelius, and Anders Hogberg, eds. 2021. *Cultural Heritage and the Future*. London: Routledge.

Jalais, Annu. 2007. "The Sundarbans: Whose World Heritage Site?" *Conservation and Society* 5 (3): 335–42.

Kammer, Alfred, Jihad Azour, Abebe Aemro Selassie, Ilan Goldfajn, and Chang Yong Rhee. 2022. "How War in Ukraine is Reverberating Across World's Regions". In *International Monetary Fund Blog*. March 15. Accessed 30 August, 2023. https://www.imf.org/en/Blogs/Articles/2022/03/15/blog-how-war-in-ukraine-is-reverberating-across-worlds-regions-031522.

Logan, Amanda L. 2020. "Eating and Remembering Past Cultural Achievements". In *The Scarcity Slot: Excavating Histories of Food Security in Ghana*, 1st ed, 158-168. Oakland: University of California Press.

Lowenthal, David. 1985. *The Past is a Foreign Country*. Cambridge, UK: Cambridge University Press.

———. 1996. *Possessed by the Past: The Heritage Crusades and the Spoils of History*. New York: Free Press.

Maskiell, Michelle. 1999. "Embroidering the Past: Phulkari Textiles and Gendered Work as 'Tradition' and 'Heritage' in Colonial and Contemporary Punjab". *The Journal of Asian Studies* 58 (2): 361–88.

Masters, Jonathan. 2023. "Ukraine: Conflict at the Crossroads of Europe and Russia". *Council on Foreign Relations*. February 14. Accessed 30 August, 2023. https://www.cfr.org/backgrounder/ukraine-conflict-crossroads-europe-and-russia.

Mazel, Odette. 2009. "The Evolution of Rights: Indigenous Peoples and International Law". *Australian Indigenous Law Review* 13 (1). 140-158.

Mohn, Tanya. 2019. "Global Shopping with UNESCO as Your Guide". *The New York Times*. November 21.

Montgomery, Alvin. 2004. "Recognizing Value in African American Heritage Objects". *The Journal of African American History* 89 (2): 177–82.

Mozaffari, Ali, and Tod Jones, eds. 2020. *Heritage Movements in Asia: Cultural Heritage Activism, Politics and Identity*. Oxford, New York: Berghahn Books.

Price, Rebecca, and Mark Shores. 2017. "Dark Tourism: A Guide to Resources". *Reference & User Services Quarterly* 57 (2): 97-101.

Schneck, Stephen Frederick. 1987. "Michel Foucault on Power/Discourse, Theory and Practice". *Human Studies* 10 (1): 15-33.

Shim, D. 2023. "Memorials' Politics: Exploring the Material Rhetoric of the Statue of Peace". *Memory Studies* 16 (4): 663-676.

Smith, Laurajane. 2004. *Archaeological Theory and the Politics of Cultural Heritage*. London: Routledge.

———. 2006. *Uses of Heritage*. London: Routledge.

Smith, Laurajane, and Emma Waterton. 2012. *Heritage, Communities and Archaeology*. London: Bristol Classical Press.

Smith, Laurajane, and Natsuko Akagawa, eds. 2009. *Intangible Heritage*. London: Routledge.

Sørensen, Marie Louise Stig, and John Carman. 2009. *Heritage Studies: Methods and Approaches*. London: Routledge.

Walker, Susannah. 2000. "Black Is Profitable: The Commodification of the Afro, 1960—1975". *Enterprise & Society* 1 (3): 536–64.

Waterton, Emma, and Laurajane Smith. 2010. "The Recognition and Misrecognition of Community Heritage". *International Journal of Heritage Studies* 16 (1-2): 4-15.

Waterton, Emma, and Steve Watson, eds. 2015. "Heritage as a Focus of Research: Past, Present and New Directions". In *The Palgrave Handbook of Contemporary Heritage Research*, 1-14. London: Palgrave Macmillan.

Watenpaugh, Heghnar Zeitlian. 2014. "Preserving the Medieval City of Ani: Cultural Heritage between Contest and Reconciliation". *Journal of the Society of Architectural Historians* 73 (4): 528–55.

Winter, Tim. 2012. "Heritage and Nationalism: An Unbreachable Couple". *Institute for Culture and Society* 3 (4): 1-14.

Winter, Tim. 2013. "Clarifying the Critical in Critical Heritage Studies". *International Journal of Heritage Studies* 19 (6): 532-545.

Young, Morris. 2004. "Native Claims: Cultural Citizenship, Ethnic Expressions, and the Rhetorics of 'Hawaiianness'". *College English* 67 (1): 83–101.

Fostering collective memory

Chapter 1

Visualization of memory in cultural practices of representing heritage: reevaluating the past in images of war and peace

Vladimir I. Ionesov

Samara Institute of Culture, Russia; International School for Advanced Research in Cultural Studies, Samara, Russia; International Organization of Folk Art, Russia; Regional Center on Urgent Anthropological Research in Samara, Russia; Samara Society for Cultural Studies, Russia

Abstract

In this chapter, I explore the cultural possibilities of visualizing memory and heritage within exhibits in contemporary peace museum activities. This study significantly pushes the boundaries of understanding within museum heritage and identifies a process of creative and communicatively rich cultural practices. I will examine some cultural bases and professional specifications in the activities of peace museums and consider how this process contributes to peacebuilding in changing culture. First, museums, and in particular peace museums, have both the ability and responsibility to present cross-cultural imaginings of what peace looks like, and how it is created and sustained. Second, peace museums must challenge traditional museum exhibit standards that focus mostly on protective-memorial issues by creating centres for communicative transformation and creativity. These museums should actively engage visitors and encourage them to define, explore, and to some extent, experience peace as it is created by different people from different cultures.

Keywords: museum, memory, visualization, heritage, artefacts, war, peace, creativity, transformation, culture, peacebuilding

***

> When things reach their limit,
> they undergo change.
>
> Old Chinese wisdom

Introduction

What is a 'peace museum'? In this chapter, I define a peace museum as a public institution for collecting, preserving (archiving), storing, and publicly displaying the most representative historical and contemporary experiences of peacemaking. Compared to traditional institutions, a peace museum predominantly exhibits the best instructive examples of cultural reconciliation and understanding, providing insight that could be successfully applied in modern society to further peaceful interactions. In this regard, the general social mission of a peace museum is to relay these samples to the public through commemorative practices and visual and interpretive forms of communication. However, the peace museum could also be a field for launching new creative peace practices (contexts, stories). Through this purposeful effort to spread a culture of peace, heritage can and should be used to positively promote peace rather than to perpetuate or glorify war. This chapter seeks to explore what the mission is of a contemporary peace museum, to highlight the cultural and political contexts for understanding and defining peace, to determine how peace is presented in the present, and to propose ways in which each peace museum can use heritage to be more effective and promote harmony, reconciliation, and greater forms of understanding.

What is the role of a peace museum?

The issue of the role of peace museums can clearly be viewed as directly related to a reconsideration of the place and role of culture in modern society, and in the re-qualification of traditional ideas about war and peace, continuity, and innovation. At the same time, the national and cultural context of museum design, which influences the optimal choice and promotion of the most effective peacemaking practices, seems increasingly important. I proceed from the fact that the effectiveness of any social institution, including a peace museum, depends on the degree of its cultural completeness, that is, on the entirety of recasting and mastering cultural values and communication narratives available to it.

Importantly, the modern peace museum can become successful in its social and humanistic mission if it manages to transform peacemaking into a practice for the cultivation of new visual strategies and contexts aimed at coupling the best patterns of the past with the urgent demands of our time. Such practices can prove once again that, to cite Gandhi, there is no way *to* peace, peace *is* the way, or as he stated directly, "if the world is to have peace, non-violence is the means to that end and no other" (Gandhi 1947, 243). This transformation will surely enable peace museums to be effective platforms for the communication of social affairs which, through peacemaking practices, illustrate the best scenarios for cultivating the nonviolent coexistence of the people of planet Earth, with their differing lifestyles, beliefs, traditions, fears, and expectations. Only in this instance will each peace museum be able to justify its social purpose and constructive mission in its cultural environment.

At the same time, it is important to understand that the museum itself is only an institution of culture—the museum's social involvement in the peacebuilding process is fully dependent on the creativity of the actions of its staff and volunteers, and on the cultural practices that connect the museum with present-day life. The best examples of peacemaking are not created to hide from war, but to master and conquer the best practices for creating peace.

A question of heritage

Heritage as a sphere for creativity: can the past be modern?

What is the visualization, presentation, and interpretation of heritage in museum practice today? In order to explore this subject, we must first of all ask what is heritage? Heritage can be distinguished as: 1) a commemorative repository of stories and values from the past, and 2) a vital substrate through which one can reflect on conditions in the modern world. In her recent study of the cultural mission of the modern museum, Claire Bishop (after Walter Benjamin 2012) (2014, 72) distinguishes between two kinds of heritage stories: the first as the keeper of sacred memory which commemorates triumphs, and the second as a way of requalifying and identifying the issues of today, seeking out "… in the past a source of the present historical moment", that is "… the determining motivation of our interest to the past. … Rather than think about the museum collections as repositories of treasures, we could rethink of them as public archives", as sorts of resource-consulting centres of culture, visualizing alternatives for development which encourage us to actively transform social practice. However, in actuality, the first of these types of heritage stories, the commemorative repository, still dominates modern museum policy. This explains the separation of the sacredly protected world of museum treasures from their use in addressing the urgent imperatives of today.

The world is constantly changing, but heritage objects and sites as valuable items of the past remain unchanged. The point is that cultural heritage objects and sites are deprived of their original historical contexts, that is, they fall out of the time in which they were created. The culture to which heritage belongs today therefore differs from the culture that produced it, and from what and to whom it originally served. Heritage objects and modern cultural institutions (museums, archives, etc.) do not relate and interact naturally because they are separated by historical epochs and were created for different purposes. This ontological temporal gap creates a contradiction. It generates a conflict between the historical experience of the past and the reality of the present, that is, between the understanding of whom and to what heritage serves and how it can be involved in the transformation of contemporary culture. In order to remove this contradiction or temporal gap, it is necessary to construct a new communicative context linking the past with the present. As a result, it can be posited that the creation of such contexts is the main mission of museums. Without this complementary context, there is no dialogue (the dialogue is impossible) and the heritage site will always be disconnected from modernity.

In other words, the question arises: how can heritage be presented in a contemporary, attractive, and creative way for the present day? For only then can history truly serve as a protective lesson and function for the betterment of a modern culture. In order to protect heritage, it must be linked to the past, the present, and the future. After all, the bygone days do not live in the past, they become the historical past for the sake of the present. Thus, the past finds its constructive function today through widespread and responsible involvement in actual practices of the present. In particular, peace is always in the present.

Importantly, museums, and especially museums for peace, can become not only institutions to harmonize and remove these contradictions, but they also can be a catalyst for positive change. Ideas and artefacts of the culture of peace give to the historical heritage of the past necessary vital dynamics, and by doing so, reveal their constructive potential for fostering modern social transformations.

It follows then that if we want to reveal the peacemaking potential of heritage, we must always be able to connect it with the present. Giuseppe Lampedusa (1961) once noted that if you want everything to remain the same, it is necessary to change something all the time. Even religious objects, including the most conservative and motionless ones, display their involvement with changing life namely by having had vivid ceremonial actions (symbolic drama) carried out around them and addressed to the welfare of those who, and for the sake of whom, they are provided. Any ideal by itself is motionless and without mobility of those whom it serves, it (this ideal) becomes lifeless and worthless. Peace museums exhibit samples of peacemaking as some ideal instructive expositions, but (unlike the church altars and icons) vivid symbolic (and creative) activities and artistic drama until now are underrepresented in them.

Objects and places do not have value by themselves, but rather they gain value only when surrounded by those who yearn and care for them. Values are not born in a museum, but outside of it in the social world. This concept enables us to assume that a museum grows with what is beyond its borders— in response to society and changes in modern life. Creative practices in museum policy must therefore have the ability to coordinate and reconcile space and time, a human and an object, traditions, innovations, and, at times, to skillfully even combine elements that were previously unconnected.

Memory without an image does not work—it is necessary to see, remember, feel, and then couple what we recall with the present. Our memories must be visualized in images of things so that they cannot be forgotten. But for all that, only to show and memorize tragic images will not be sufficient to protect society from cruelty and violence. Perhaps Susan Sontag (2003, 89-90) is right when she states we assign too much value

> ... to memory, not enough to thinking. Remembering is an ethical act, [and] ... is deep in our natures as humans. And too much remembering embitters. ... It is desirable that the account of specific injustices dissolve into a more general understanding.

When the exhibits do not raise questions, do not excite or stimulate thoughts, but instead present simplified historical battles and provide ready-made answers to previously unpacked questions, visitors find themselves in situations where everything has already been decided for them. In this position, each visitor is deprived of the choice, in fact the right, to question and doubt. All dialogue is interrupted and not encouraged.

Furthermore, the presentation and visualization of war images and documentary evidence of violence cannot only convince the museum visitor to reject war but can also cause and promote in him/her a feeling of hatred and revenge against others. Unfortunately, "being a spectator of calamities taking place in another country is a quintessential modern experience" (Sontag 2003, 16).

The aim of a peace museum exhibit should be to touch and capture the feelings of the viewer, that is, to some extent, to subjugate itself. For example, while exposing images of victims of violence and traces of war crimes through an exhibit, it must not be forgotten that the expression and drama of the historical conflict are convincing only through its documentary nature. But the presentation and visualization of violence and suffering, as well as the viewer's sensory perceptions of it, does not in itself add to peace, mutual understanding, or bring peoples and cultures closer together. Moreover, a direct view of suffering may result in detachment from it and thus remove personal responsibility for what has happened. This is how Susan Sontag (2003, 79-80) reasons the visualization of suffering:

> The imaginary proximity to the suffering inflicted on others that is granted by images suggests a link between the far-away sufferers—seen close-up on the television screen—and the privileged viewer that is simply untrue, that is yet one more mystification of our real relations to power. So far as we feel sympathy, we feel we are not accomplices to what caused the suffering. Our sympathy proclaims our innocence as well as our impotence. To set aside the sympathy we extend to others beset by war and murderous politics for a reflection on how our privileges are located on the same map as their suffering .... [It] is a task for which the painful, stirring images supply only an initial spark.

All this also applies to the practices of museum exposure to the legacies of war and peace. In the purposeful excessive proximity and pressure of the exhibits on the viewer, there is no room for reflection. In this way, thought seems to be immobilized and subordinated to the contemplated object itself through a specific and concrete one-dimensional presentation perspective. This excessive closeness removes the boundary between life and death, movement and inactivity, good and evil, peace and war, dialogue and silence, responsibility and impunity. Values are blended and mutually eliminated. There is more dictate than democracy in the dialogue between the exhibit and the viewer. Hence, "a passivity emerges that dulls feeling" (Sontag 2003, 101).

Looking at modern peace museums, one cannot but agree with J. Baudrillard (2006, 130, 134) that "our culture is a culture of despondency and suffering", and that "happiness and unhappiness, depression and ecstasy are connected … exclusively with objects". As the French philosopher shows, the borderline that has divided good and evil, and that has divided objects, is the same.

War and peace as the challenges of modernity and values of culture

Indeed, there are too many themes of war and violence in peace museums and too little of beauty, goodness, and peacemaking. In this projection, it is apparent that peace strongly resembles what it opposes, turning the peace museum into a museum of war, conflict, and violence. Therefore, it is necessary to make a distinction between 1) museums for peace/containment of war and 2) museums for peacemaking/culture of peace. No matter how different their histories, collections and functions, peace museums have one current and urgent task: to let into museums as much peace as possible, and through their displays and culture construct within each venue an atmosphere of real peacemaking, creativity, and communication. I think this task is applicable to any museum, but it can be implemented in different ways, depending on its profile and the specifics of museum artefacts.

It has thus become a necessity to transform museum exhibits into a lively dialogue using present communicative practices to expand the boundaries, knowledge, experience, and sheer determination of peacemaking efforts. To achieve this, there must be a shift from the routine acceptance of peace artefacts as museum specimens and symbols into items used for developing a lively new cultural design for the world order, in other words, for that culture of peace which was enshrined in the United Nations documents as a strategy for change (UN/UNESCO 1997-2010).

How can the move away from the passive conception of an exhibition piece to that of an object actively used for serious socio-cultural involvement be achieved? This could be achieved in two ways: 1) by incorporating museum objects into peace projects with social activities beyond the museum itself, and 2) alternatively, by bringing to the museum relevant peace examples from everyday experiences occurring outside the museum.

Historically, a considerable number of museums for peace owe their origins to events that are far from actually peacebuilding activities. At the heart of their expositions are 1) a history of violence, 2) chronicles of combat victories and defeats, 3) evidence of war crimes, and 4) demonstrations of the victims of armed conflicts. The images and plots of the primary museum showcases are designed to show the depth of human disunity and the endless social cataclysms within the history of society. Of course, despite the striking differences in the sectoral specifics and the thematic focus of each of the four types of exhibitions, all of them, in one way or another, are ultimately concentrating on cultivating the values of nonviolence, mercy, concord, and peace. They are, after all, in museums of peace.

However, the ideas of peace and humanism are often expressed in contrast to the destructive consequences of wars and violence. In the discourse of this visual contradistinction, peace itself is not the focus. Peace is only shown as the projection of the military paradigm and is understood as a continuation or absence of war and deterrence of violence.

This type of exhibit can be viewed as a memorial peacekeeping presentation. The importance of a memorial peacekeeping practice, or of the modern culture of opposition to war, is beyond any doubt. But it is also important to the extent that the United Nations Peacekeeping Forces are significant, that is, for the cessation and containment of war, which in the interpretation of the Charter of this international organization is a specialized military contingent with the aim of preventing or eliminating the threat to peace and security through joint enforcement actions (military demonstrations, military blockades, etc.).

Thus, museum peace*building* practices often act as certain peace*keeping* forces to relieve military tensions and to tame violence. In this way, peace is positioned in museum presentations rather in the form of a triumphant end to a war, or in acknowledgement of a victorious event or a meaningful truce. Here the value of peace is involuntarily replaced by the value of war. And this is understandable, for the voice of war is loud and intrusive.

However, violence does not stop in a turbulent world and it can turn into attacks on heritage and cultural symbols; thus crimes are committed not only in relation to people, but also with regard to monuments. In this way, the past is increasingly being targeted by the present. Examples include the destruction by the Taliban of the monumental Buddha statues in Bamiyan (Afghanistan, 2001), the barbaric destruction by ISIS militants of the World Heritage sites in Palmyra (Syria, 2015), the devastation of the Mosul Museum (Iraq, 2015), the bulldozing of the ancient city of Nimrud (Iraq, 2015), and many others acts of vandalism. The struggle against the continuation of cultural heritage, or the history of modern vandalism, through the destruction of facts, chronicles, conceptualizations and presentations should be also cleverly (advisedly) documented and picturized (presented/ screened) in current museum practices.

One of the most dangerous challenges to modern culture is the globalizing syndrome of value disorientation. Modernity is increasingly being positioned as an era of substitution, mixing, and destroying values. Moreover, in this process of the total mixing of values, the promotion of peace is often accompanied by the expansion of what can be considered the 'culture of war'. Value disorientation is a "crisis of differences" as stated by René Girard (1972), when meanings are blurred, concepts are substituted, and values (meanings) are distorted. This refers to the loss or violation of guiding values, morals, customs, etc., which are the basis of society and civil action. This is vividly expressed in dominant museum practices depicting war and peace. People think of peace through images of war, and they subsequently turn to war by recalling images of peace. All of this confuses museum visitors. Peace perceived only as the other side of war is guided by the principle '*Si vis pacem, para bellum*' ('If you want peace, prepare for war'). In this statement a path to security and well-being is proposed, but as a trap for a peace based on Baudrillard's ideology of a happiness that is, in fact, absolutely unhappy. Thus the representational and cognitive distortions of our conditioned consciousness are always guided in current museums of peace by images of war and violence. Here, it is not peace but war that is presented as a more spectacular and exciting type of activity and museum display, although it should be the other way around.

In fact, currently, images and stories of war significantly prevail in modern culture over peacekeeping pictures. Proof of this can be found in the fact that the number of internet queries (by Google) with the words *war* and *military* exceeds almost 2.5 times the number of queries with the words *peace* and *peaceful,* and there are far more museums of war and victims of violence than museums dedicated to the culture of peace. For example, the European Museums Network[1] lists 4175 Military and Army Museums versus only 951 Peace Museums (the results of online search queries). In addition, even peace museums included in these searches traditionally present mainly scenes of war and violence in their exhibits.

Nonetheless, there are museums truly dedicated to the culture of peace. With regard to the museumification of the culture of peace, it is necessary to distinguish between two important divergent and simultaneous attitudes and actions: 1) collecting and presenting constructive examples of peacemaking allows the peace museum to retain positive experiences of the past (heritage), whereas 2) the deployment of heritage in the direction of modernity—through exhibitions to the public/audience—makes it possible to generate new values in order to address the pressing problems of contemporary culture. The dual focus of museum activities—in the memorial past and the actual present— makes the peace museum not only a platform for versatile and effective cooperation between groups, but also an extremely important and effective tool for social transformations.

After all, when social and cultural practices change, that which does not change grows in value, and often becomes heritage. When everything in society is split, disrupted, and fragmented, those elements of heritage that connect people provide comfort and thereby grow in value. In other words, there are human aspirations to get closer and cooperate with each other, and in times of crisis, elements of shared communal heritage support resilience. In the design of museum peacemaking activities, it is therefore necessary to show two sets of values: those which perform functions for the *retention* of culture (values of constant significance) and those that perform functions for the *promotion* of culture (values of innovative nature/ character).

The values of constant significance include both the tangible and intangible. They are associated with, for example, memorial artefacts, collections, archives, traditional representation within exhibits, knowledge and experience, universal human values, ceremonial-symbolic actions, social stereotypes of behaviour, and customary functional-target settings. Alternatively, the values of innovative nature/character are intangible, and include, among other practices and programs, creative actions, form-building visual-communicative experimentation, subject-attributive openness and mobility, new dialogues with artefacts, broad social involvement, principles of participation and co-participation, new information and technological methods of object screening, art-design solutions, language, and event design.

In such a splitting of cultural values, it is important to compensate for the loss of cultural property (including heritage lost through war) by "increasing the value of what did not have it before" (Groys 2015, 134). This is a process of value regeneration and it allows curators to talk about two vectors in the cultural valuation of peacemaking artefacts: 1) peace museum objects (artefacts of heritage) that have been incorporated into collections, and which were attached to everyday life pre-war, and 2) those samples of contemporary everyday culture which are now attached to the peace museum, thus acquiring a new status with a cultural value. Collections can therefore take on new meanings when being presented through innovative peace museum exhibitions. In other words: even though the past may be filled with death, in museums the future can be seen as positive, with new cultural values generated. And all of these values should focus on peace, not on war.

Methods and background in the study of peace museums and heritage

The theoretical proposition: question formulation and basic proposals

The modern peace museum strives to be a communicative laboratory and institution for the preservation and cultivation of successful visual practices for the exhibition of and instruction in experiences of the past. However, there is a need to highlight the cultural meanings within visualizing memory, especially those that are revealed through creative communication strategies. Such a communicative shift would significantly expand the boundaries of usual museum activities and thereby carry out a transition from the narrow framework of only display in cases to actual projects of live visual creativity, all in order to appeal to a wider audience and to be more effective in the mission of promoting peace. Such a re-formulation of presentation allows us to put forward a hypothesis that a modern peace museum can become more successful in its socially representative mission through new innovative, actual creative practices. To accomplish this, it's important to transform the meaning of museum objects by cultivating new communicative strategies and visual contexts aimed at linking together the best patterns, ideas, and concepts of the past, including the need for peace, in order to face the urgent challenges of modernity.

This change is very timely. At present in modern museum design, there is a post-conceptual paradigmatic shift towards a culturalization (i.e. filling with culture) of the concept of peace. Here we can observe practices where each artefact is part of a great story, is an element in a historical narrative, and is also a provider of and inspiration for cultural meanings (texts). This post-conceptual intellectual turn, a new understanding of peacemaking, has freed the artefacts used to promote peacemaking from their habitual specific existence

(Peter Osborne 2013) and disavowed their sacral symbolic confinement, extending the subject-aesthetic and socio-communicative properties of things to the entire system of the life activity of culture. If in the past a museum exhibit was perceived only as a group of static, sacral, elite artefacts within an exhibition presentation, then today the same exhibit may be increasingly positioned as a communicator, a recorder of important messages and a participant within an actual conversation: in effect, a co-creator and transformer. Exhibits within a museum in this case are storytellers, initiators, and designers that motivate viewers, prompting audience members to absorb and interpret stories through their own experiences and social creativity.

In peace museums in particular, it is important to pose the question of how peace is actually introduced within the museum itself, and by what object articulations, ideological discussions, discourses and narratives is peace presented and promoted in the modern museum space? And how can peace museums better present the concept of peace to promote peace? The answer is to creatively and innovatively present and visualize the culture of peace through new exhibition technologies.

The peace museum as a cultural reality and a subject of knowledge

The concept of a peace museum should be viewed as a cultural reality in which the artefacts of peacemaking are gathered into a certain memorial-specified visual composition. This composition is built into a collection of stories, events, and portraits which serve as a way of publicly demonstrating and relaying socially significant messages. In this way, a peace museum is a specific social institution for the cultivation of knowledge, experience, and values of peacemaking, as well as for providing instructive examples of ways of viewing historical events and overcoming modern wars and conflicts. Each peace museum is unique in that it is created in a specific society and functions in a specific cultural environment in accordance with the prevailing mental attitudes, stereotypes of perception, and behaviour. For this reason, every peace museum cannot be understood outside of the cultural and national contexts. Without taking these contexts into account, a modern peace museum cannot achieve operational effectiveness.

It is not just peace museums that are and should be changing. Peace museums are part of a greater transformation in the museum world. The modern museum is undergoing radical transformations in the ways and practices for the presentation and interpretation of artefacts, including in exhibition strategies. The transition to a new communicative space is being traced (seen/ targeted) in which museum exhibit pieces (artefacts) will perform not only memorial and educational functions but will also be included in a more complex process of object-symbolic exchange and artistic design. In this process, the status of a thing changes and the imperative of creativity of action comes to the fore (Bishop 2013; Groys 2015; Harman 2005; Ionesov and Ionesov 2015; Norris and Tisdale 2013; Simon 2010). The most sensitive to these ongoing changes are those museums that are called upon to articulate and relay through their exhibits socially significant topics, including war and peace, violence and peacemaking, crisis and viability. In their efforts, there is a need to clarify what is meant by the culture of war and peace, and how to manage the artefacts of peacekeeping in relation to modern museum practices. These issues have already been the subject of consideration for many researchers of museum peacemaking practices (Anzai, Apsel and Mehdi 2008; Apsel 2016; Barrett and Apsel 2012; van den Dungen 2016; van den Dungen and Yamane 2015; Yamane, 2006).

The task posed is to re-qualify the concepts of war and peace in the context of cultural knowledge (Apsel 2016; Barrett and Apsel 2012; Bedford 2014; Ionesov and Ionesov 2015, 2017 Ionesov 2018a, 2018b, 2019; Jenkins 2006; Pachter and Landry 2001; Schirch 2004; Simon 2017). Researchers, in general, emphasize the need to progress to new communicative strategies in designing the peacemaking process, and to utilize the relevant technologies of visual modelling in the creative representation of peace as a cultural value. Numerous authors further point out the significance of expanding the art-object and eventful screening of the communication continuity in which things and people will act as participants of a big conversation about the pressing needs of the present (Bensaid 2011; Carey 1989; Engelkamp, Roepstorff and Spencer 2020; Harman 2005; Genoway 2006; Ionesov and Ionesov 2015; Norris and Tisdale 2013; Roberts 1997; Schirch 2004; Simon 2010; Smith 2006; Sontag 2003; van den Dungen and Yamane 2015; Yamane 2009). In particular, numerous academic studies focus on the social aspects of multicultural creativity in education and communication, and the need to provide techniques for relating to contemporary society (Anderson 2012; Groys 2015; Hein 2012; Ionesov and Ionesov 2014; Yamane 2006).

The publications and projects of the main strategist and coordinator of museum activities in the field of peacemaking—the International Network of Museums for Peace/INMP (see https://www.inmp.net/)—significantly contribute to the study of the museumification of peace. The INMP's activities unite many museums and organizations from around the world in cultivating ideas of peace and non-violence by accumulating both theoretical and practice-oriented research concerning the problems of peace, and regularly holds international forums and thematic discussions on the development of museum peacemaking movements. Importantly, the INMP has managed to form and present its culture through its recognizable image, its philosophy of the world order, its traditions, social and artistic practices, educational projects, publications, symbolic attributes, and even its language of professional creativity. The creation of INDP's unique culture is in itself a great asset because the organization has developed necessary and effective tools for the implementation of its peacemaking mission and for the promotion of socially significant initiatives (Ionesov and Ionesov 2017; van den Dungen and Yamane 2015).

Peacemaking in museums and peacemaking for bridging cultures

What can or should be the role of peacemaking in museums? Peacemaking, the process of bringing about peace, can involve the museum through a variety of relevant social projects. These projects start a conversation about the pressing challenges of our time and invite the museum to participate in their solution. Thus, peacemaking as a culture of peace not only expands the communicative space of a modern museum, but also enriches the museum with new social practices and valuable experiences for the rapprochement of cultures. For example, every transformation in the relationship between object and human has several semantic projections. Every heritage artefact exhibited in a museum contains at least two instructive (cognitive) stories. *The primary story* is the main one; it talks about the genesis and existence of the artefact in a specific historical culture (time). *The secondary story* describes the process of regeneration and the transfer of the artefact into a museum space (transformation of historical artefact into exhibit). Each of these stories is filled with a series of events and experiences, often dramatic and educational. Therefore, every exhibition artefact has its own unique stories of peacemaking, which together can inspire new dialogues and subsequently build bridges between cultures.

The diversity of cultures is a necessary condition for such interactions. These interactions enable people to transmit to one another the best social knowledge, experiences, values, and practices of their culture. Yet each nation has its own visions, interests, manners, and ambitions, which are very unique and often do not coincide with others (Lewis 1996; Triandis 1994). Globalization through technical expansion and world market order has levelled out national differences yet has led to a resistance of cultures (Ionesov 2014), to a clash of civilizations (Huntington 2011), and to a crisis of differences (Girard 1972). These conflicts have divided people even more. In these conditions and situations, it has become necessary to look for new ways of bridging cultures and for peacebuilding. In this process, the creative abilities of national cultures are very valuable, and are best employed for peacemaking practices. However, social interaction between cultures is useful only when it cultivates peace in all its diverse and mutually beneficial social projections. Peace which is poorly visible can't be effective. It is heritage artefacts that can and should act as a powerful means for the presentation and visualization of cultures and that can perform as symbols for peace. A museum includes the best examples of heritage in its communication space, and in this way, has the potential to promote the rapprochement of cultures through dialogue and the co-creation of diverse traditions, visions, and attributions.

Obviously, there can't be the same patterns for the cultivation of peace within different societies. Indeed, ignoring the variations within different ethnic groups' perceptions of cultural values can have the opposite effect from the given intention, and such oversights can lead to disappointing results. As Clotaire Rapaille (2015, 17, 20) notes:

> Cultures differ from country to country. But not many people understand that this is why people from different cultures perceive the same information differently. The imprinted images vary from culture to culture. And if you find their source, somehow decipher the elements of culture and discover what emotions and meanings are hidden behind them, you can understand a lot about human behavior and cross-cultural differences.

The differences in values can be illustrated through a contrast between Anglo-Saxon and Central Asian[2] understandings. The Anglo-Saxon world (for all the cultural specificity of its peoples) is dominated by living experience and values based on European tradition (Roman Law): what is legal is desirable for a person (Triandis 1994). The European mentality (despite the obvious cultural differences with Central Asia) is largely based on Enlightenment ideals. Here, peace is used instrumentally and pragmatically as a social principle of conflict resolution. Peace acts as a registrar of taming violence, overcoming hostility, and ending war.

In contrast, the mentality of Central Asian peoples offers a different order of priorities: what is recognized as a custom and therefore desirable is legal. That is, central to social relations and cultural order are traditional customs and their symbolic values. This difference is due to Central Asians' historical experiences and social adaptations, religious traditions, and mental perception of life order. In this geographic area the peacekeeping process will be effective if it is accompanied by vivid aesthetic articulations and ceremonial actions, as well as if it is confirmed by examples of collective experience and recognition. Ceremonial mediation provides the necessary detachment and distance from life's vital problems and thus softens for people a direct confrontation with conflicting reality. Here, everyday cultural reality surrounding a person is not perceived directly, but through images of peace—by means of metaphors, allegories, and symbolism (Ionesov 2019, 341-342).

Alternatively, for people from the Indian subcontinent and their unique cultures, peace is what pleases and inspires the here and now. Peace appears to each person not as something purposefully transformed, but as something immutable, recognized and protected. All of these examples demonstrate elements that must be taken into account when promoting trans-cultural practices of peacekeeping in Asian communities.

Nonetheless, even an impeccable knowledge of another culture does not always allow the correct emphasis and understanding of specific values and perceptions of its nature, and quite often misunderstandings may lead to semantic distortions and false conclusions. The wrong arrangement of exhibits, an arbitrary combination of historical and thematic plots, an ill-conceived colour palette, and violations of the principles of spatial perception of museum objects, are all among the possibilities of issues that may conflict with the traditional experience in the worldview of a particular ethnic group and lead to incorrect decisions. For example, at the Museum of Humanistic Anthropology at the Samara Institute of Culture, the representatives of the local Uzbek community were invited to visit two halls with identical peacemaking materials but decorated in different ways. The first hall was decorated in bright ornamental traditions of *suzani* (embroidered decorative textiles) and quaint but interrelated artistic subjects. In the second hall, there were strict geometric and disjointed figures—separately standing triangles, squares, and trapezes. Visitors were asked to evaluate which hall had more to do with peace, goodness, and creativity, and which one caused anxiety. Almost all of the representatives of the Uzbek community definitely chose the first hall—the one with plant (floral/vegetable) motifs contrasting but connected with each other and ornamented in a colour combination of dark pink and black on a white background. These colour and ornamental compositions were associated in their minds with the comforts of house and home as the collectivist mutual warm colours of *suzani*. Whereas the second hall—the one with cold and monotonous geometric shapes—rather caused anxiety, loneliness, and protest. We see the same differences in the external design of medieval architectural structures in Central Asia. They are distinguished by bright external decorativeness reminiscent of *suzani* plots (in contrast to the stricter external design of buildings in Western European architecture). These designs can be found on walls, minarets and domes, which are all decorated with ceramic tiles of various colours and ornaments. A good example of this style can be found on the richly decorated external walls of Shah-i-Zinda ensemble in Samarkand.

These are examples that expressly link ornamental motifs with cultural identity. In a further study, we tested the perception of ornamental compositions (taken from the original samples of traditional clothing) by various ethnic groups in Samara. Pictures with different ornaments were distributed to students representing Mordovians, Tatars, Chuvashes, Russians and Kalmyks. As it turned out, the preferred choice of students in most cases coincided with the original historical ornaments belonging to their ethnic group.

Another study further confirms my findings. At the Samara Society for Cultural Studies, the participants in the multicultural training "Culture and social behavior" represented two national groups—the Tajik and the Kazakh. They were asked to choose from a large set of subjects and things that in their perception are associated with peace and well-being. The Tajik group selected artefacts with predominantly floral images (motifs), whilst the Kazakh group preferred zoomorphic images. Each group chose exactly the subjects that are fixed in their ethnic consciousness and archetypes of the worldview. Horticultural scenes (trees, flowers, cereals, leaves, fruits, etc.) appeared to be closer to Tajiks as sedentary farmers. The animal world of horses, sheep, deer, birds etc. is more understandable and more akin to Kazakhs as nomadic pastoralists.

While promoting museum practices of the culture of peace through new experiences and communicative-symbolic design, it is advisable to compare and synthesize the various traditions of peacemaking since no one culture has all the necessary set of conciliatory means. Often what is lacking in one society can be found and taken from another. Mastering the lessons of social reconciliation between cultures through this process not only enriches the arsenal of peacekeeping tools for each, but also is a useful tool for the prevention of xenophobia and to develop a culture of dialogue and tolerance. This is also true for individuals. In cross-cultural communication, a person, comparing himself/herself with other people, is better aware of his/her individuality, and the identity of his/her culture. He/she may feel the possession of something, some value, concept, or idea that can be useful to him/her and others in their search for peace and harmony. After all, our own culture is always better seen from the other side. Just as in order to see your side of the road, you need to look at it from the other side. In this perspective, different cultures are similar to traffic on the road—to see the way on your left, you have to go to the right side and vice versa. Here, the native becomes such on the side of the alien. By appreciating the other, peacebuilding processes can inspire and educate cultures from different countries in the instructive practices of rapprochement and reconciliation of peoples. For instance, the life experiences of the peoples of Central Asia can teach individuals from other regions to contemplate and pacify culture through beauty, rituals, and customs, and European cultural values can be transferred to many Asian communities and be useful for the creativity of action, appreciation of diversity, sparking individual creative activity, and instilling greater levels of freedom.

At the same time, the museumification of peace is an extremely specific and delicate process. Here it is impossible to ignore the specifics of each individual region, national mentality, value preferences, and ethnic stereotypes of the behaviour of people, by whom and for whom, first of all, the museum has been created. Plus, what has been accepted in traditional cultures is often rejected in the technogenic society—that which reconciles people in the Central Asian communities can be alarming, divisive, disconnecting, and unacceptable to individuals in European culture.

This is likely to be the case in other places as well, given that each culture has its own vitality and set of tools for survival. Therefore, the best tools for overcoming obstacles to understanding should be mastered by different cultures. As Mahatma Gandhi (1921, 170) accurately remarked: "I do not want my house to be walled in on all sides and my windows to be stuffed. I want all the cultures of all lands to be blown about my house as freely as possible. But I refuse to be blown off my feet by any".

Two functions of peacebuilding activities in a museum

The presented theoretical provisions are necessary for understanding what modern peacekeeping practice is, what is happening to peace museums today, and how to make the peace museum a real participant in cultural transformations. With regard to the social-cultural context of the topic under development, and taking into account the above, it is important to further define the basic principles that are necessary to consider the place and role of museum practices in promoting the culture of peace and non-violence.

The social mission of peace museums is determined by the two functions of peacebuilding activities: *protective-memorial* and *creative-transforming*. The *protective-memorial* function directs the peacebuilding practice of preserving the memory of the war and its victims and on relaying information for an instructive experience. Here, the museum peacebuilding practice seemingly keeps time, inherits culture, warns about the danger of the recurrence of wars, and teaches lessons from history, all with the purpose of transferring valuable knowledge to the next generations. The *creative-transforming* function is aimed at generating and promoting a culture of peace in all its diverse and socially significant projects. Through these functions, peacemaking acts as an actual cultural practice enabling the peace museum to become a real participant in the essential need of social transformation. Modern museum peacebuilding practices themselves can be examples and catalysts of social change only through communicative shifts and the construction of new ways for participation in communication with society. According to the American museum expert Nina Simon (former Executive Director of the Santa Cruz Museum of Art & History), museum participation provides valuable civil and cognitive experience. "Participation is a strategy that addresses specific problems" (Simon 2010, iii; 2017, 421). The combined efforts of thousands of institutions utilizing participation as a strategy for peace can change the world.

Necessary conditions for the effective promotion of peace in museums

The necessary condition for the effective promotion of the museum-exhibition culture of peace is a transition to new informative and art-communicative techniques for the visual and interpretive presentation of the artefacts of peacemaking. The museum, in this case, not only must create a new space for a meaningful dialogue with exhibits for visitors, but also must include museum visitors in its co-creation, offering them an opportunity to share their empathy and experience and become participants in the live peacebuilding process. But in order to realize and experience peace, first of all, they must understand the conflict depicted. No matter how horrifying the perception of the images of war, each visitor will remain helpless without understanding what lies behind it. "We truly can't imagine what it was like. We can't imagine how dreadful, how terrifying war is; and how normal it becomes. Can't understand, can't imagine", writes Susan Sontag (2003, 97- 98).

Peace museums must create new dialogues between objects and viewers

Each peace museum, one way or another, embodies examples of dialogue and interpenetration of cultures since a museum is a place where people interact with the artefacts of culture. It is important to be able to release these examples (museum exhibits) from physical imprisonment, to awaken their voices, to fill them with text, to hear their stories and to translate them into the solution of urgent tasks of our time. However, this process should create new communication continuity (distance) between a person and things as exhibits of an exhibition presentation. Yet Jean Baudrillard, following Régis Debre, believes that "we live in a completely new environment, and we are threatened not by the loss of connection with the world or alienation from it, but, on the contrary, a total immersion in reality" (2006, 86). He continues that excessive proximity to a thing destroys its symbolism and does not allow it to properly communicate with the viewer, distorting its meaning and purpose. According to Baudrillard (2006, 24):

> We live in a society that does not completely separate the substance from us, and we experience alienation, not because we are allegedly separated from it … Our misfortune to which we have condemned ourselves consists, on the contrary, in excessive proximity to things, as a result of which in our society everything—both they and we—appears to be an immediate reality. And this excessively real world is obscene.

The point is that there is often now no communicative field for effective dialogue between the object and the museum visitor. There is an object addressed to the viewer, and there is a viewer addressed to the object. The lack of context between them eliminates the necessary distance between them and thus does not allow them to conduct a dialogue. When you get too close to the screen, the shapes and plots blur and become indistinguishable. The movement stops. Obscenity here is the washing out, the denudation of meaning, sense, distinction, that is, of touching a pure, immovable substance. There must be a cultural context between a person and an object that connects the past (historical exhibit) and the present (urgent experience, knowledge and feeling). This context is created by means of art, communicative participation, and exchange. Thanks to this coupling, the visitor's meeting with the object becomes an event, i.e. a co-being, a meeting of two communicators—the exhibit and the viewer.

Meanwhile, in modern culture people and things are in unprecedented proximity to each other. This is especially noticeable in the museum space. The visitor to the museum of the culture of peace at times is overwhelmed by so many exhibit objects on socially sensitive themes that when he/she comes into contact with them, not only are the instructive images and plots of historical events erased, but also the voices of the artefacts of peacemaking—their voices, messages, texts—are disregarded. Because where there is no distance, there is no boundary line (line of demarcation), and that is necessary (required) for distinction and communication. The consequence is a blurring of values and a cessation of communication. However, with space for interpretation, the communicative-symbolic nature of an artefact will allow it to be in demand in the process of transformation, and valuable in modern experiences for the re-qualification of culture.

Peace museums as centres for cultural activities and creative practices

There are several reasons to consider a peace museum as both a cultural activity and a creative practice. First, a peace museum acts as an institution for the cultivation of experiences and social practices by incorporating the artefacts of peacemaking in a dialogue with people. Second, unlike standard interpretations, the object expositions of a peace museum can be useful to society only when they manage to creatively link to the past and update it with current experience. Third, leaving and exposing the artefacts of peacemaking as only exhibits of the past, we, thus, conserve and even sacrifice them, depriving them of vital communion with modernity. We are speaking about a dangerous syndrome of the discharge of a commemorative thing from life's daily practice.

The problem is that museums design museum changes slowly, and therefore many new exhibits quickly lose their relevance and become outdated. Thus, the artefacts of peacemaking may form a lifeless environment and a communicative gap can emerge in the dialogue between visitors and the museum exhibit.

However, artefacts are capable of transforming the space themselves, but only if they are creatively curated in the context of communication (Popova 2002).

In the opinion of Graham Harman (2012), two entities influence one another only by meeting on the interior of a third where they exist side by side until something happens that allows them to interact. That is, a museum exhibit should not be shown statically, but through various communicative and historical contexts in dialogue with the viewer. And this is particularly relevant for museum exhibits in which samples of a culture of peace and non-violence are displayed. After all, there is nothing that so strongly distorts the sample's virtue as an inappropriate and arbitrary presentation. Any gap between the artefact of peacemaking, visual image, aesthetic form, context, and presentation method leads to a wrong, distorted perception and creates the very "gap, through which enters cruelty and violence" (Pomerants 2013, 10).

The culture of non-violence and of peacemaking is addressed to the innermost human feelings, to the living contact between the past and present, national and universal, social and artistic, personal and planetary. Thus, modern communicative practices appear in a creative society in the form of new dramatic arts and as a culture of participation. The multimedia revolution adds to this by putting forward not only efficient technologies of interaction between subjects and objects of culture, but also by constructing for them trans-subject narratives and scenarios for participation in events, thus offering various combinations of interactivity and motivating a search for new forms of creativity and transforming alternatives (Pachter and Landry 2003).

It is critical to move from the symbolic sacralization of peace to a cognitive and creative understanding of peace: from peace as a metaphor, trite and unheeded, to peace as a critical urgent necessity for humanity. The question is how can this be successfully achieved? Perhaps, in search of a response to this question, we should appeal to innovative technologies of peace museum representation and ability as a new creative strategy of visual communication.

How can museums make the concept of peace more accessible, more interactive? What concrete steps are necessary in order to achieve that? Experience shows that it is more successfully brought about through art and new technologies—art-cultural installations, peace-performances, visual phenomena, peace-marketing, media projects, virtual reality, etc. Effective practices of peacemaking activities are the creative projects of the Peace Museum in Vienna, and for example, its social art project "Windows for Peace". This so-called street museum is open 24 hours a day for residents and guests of the Austrian capital. Windows for Peace displays various art posters and photos with brief biographies of peacemaking heroes who changed the world for the better. It is a kind of peace message for everyone and an inspiring stimulus to believe in oneself and become a participant of social transformation. In this instance, the experience of the past becomes an incentive for the present.

What are better examples of peacemaking through museumification? The creative activity of the International Red Cross and Red Crescent Museum's "The Humanitarian Adventure" is an exceptional example of how the contemporary peace museum can be an active stimulation for social transformations.[3] In this museum, the values of peace are being created and displayed in a large, architectonics section of the exhibition complex. Peace is not the only concept exhibited, as there are other themes presented, such as aesthetic landscapes, the interaction of people and objects, new colour palettes, innovative planning solutions, and even explanations of the properties of construction materials. In this museum, creative communication begins with architecture that includes approaches to the museum complex itself. Inside, the museum has a pleasant environment, and the exhibition space has been well utilized, with detailed information provided about the exhibits in a variety of interesting ways, all in an effort to generate greater responses from visitors. Here is what can be deemed 'a communication mobility in action' as a variety of types of open and lively conversations—responsive and visual—are in actual dialogue with the public.

Museum peacemaking experiences in various cultural practices

The social imperative of the museum's communicative strategy is to provide the general public with access to artefacts in order to use them in their creative activities. Such an approach allows museum visitors to become involved in co-creation, express what they are concerned about, give themselves the opportunity to change what they want, and eventually be able to see and implement it in the context of their most serious individual experiences.

This appears to be relevant to the Wing Luke Museum of the Asian Pacific American Experience (Seattle, USA), which functions as a public platform for participation and change. The exhibitions are designed according to the method of co-creation, thus maintaining a sense of co-participation, belonging and co-ownership. In this museum, the process of co-creation begins with the development of an open model of the exhibition. Initially, each visitor to the museum offers their own project, which the museum staff then consider according to its importance and social significance. The goal is that the final exhibit design should represent a social value and be accessible and useful for the widest possible audience (Simon 2017, 322-326). It refers to the so-called open museums (using the practice of visual-communicative scaffolding), in which the artefacts of co-creation acquire their status of museum exhibits by means of their transfer from the present (made by the hands of visitors) to the past (museum piece). In other words, here the artefacts do not translate history into modernity (the practice of conventional museums), but the modern items, which are actually created, are interpreted into the field of the commemorative as valuable, socially important life experiences that need to be preserved in order to be passed on to others.

The political and cultural context of heritage for understanding and defining peace

Artefacts of peacemaking, in particular, express experiences of the culture of nonviolence and reconciliation, and therefore they become more important in urgent and dramatic situations. For what is peace if not an approximation of reality? For this reason, it is important that museums should not narrow but expand their presentations of the diversity of life. This allows the museum visitor to comprehend the concept of *peace* with lively aesthetic images and experiences, to make it attractive and recognizable, and to encourage imaginative thinking and creativity. Examples of this are several new creative initiatives of the Samara Society for Cultural Studies "Artefact—Cultural Diversity": the project "Smells of Peace", where visitors to the exhibition are invited to find an aroma combination to various peacemaking themes and landscapes. It turns out that different manifestations of *peace* can have not only different colour compositions, but also aroma associations. Another project was the creative experience "Create your own street of the Peace". Here young people virtually build into the famous places of the city of Samara, thematic avenues, streets, parks, lanes, and squares with corresponding names, such as "Music of the Peace", "Humanistic Order", "Expected Harmony", "Faces of the Peace", "Diversity in Unity", etc. Such cultural practices are becoming in demand outside the museum itself: they are often included in the creative industries to ennoble the multicultural urban environment of a modern city. Other art-social and educational-cultural projects can be useful examples of effective practices: "The Peace Autograph" (by Samarkand Museum of Peace and Solidarity, Uzbekistan) (Ionesov and Ionesov, 2014); "Artefacts that Change the World: from Small Steps to Big Changes", "The Games that Reconcile Us", "Culture of Peace's Personalities: People Who Changed the World" (by Samara Cultural Society "Artefact—Cultural Diversity", Russia), "Peace Mask Project / Japan-Korea)", "What color is peace" (Kyoto Museum for World Peace) and a number of creative projects initiated by the International Network of Museums for Peace (Ionesov 2018a).

  Despite the fact that the museum is a fairly closed space, its goal is to exhibit the achievements and experiences of people. To do so it must correspond to the diversity of life, linking cultures and traditions through dialogue with past and present. Such diversity is impossible without the democratization of history, memory, and heritage, just as diversity is impossible without diversification of functions, methods, and contents of museum activities. It is critical, therefore, that the culture of peace, launched and proposed by museum practitioners, re-work and re-present the reality of life in all its diversity. For this reason, peace museums, in particular, must be more direct and intentional in trying to match the diversity of life. Importantly, the more culturally diverse specifications are represented in peace museums, the more effective will be their influence in responding to the political challenges of a changing world.

A good example of the cultivation of peacemaking practices by means of art is the project "Missing Peace Art Space"[4] that has been developed by the *Creative Resistance* group since February 2014, in Dayton, Ohio, United States. The project participants are invited to provide the missing elements in the work of art put before them, so as to inspire another artist to continue their creative work. An example of this is beneath a picture of a soldier, someone added the words "You are not my enemy". Visitors take great interest in this method of promoting peace as it highlights the contradictions and divisions in humanity's fractured society at the same time as encouraging pursuance of ideas of co-operation, understanding, rational thinking, and acceptance that we are but one people, one human race.

Other examples of the appeal to a culture of peace in museum designs through the representation of diversity are also noteworthy. The Samarkand Peace Museum has been transformed using a variety of creative practices, expanding not only the geography of international relations and professional cooperation, but also inspiring its partners to new peace-building actions and scientific forums. In this regard, it is also worth mentioning the scientific-educational Russian-Uzbek project "Heritage and Modernity in the Dialogue of Cultures from the Volga to the Zeravshan: Samara and Samarkand" (2016-2017). This project is a continuation of the previously presented edition of *A Concise Encyclopedia of Foreign Samarkandiana: Culture Linking the World"* (Ionesov and Ionesov, 2014). The main mission of this forum is to promote rapprochement and reconciliation of cultures, relying on historical and modern artefacts of the peacemaking of the two cities, Samara and Samarkand.

Useful cultural developments can also be considered, such as socio-educational projects, as demonstrated by Samara cultural experts through the "Museum of Home Collections", "Ethno Look", and "Teach Me Peace". Thanks to these initiatives, various peace-building presentations, exhibitions and performances in cultural studies are regularly held at the museum sites of Samara City. For example, the "Museum of Home Collections" acts as a temporary exhibition based on family stories and shows how to build peace and harmonize with difficult relationships among people. "Ethno Look" is an annual festival of ethnic cultures, where participants, using various artistic techniques (songs, dances, stories, performances, etc.), share humanistic traditions (images and stories of beauty, virtue, and appeasement) of their national community. And "Teach Me Peace" is a cultural project for students in which each participant not only prepares an example of a visual description of a real conflict, but also develops scenarios of its taming, offering techniques for preventing violence and reconciliation of cultures.

The partnership project "Flowers of Peace" and the accompanying annual flower festival (2010-2015) in Samarkand became a new experience in the design of the aesthetics of peacemaking. The concept of peace here was interpreted through a festival, which like a cultural plant, must be patiently cultivated and protected. In this project, a museum took on a partner—the House-Museum of the poet and educator Orif Gulhani—which prepared, especially for the festival, over 4,000 copies of 30 varieties of flowers and ornamental plants—and the plants, as seeds of peace, were distributed free of charge to all comers. Yet the plants came with an indispensable condition—the participant should promise within the next year to give plant shoots to ten of his/her acquaintances. Does this not remind us of the specifics of the peace-building process: if you do not transfer peace to another person, it will not come to him/her by itself? Here comes to mind the Eastern wisdom: take what is given and give back what could not be taken (instruction of Sufis). It's necessary to learn to cultivate peace like flowers, to notice it, artistically decorate it, and give it to others. To some extent, peace attracts reality through beauty (Ionesov and Ionesov 2015).

Thus, peacemaking as a social practice has its own recognizable and attractive attributions—lines, contours, colours, shapes, smell, style, manners, experiences—in other words, its own social-artistic language, its own culture. Why not deploy all these benefits (opportunities) and resources in the sphere of museum design? The culture of peace is not a process of passive contemplation, but an active, life-affirming practice. Its mission is to generate new values: a word that acts; a smell that has a shape; a colour that sounds. In this regard, there is a need to create new peace museums that could capture the most diverse social and aesthetic values of human life. Such new peacemaking platforms could be, for example, museums of charity, museums of virtue or goodwill, museums of generosity and hospitality, or museums of universal responsiveness. Provided that they will function not as sacred memorials, but as open laboratories for creativity of action, co-participation, and co-creation for addressing the urgent problems of our time and thereby promoting peace.

Conclusion

Our overall perception of what a modern peace museum is and its possibilities to change the world for the better are evolving. A new vision is emerging of peace museums that not only possess unique historical collections of artefacts of peace and provide vast experiences for taming violence, but that also focus on the most sensitive topics of peacekeeping activity.

This is very meaningful, since is known that our surroundings influence our behaviour. In museum communications, it is therefore important to distinguish, interpret and transform the world of objects into a dialogue with the viewer. Through this dialogue of peacemaking, a museum exhibit acquires a different status than just a collection of material substances. Exhibits become speaking characters, broadcasters of important social messages, that invite museum visitors to think, compare, connect and create.

Museum exhibits should, as a result, not contain passive and static objects which are displayed for contemplation. It is important from time to time to set them in motion, to build a new composition, to transform the context, and fill it with art design and social dramaturgy. The artefacts should be rediscovered each visit by the viewer through communicative shifts, visual interconnecting, and mobile art installations. According to Nina Simon, such constant change of an exposition will supersede the traditional storage and demonstration of exhibits, and multi-voiced content will appear in the place of the didactic catalogues (2017, 420).

Significantly, presentations in the museum should not be simply to be looked at—their purpose should be to encourage observers to empathize, to keep historical events in memory, to connect the past and the present, to understand and respect others, to respond to the challenges of our time, and to take responsibility for what is happening today.

It is hopeful that the role of communicative practices for co-participation and co-creation in peace museum activities will further increase in the future. These new practices can serve as valuable routes toward better forms of communication, tolerance, and mutual understanding, creating platforms for the removal of social phobias and prejudices. And how and to whom heritage will be of value will depend on how the modern peace museum presents the information, and, ultimately, how their endeavours will impact peace in our turbulent world. The proposed ideas and specific examples of effective peacemaking activities detailed in this chapter have led to a formulation of the following practical recommendations for the management of museum heritage:

1. *Make the idea of peace heritage an attractive and creative ambition in commemorative politics.* In the face of a rapidly changing world and its increasing turbulence, there is a need for effective creative practices of visualizing memory by generating new social and aesthetic experiences whereby, for example, a word begins to act, a smell

becomes visible, a colour is filled with sound, a thing gets a voice. Through this creative action and artistic transformation, along with the acceptance and use of changing values, it will be possible to promote a wider resonance of thoughts about peace among an increasingly alarmed population

2. *Be closer to life, move peace towards where it doesn't exist yet.* Be realistic with regard to the diversity of life, culture, and thinking and strive to promote peace heritage everywhere. The task is to spread a fresh cultural field of peacemaking in which peace museums will effectively demonstrate the humanistic potential of their heritage in order to encourage peacemaking thoughts and actions among a wider audience, thereby giving value to what it did not have or what still remained not obviously significant for the museum efforts. This could be achieved in two ways: 1) incorporating peace projects with social activities and areas beyond the museum itself, and: 2) alternatively, bringing to the museum-relevant examples regarding the subject of peace from everyday experiences occurring outside the museum and combining the best of them with those of the museum (Ionesov 2018a).

3. *Merge the best past practices with the best arising innovations.* Preserving the old, thinking about the new. The effective documentary and historical work of the peace museum is evidenced by the museum's ability to creatively combine tradition and innovation. After all, in order to remain relevant and valuable to people, heritage must be lively and dynamic, allowing it to change in response to stimuli, in accordance with needs or challenges in a changing environment. Artefacts of peacemaking and the strategies for their museum presentation that do not incorporate contemporary innovations nor take them into account will be ousted from cultural memory (Groys 2015, 143).

4. *Expand the art of communication in its most powerful and positive manner.* Peace is an environment and conversation. To attract and capture the interest of visitors the peace museum must present attention-grabbing exhibits that are well documented and meaningful. This will be an encouragement for individuals to question and debate various aspects of the case for peace. The museum exhibits are not performing their intended function if they do not make a positive impression.

5. *Give the culture of peace a chance to make a difference.* We should think, first and foremost, not about how to protect peace as such (with only this aspiration, as experience shows, we will never preserve it),

but about how to use its cultural heritage so that the culture of peace protects us and supports our desire to change the life for the better. The question is how to make culture of peace heritage turn into a solution for the most vital challenges of our time (Ionesov 2018a). Heritage is the application of memory to meet the current needs of a contemporary individual or community.

The practical experiences of some peace museums demonstrate that these tasks can be solved very effectively, and that good progress has been made in publicizing the urgent need for a peaceful world. Indeed, the peace museum can be a leading force in bringing about the monumental achievement of global peace. Together with promoting the case for a peaceful world, the museum should emphasize the massive benefits for humanity of a world without war. Throughout human history, wars have brought about death, destruction, and misery for millions. There must be an in-depth discussion and consensus about the cause of warfare in the present era because without rooting out the cause there will be no peace.

Thus, perpetuation of peace heritage is always a test and a challenge. We should not oversimplify the problem or excessively romanticize it. We are not yet quite ready to separate the culture of peace from the culture of war. War tends to be dressed in the clothes of a peacemaker. And sometimes, under the guise of peace, we unintentionally promote the culture of war and violence. There is too much of war in our thoughts, actions, desires, and values.

"Counter-path, that is peace, isn't it ...?" once remarked the outstanding French philosopher Jacques Derrida in his message (30 July, 2000) to the Samarkand International Museum of Peace and Solidarity. However, who said that the path against the current is impossible? After all, peace has one absolute advantage: it gives a human being a chance for salvation.

Notes

[1] http://museums.eu.

[2] I use the terms "Anglo-Saxon", "European", "Asian" and "Eastern" without any connection or hint to Orientalism as understood by E. Said or essentialist statements. For me, these terms are merely cultural concepts that characterize the lifestyle in a vast geographical area without any post-colonial, preconceived or evaluative context. We should not overestimate the meaning of such ordinary concepts ("Eastern" or "Western"), just because in some cases they are used by someone in a biased and speculative manner. I understand "Central Asia" as a recognizable cultural reality, and not as representative and ideologically opposed to the West's social reality. I use the term "Central Asian" or "European" only to describe the cultural world of the Middle East and Europe: East and

West have their own historical and cultural specifications and unique historical experiences, but they can complement each other (Triandis 1994).

³ https://www.redcrossmuseum.ch/en.

⁴ https://www.missingpeaceart.org/.

Bibliography

Anderson, Gail, ed. 2012. *Reinventing the Museum: The Evolving Conversation on the Paradigm Shift.* Lanham, Md.: Plymouth: AltaMira Press.

Anzai, Ikuro, Joyce Apsel, and Syed Sikander Mehdi, eds. 2008. "Museums for Peace: Past, Present and Future". *The Organizing Committee of the Sixth International Conference of Museums for Peace.* Kyoto (Japan): INMP, Kyoto Museum for World Peace, Ritsumeikan University.

Apsel, Joyce. 2016. *Introducing Peace Museums.* London and New York: Routledge.

Barrett, Clive and Joyce Apsel, eds. 2012. *Museums for Peace: Transforming Cultures.* Hague (The Netherlands): INMP.

Baudrillard, Jean. 2006. *Paroli. Ot Fragmenta k Tselomu* [Passwords. From the Fragment to the Whole] (In Russian). Yekaterinburg: Faktoriya.

Bedford, Leslie. 2014. *The art of museum exhibitions: How story and imagination create aesthetic experiences.* New York: Left Coast Press.

Benjamin, Walter. 2012. *Ulitsa s odnostoronnim dvizheniem. [Einbahnstraße].* Moscow: Ad Marginem Press.

Bensaid, Daniel. 2011. *Le Spectacle, stade ultime du fétichisme de la marchandise.* Fécamp, France: Éditions Lignes.

Bishop, Claire. 2013. *Radical Museology, or What's "Contemporary" in Museums of Contemporary Art?* London: Koenig Books.

———. 2014. *Radikal'naya muzeologiya, ili Tak li uzh "sovremenny" muzei sovremennogo iskusstva [Radical Museology, or What's "Contemporary" in Museums of Contemporary Art?].* – Moscow: Ad Marginem Press.

Carey, James W. 1989. *Communication as Culture: Essays on Media and Society.* London: Routledge Press.

Engelkamp, S., K. Roepstorff and A. Spencer. 2020. "Visualizing Peace – The State of the Art". *Peace and Change. A Journal of Peace Research* 45: 5-27.

Gandhi, Mahatma. 1921. Young India. Accessed 10 November, 2023. https://www.mkgandhi.org/momgandhi/chap90.htm.

———. 1947. *Harijan Journal.* Ahmedabad : Navajivan Trust.

Genoway, Hugh H., ed. 2006. *Museum philosophy for the twenty-first century.* Lanham, MD: Altamira Press.

Girard, René. 1972. *La violence et le sacré.* Paris: Éditions Bernard Grasset.

Groys, Boris. 2015. *O Novom. Opyt Ekonomiki Kultury /* [About the New. The Experience of Cultural Economics] (In Russian). Moscow: Ad Marginem Press (Garage Pro).

Harman, Graham. 2005. *Guerrilla Metaphysics: Phenomenology and the Carpentry of Things.* Chicago and La Salle, Illinois: Open Court Publishing.

————. 2012. *O zameschayuschei prichinnosti* [About substitute causality]. *Novoe literaturnoe obozrenie* 114 (2): 75–90.

Hein, George. 2012. *Progressive Museum Practice: John Dewey and Democracy.* Walnut Creek, CA: Left Coast Press.

Huntington, Samuel P. 2011. *The Clash of Civilizations and the Remaking of World Order.* New York: Simon & Schuster.

Ionesov, Vladimir I. 2014. "Soprotivlenie kultur: k osobennostyam nashego vremeni" [Resistance of Cultures: Particularities of Our Time]. In *Modernization of Culture: Ideas and Paradigms of Cultural Changes*, edited by Svetlana Solovieva and Vladimir Ionesov, 167-173. Samara: Samara State Institute of Culture.

————. 2018a. "Can Peacemaking be a Peace Maker?" *Peace Review. A Journal of Social Justice* 30 (4): 527-536.

————. 2018b. "Slipping Culture: Borders and Transitions in the Turbulent World". In *Facets of Culture in the Age of Social Transition*, 135-140. Proceedings of the All-Russian Research Conference, March 23-24, 2018. Yekaterinburg, Russia: Ural Fed University.

————. 2019. "Ideas on Peacebuilding in Asia: How to Create Peace in the Region (Reflecting the Experience of the Samarkand International Museum of Peace and Solidarity and Its Partners)". *Ristumeikan Journal of Kyoto Museum for World Peace* 20: 48-63.

Ionesov, Vladimir I., ed. 2019. *The Art Paradigms in the Time of Social Turbulence, Vol. 1-2.* Moscow-Samara: SGIK, Press House.

Ionesov, Anatoly I. and Vladimir I. Ionesov. 2014. *Malaya entsiklopediya zarubezhnoy Samarkandiany: kultura, ob'yedinyauschaya mir* [A Concise Encyclopedia of Foreign Samarkandiana: Culture Linking the World]. Samara-Samarkand: Vek #21.

————. 2015. "Muzey kak mirotvorchestvo: sposobny li artefakty kultury nas primirit?" [Museum as peacemaking: can the artefacts of culture reconcile us?] *Vestnik Chelyabinskogo gosudastvennogo universiteta*, 2: 75-82.

————. 2017. "What Can Be Done in 25 Years or the Organization that Gave Peace a Chance". *INMP Newsletter*, no. 18 (March): 59-60. Special Issue, International Network of Museums for Peace, Hague.

Jenkins, Henry. 2006. *Convergence Culture: Where Old and New Media Collide.* New York: New York University Press.

Lampedusa, Giuseppe Tomasi di. 1961. *Leopard.* Moscow: Inostrannaya literatura.

Lewis, Richard D. 1996. *When cultures collide: leading across cultures.* London: Nicholas Brealey Publishing.

Norris, Linda and Rainey Tisdale. 2013. *Creativity in Museum Practice.* London and New York: Routledge.

Osborne, Peter. 2013. *Anywhere or Not at All: Philosophy of Contemporary Art.* London: Verso.

Pachter, Marc and Charles Landry. 2001. *Culture at the Crossroads. Culture and Cultural Institutions at the Twentyfirst Century.* Comedia.

Pachter, Marc and Charles Landry. 2003. *Kultura na pereputie. Kultura i kulturnye instituty v XXI veke* [Culture at the Crossroads. Culture and Cultural Institutions at the Twentyfirst Century]. Moscow: Klassika-XXI.

Pomerants, Grigory. 2013. *Sobiranie sebya* [Picking of yourself]. Moscow; Sankt-Peterburg: *Tsentr gumanitarnykh isslidovanyi.*

Popova, Yulia. 2002. "Likvidator" [Liquidator. Interview with Karim Rashid]. / *Vesch [Thing]* / *Expert*, 4 (28): 8-12.

Rapaille, Clotaire. 2015. *Kulturnyi kod* [The Culture Code]. Moscow: Alpina Publisher.

Roberts, Lisa. 1997. *From knowledge to narrative. Educators and the Changing Museum.* Washington, DC: Smithsonian Institution.

Schirch, Lisa. 2004. *Ritual and Symbol in Peacebuilding.* Bloomfield, CT: Kumarian Press.

Simon, Nina. 2010. *The participatory museum.* Santa Cruz, California: Museum 2.0, 2010.

———. 2017. *Partitsipatornyi Musey / The Participatory Museum* (In Russian). Moscow: Ad Marginem Press (Garage Pro).

Smith, Laurajane. 2006. *The Uses of Heritage.* London: Routledge.

Sontag, Susan. 2003. *Regarding the Pain of Others.* New York: Farrar, Straus and Giroux.

Triandis, Harry. 1994. *Culture and Social Behavior.* McGraw-Hill.

van den Dungen, Peter. 2016. "Abolishing Nuclear Weapons through Anti-Atomic Bomb Museums". *Peace Review* 28 (3): 326-333.

van den Dungen, Peter and Kazuyo Yamane, eds. 2015. "Special Issue: Peace Education Through Peace Museums". *Journal of Peace Education* December: 213-284.

Yamane, Kazuyo. 2009. "Peace Education through Peace Museums". In *International Security, Peace, Development and Environment,* Volume II, edited by Ursula Oswald Spring 94-164. EOLSS Publications/ UNESCO.

Yamane, Kazuyo. 2006. *Peace Museums in Japan: The Controversial Exhibits on Japan's Aggression at Peace Museums and Citizens' Efforts for Peace and Reconciliation.* University of Bradford, Department of Peace Studies, PhD Thesis.

Chapter 2

Sensing the city: historic landscapes empowering future communities

Kelly M. Britt

Brooklyn College and The Graduate Center,
City University of New York, United States

Abstract

Sensory experience of place provides an experiential practice that illuminates an understanding of history not accessed through traditional archaeological narratives. This experience is informative for community-based archaeological projects to actively shift historic power relations in the present by harnessing the power of collective action. The historically African American community of Bedford Stuyvesant, Brooklyn, NY is home to the United Order of Tents Eastern District 3 headquarters. The Tents are the oldest Black women's benevolent society in the US and was founded by two former enslaved African women at the end of the Civil War. The Tents are trying to keep membership moving forward and preserve the materiality of their 19th-century structure in a rapidly gentrifying neighbourhood. This chapter contemplates whether somatic explorations of place can be harnessed to better understand the history of the organization and the neighborhood, and empower the community to preserve the landscape moving forward.

Keywords: activism, advocacy, city, community, urban archaeology, gentrification, heritage, historic preservation, landscape, memory, phenomenology, place/placemaking, sensory archaeology, social justice, space

***

> History, as nearly no one seems to know, is not merely something to be read. And it does not refer merely, or even principally, to the past. On the contrary, the great force of history comes from the fact that we carry it within us, are unconsciously controlled by it in many ways, and history is literally present in all that we do. It could scarcely be otherwise, since it is to history that we owe our frames of reference, our identities, and our aspirations.
>
> James Baldwin

Introduction

A sensory experience of place and placemaking in cities provides an experiential practice that illuminates an understanding of history not accessed through traditional archaeological narratives that focus on tangible objects. Yet, this sensory knowledge is informative for community-based archaeological and historic preservation projects working directly with local communities or diaspora. Combining tangible and intangible knowledge of the past, particularly those directly tied to power relations in the present, provides a unique opportunity to trace these power dynamics from past to present. This chapter will explore the effect of a sensory experience of placemaking on generational memories of the past. With this, the chapter argues that experiential moments with the past can foster an emphatic response in the present in the form of activism and advocacy work.

Research into this topic employs phenomenology or sensory archaeology, historic preservation, and memory studies to explore the effects the experiential can have on individuals at sites of heritage. Somatics, or the way one experiences the self in the present, play a key part in bridging the philosophical bases between these research fields, making the encounter with historic sites an individual, multi-sensory, relational experience of space in the present. Additionally, as this chapter will illustrate, as the past is embodied through first-hand or empathetic experiences in the present, an opening, or opportunity, is created to actively shift historic power relations through harnessing the power of collective action. While experiential opportunities can be created at any historic site, the effect of such interactions can have profound impacts on those witnessing sites associated with erased or silenced history from marginal communities, or those associated with historic places of trauma, and consequently serious and meaningful repercussions for site valuation, interpretation, and preservation. Evidence of this can be observed in heritage sites of the African diaspora across the United States, from rural to urban, with many being places of either confinement and trauma or freedom and mobility. Using interdisciplinary, theoretical lenses with examples from urban historic site contexts, mostly from New York City, this chapter illustrates how historic places are embodied sensorially, and how that embodiment directly affects political action in the present.

To understand the importance of a sensory experience of place when it comes to evaluating significance in the historic preservation process, the chapter will first examine how historic preservation's rigid system in the United States deems what is considered important, integral, and authentic, and then investigate how this system has left a disparity in the material heritage from marginal communities that has been officially preserved for the public. This topic is particularly complicated in urban settings where the mere process of urbanization and the developmental desires for newness, combined with political desires for economic growth, mire the historic preservation process. While the gap in this discrepancy is slowly closing, it is still quite wide in the United States. The United States and many western polities prioritize the visual as it relates to a classical aesthetic and the written archive and downplay other sensory experiences and knowledge production like oral history. The combination of the sensory and the memory can produce an empathic correspondence to a place, which in turn can impact an individual or community's physical response to place. These responses can galvanize a variety of reactions in people from apathy to direct action. This chapter hopes to illustrate how these somatic responses to place can be harnessed into direct action by individuals as well as the wider community. These actions can be seen in a variety of outcomes from successful material preservation initiatives of the built environment, to changes in policy at local levels that can influence state or national initiatives.

I will explore a few historic sites to illustrate my goals, however, the focus of my research is on the historically African American community of Bedford Stuyvesant, Brooklyn, New York. The community is home to the Eastern District Grand Tent #3 of the United Order of Tents, JR Giddings and Jolliffe Union, also known as "the Tents", and their nineteenth-century mansion, which is in desperate need of preservation. The Tents is the oldest Black women's benevolent society in the United States and was founded by two formerly enslaved African women at the end of the Civil War. As the Tents begin to preserve the materiality of their structure in a twenty-first century, rapidly gentrifying neighbourhood, I explore if somatic explorations of urban space can be harnessed to not only better understand the history of the organization and the neighbourhood, but also to inspire the activism needed to preserve the landscape and empower the community toward moving forward.

Theoretical lenses

The embodiment of memory and displacement

At the heart of this chapter's inquiry are the politics of memory and displacement and a struggle for social justice. While the theoretical investigation of memory, displacement, and social justice through materiality has guided much of my work (Britt and Gregory 2019; Britt 2023; Britt and George 2023), recently I have found my personal experiences influencing my research methodology and theoretical thinking in reflexive ways. As a former performing artist and current yogi, I have always found movement through space directly yokes the body to place and the present moment. Therefore, it is not surprising that I found inspiration in a twentieth-century dancer, Pearl Primus, a Trinidadian-born artist who moved to the Bedford Stuyvesant neighbourhood in Brooklyn in the early twentieth century, as the impetus for exploring a somatic perspective for this project. She used movement, a full sensory experience, as a means of communicating social justice. Historian Farah Jasmine Griffin captures the essence of what Primus embodied in her 2013 book *Harlem Nocturne: Women Artists and Progressive Politics During World War II:*

> ... Primus was able to portray the challenges and restrictions of segregation ... In these choreographed gestures she embodied a particularly black paradox: forced confinement *and* forced mobility. While the major experience of black diasporic communities has been one of mobility, migration and dislocation, these populations have also experienced forced confinement in various forms of segregation, imprisonment, and enslavement (27).

The concepts of confinement and mobility highlighted in Primus's choreography are two excellent ways to explore the past and one's relationship with it, for they both can be experienced spatially and embodied physically. One can witness confinement and mobility materially through the built environment, objects, artefacts, and historical records, and also experience them through all the senses. Therefore, dance provides a wonderful way to enter a discussion about preserving the past through somatics of movement. Somatic studies of dance have accentuated experimentation over replication with multiple modes of reflection (Lester 2015 in Ferris 2018). Historic sites mirror this through the production of multiple ways of reflecting on the past. This is especially true for historic sites located in urban spaces, for the process of urbanization itself creates a placemaking cycle of production and reproduction, providing a need to reflect and re-reflect. This is particularly true for the focus of my study—the Tents home and headquarters. Primus's paradox of multiple modes of being in space, forced confinement and forced mobility, seems to be at the centre of the urban community in which I live and research and is experienced individually and collectively by community members. The forced confinement can be seen physically through the historic, racist housing policies such as redlining, which bounded who could live where. Additionally, it can be seen socially, particularly in the Tents' organization itself. As it began in the mid-nineteenth century before emancipation, the organization's need for secrecy was imperative for the safety of the members of the organization. This confinement was a unifying form of protection. The slow unfolding of these confinement narratives is set against the backdrop of urbanization. While urbanization almost requires a continual cycle of change, the late twentieth and early twenty-first century experienced rapid transformation in the shape of various forms of gentrification, dislocating, and displacing those that were once confined to a space, which over time has become home.

Building on phenomenology and sensory discourse in an archival activist framework (Carney 2021; Finn 2011; Tilley 2010; Van Dyke 2014), this chapter explores the use of somatic mapping of urban space to understand historic sites and their meaning to the diasporic communities they represent in the present. Interpretation of the past is tied to politics and ideology of the present, and in urban settings, this correlates also to place and placemaking. Using a Participatory Action Research approach to a community-based archaeological project, my goal is to better understand how members of historically underrepresented communities experience a historic site somatically, if that experience shapes how they interact with the site, and how they react politically. Therefore, what this piece does not do is explore somatics or sensory experiences *in* the past. Rather, this paper builds backwards, taking somatic place-making experiences in the present to explore how they influence the preservation, interpretation, and understanding of the past in the present. While this project is in its early stages of inquiry due to the setback caused by the COVID-19 pandemic, many interdisciplinary theoretical lenses have and continue to influence this research, including somatic psychology and movement studies. However, for this chapter, I will be focusing on two central influences: historic preservation policy and scholarship, and sensory or phenomenological archaeology studies. Michael Allen's challenge to historic preservation in the United States to be "more than an exclusionary bureaucratic consensus" (2016, 44) and Laurajane Smith's notion of Authorized Heritage Discourse (2006) assist in understanding the present moment of heritage studies and policy. Christopher Tilley's (2010) use of phenomenology in landscape studies, particularly urban ones, along with Stephen Greenblatt's (1990) notion of resonance and wonder with person/object relationships, will anchor my thoughts and examples in this chapter on the sensorial impact of space on an individual or community.

Historic preservation: historical consciousness, authorized heritage discourse, and memory

The collective and social memories tied to places hold power. Collective memory, a term coined by Maurice Halbwachs (1992), in the 1930s is a socially sanctioned public memory comprised of family, religious, and national narratives. It dictates what gets remembered and why. This notion is important to understand, for not everything is remembered or sanctioned to be remembered; rather, a more calculated silencing of the past can take place (Trouillet 1997). The power, therefore, lies in the development of dominant, politically sanctioned narratives of history or as Laurajane Smith (2006) calls it, the Authorized Heritage Discourse (AHD).

National aspects of history that de-centre the local create a hierarchy of values of heritage (Smith 2020), thus playing a part in which narratives are tied to place and serving to determine which sites are remembered or not. Yet the questions remain of why some sites of local value slip from the larger collective memory? How does trauma and the AHD become tools for this? And is there a way to resurrect the historical memory tied to place through a phenomenological or sensory approach, to help heal past traumas or inspire present action for change? These are questions that I ponder as I have worked across a variety of historical sites tied to the African diaspora in the urban northeast United States. These questions are not new. Many historians and archaeologists have written about the silencing—the forced forgetting (Shackel 2001; Trouillet 1997). What this chapter will explore through a phenomenological/sensory approach is how the re-remembering of these sites, places, buildings, memorials, and landscapes, among other important and meaningful places, may empower individuals and communities to not only change the AHD of a given history, region, or event, but perhaps also contribute to direct action in larger social justice causes.

These national narratives of sanctioned AHD play a role in local historic preservation politics and policies within the United States and many western countries (Smith 2020). As Smith (2020, 10971) has stated

> The consequences of the AHD are that it tends to regulate and confine professional and academic debate about the nature and meaning of heritage and the way it can be managed, preserved, and interpreted. This means that it also tends to validate the bodies of knowledge and values that contributed to it—it is by definition self-referential. It also excludes those understandings of heritage that may sit outside of the framework defined by the AHD.

National, state, and local preservation policies in the United States have been built on these national AHD models to determine the significance of a place, structure, or object based on the emphasizing of aesthetic aspects, and/or the authenticity of a built structure as seen in its 'integrity', meaning the less modification that has been done to the structure, the more meaning it has. These policies, particularly in urban spaces where building and rebuilding are constantly happening, directly affect what is preserved and what is not. Many structures that hold meaning to the community but do not meet the requirements of preservation policies have been demolished and lost, disregarding whether or not they hold meaning to the community in which they were built. Heritage, by nature, is constantly evolving in meaning. As Barbara Kirshenblatt-Gimblett (1998, 149-150) defines heritage, "it is a mode of cultural production that has recourse to the past", therefore it is constantly being invented and re-invented, giving a place, structure, and object meanings again and again. Yet most preservation policies, ironically, are static, and primarily based in aesthetics that support the AHD. For preservation policy to evolve with and for heritage, new modes of attributing significance to a place need to be sought out. This is where I see phenomenology and resonance playing a role.

Phenomenology: sensing the past, remembering (in) the present

Christopher Tilley (2010, 25) notes that "phenomenology allows knowledge of landscapes, either past or present, [to be] gained through perceptual experience of them from the point of view of the subject". He states "landscape is fundamental for human existence because it provides both a medium for an outcome of individual and social practices. The physicality of landscapes grounds and orients people and places within them, it is a physical and sensory resource for living and the social symbolic construction of life-worlds" (Tilley 2010, 26). While much phenomenology work in the discipline of archaeology has situated itself among sites of deep time in rural settings, the embodiment of the landscape can be experienced in rural and urban settings, among natural and human-made places associated with more historical or contemporary sites, as well as those dating back millennia. They physically connect the past to the present through the human sensory experience, shaping a person's identity or a collective one. As Tilley goes on to state, "places and monuments are always a form of presencing the past in the present and in their mute way objectifying a story of the generations who used and inhabited them" (Tilley 2010, 34). As people shape places, places shape people; and memories, whether individual or collective, are formed and reformed, at times passed down to generations via oral histories and narratives, or through the physical engagement with the place itself. Places are made from spaces.

Resonance and wonder

Borrowing from Stephen Greenblatt's work on the essence of resonance and wonder of art objects, where he poses that resonance can be achieved via an "awakening" within a person of a notion of cultural and historical essence via exchanges through representational practices (1990, 45), I would like to extend his thoughts to reflect not just on art objects, but to the built environment as well, particularly to heritage places. We can see the resonance that is emitting from some historic places via visitor responses. In communities whose history has not been part of the dominant historic narrative, or has been erased, silenced, or is not easily accessed, such as African American history in the United States, the historical sites of these communities take on a particularly important meaning, tying personal and collective memories to present and future realities. This chapter hopes to illustrate the unsilencing of one of these places that holds a powerful place in a community in Brooklyn, New York: the site of the United Order of Tents Eastern District #3 Headquarters.

Methodological movements

At the heart of this inquiry are the politics of memory and a struggle for social justice. Using a Participatory Action Research (PAR) approach to a community-based archaeological project, my goal is to better understand how members of historically underrepresented communities experience a historic site somatically and if that experience shapes how they interact with the site and impact its preservation.

Emancipatory PAR methodology provides the framework for this translation from resource to people and is at the heart of my project with the Tents project. Participatory Action Research (PAR) is a non-traditional research methodology designed for researchers and participants to work together in a collaborative research design to challenge inequities and strive for social change. Rather than telling, PAR seeks collaborative knowledge production. An emancipatory PAR method uses a critical theory paradigm (Jacobs 2018, 42) grounded in action and based on critiques of social inequities and structures of power to promote change (Jacobs 2018, 42).

The framework for this translation from resource to people is the Emancipatory PAR methodology with an archival activism design. Archival activism, or "radical history-making activities performed by ordinary people" (Carney 2021; Vukliš and Gilliland 2016; Zinn 1977), fits into an Emancipatory PAR approach to a community-based archaeological project because it is a non-traditional research methodology designed for researchers and participants to work together in a collaborative research design to challenge inequities and strive for social change. Megan Carney (2021) notes that Andrew Finn (2011), a professor of archival studies and oral history, sees "archival activism occur[ing] outside of institutions of power, such as government or the private sector. It requires broad participation by diverse communities to address historical gaps. Instead of relying only on official published records or other types of written accounts, a decolonial and activist approach might include oral histories, works of art, photographs, everyday objects, or other sources within archives".

Carney's recent work in Palermo, Italy, with migrant filmmakers, illustrates the power of media storytelling aimed toward a larger public to create an awareness of the social struggles of a migrant community. The non-profit organization Zabbara provided a space for the collaborative film laboratory FunKino to create narratives and disseminate them to alter the misinformation spread regarding migrants (Carney 2021). According to Carney (2021), these anthropological stories are archival activism, for it is ordinary people who are performing these counter-narratives of history. My research builds upon existing archival activist scholarship with the addition of materiality and place. Global Heritage Fund's Donovan Rypkema describes place as "'the vessel within which the 'spirit' of the community is stored.' Community is [therefore] the catalyst for making a place a product not just of individuals but of a society" (Hosking 2018). Thus, the process of placemaking ties people to place through memories and emotions, particularly on a community level. Heritage sites link the past to the present through the materiality of place and shape community identity, but due to AHD, many heritage sites significant to communities slip from the dominant historical discourse through forgetting, erasure, and silencing.

A decolonial and antiracist approach is needed for an archival activist project approach to knowledge production, which means rethinking whose stories get included, referenced, and highlighted in any record of the past (Atalay 2012; Flewellen et al. 2021; Mbembe 2015; Rizvi 2016, 2020, 2022; Yako 2021). While decolonial practices have been critiqued and calls elicited for these practices to go beyond a mere metaphor (Tuck and Yang 2012), decolonial engaged practices as a system of caring (Rizvi 2016; Supernant et al. 2020) can be grounded in more equitable forms of knowledge production, by building *with* not *from* the community in which research is being conducted. Examples of this can be seen in public archaeology programs and projects working with descendant or diaspora communities (Archaeology in the Community, n.d.). To do this effectively, the research must be grounded in antiracist methods of data acquisition (Dei and Johal 2005; Boston University Center for Antiracist Research, n.d.). The University of Minnesota Libraries (2022) "Conducting Research through an Antiracist Lens" provides a guide to researchers across disciplines on how to conduct such research which includes: decentring whiteness in primary and secondary research, acknowledging data is not objective, and that scholarly publishing, research algorithms, and cataloguing systems are racist. This chapter acknowledges all the inherent biases immanent in the project, including the academic portion which is led by a female white researcher; however, decentring the academic aspect of the project through an engaged approach places the collaborative knowledge production with the members of the Tents to the forefront and strives to disrupt the biases that are present. Data collected is not objective but rather transparent, acknowledging the subjective biases that exist in research data collection. The nature of the project working in an archival activist framework provides an opportunity to disrupt the racist aspects of algorithms and cataloguing.

While I strive to conduct this project with a subjective perspective, the personal and self-reflexive weaves in as well. As a community member of Bedford Stuyvesant, I bring personal experience from living in the area and being a witness to, as well as part of, the changing landscape. This includes my impact as a white woman on the gentrification process within the community, one complicated and exacerbated due to the recent COVID-19 pandemic. This personal connection to the area brings with it a responsibility to try to understand these processes and address the dislocation associated with this changing landscape, including my actions in this process. Lending my services and knowledge in historic preservation as a Friend to the Tents is part of the process of reflecting on my role in the gentrification process.

On a more personal note, I am a mother to a child with a multi-racial ancestry, one tied directly to the African diaspora and Underground Railroad history, thereby in many ways connected to the legacy of the Tents. Thus, I also feel a personal responsibility to understand and protect this history for her, to not only comprehend the intangible but to actively preserve the tangible and its effect on the urbanization process. I strive to carry out my work with the Tents considering these concerns, being continuously mindful of my positionality within the community and racialized socioeconomic structures more broadly.

Urban perceptions: historic sites in Brooklyn, New York—Black history matters

The United Order of Tents Eastern District #3

After moving with my family to the Brooklyn neighbourhood of Bedford Stuyvesant in 2011, I soon took interest in 87 MacDonough Street, a seemingly urban ruin located about two and a half blocks from my apartment. Located on a lot measuring 100' x 200', which is large by New York City standards (usually 20' x 100'), a house and grounds stand which run from Macon Street south through to MacDonough Street. The house seemed to speak to those who walked by, including myself. The external facade spoke in phrases, indicating there were longer stories to tell. Some windows were broken or missing panes of glass, while tattered curtains flowed through the spaces. The exterior paint showed signs of wear with its peeling and different shades. The chipped paint sign above the door that reads "1888-1988 EASTERN DISTRICT GRAND TENT #3 GRAND UNITED ORDER OF THE TENTS OF BKLYN. JRG JU", and the energy-savings LED lightbulb above the front door, led me to believe this was not a ruin, but rather a well-worn building with stories to tell. Finding those stories became a difficult task, for most people I met who grew up in the area knew the house but not of the Tents—what the organization was, and if they were still active (Britt and Gregory 2019).

I was introduced to the Tents, as they are known, in 2018, and learned more about their history, legacy, and plight for the preservation of both their membership and the building that membership called home. The Tents are a women's fraternal order dating back to the mid-nineteenth century that is rooted in Christian missionary work, providing food, places to bathe, and nursing care to those in need. The founders were two formerly enslaved African women, Annetta M. Lane and Harriet R. Taylor, who were supported by two abolitionists. While formally organized after the Civil War with four Districts across the eastern seaboard, Tents' legacy states that the fraternal lodge began as a stop on the Underground Railroad—"Tents of Salvation", with actual tents set up to assist the enslaved escaping north and provide aid to those in need (The United Order of Tents n.d.).

Like with many fraternal orders, the Tents' organization was conducted in secrecy, with rituals and details only shared with members. This secrecy was even more important for Black fraternal organizations, particularly during the Civil War, Reconstruction, and Jim Crow eras, when persecution of African Americans through racist policies and programs was at an extreme high, and lives were in constant jeopardy. The building the Tents call home, or their headquarters, is located at 87 MacDonough Street in Brooklyn, New York, and was originally built in 1863. It is made of brick in Italianate and French Empire style and has been listed on the National Register of Historic Places since 1996 (USN 04701.004141). It is also noted as a contributing element of the listed Stuyvesant Heights Historic District. The aspects of design, and listing, play an important part in preserving the physical aspect of the home, for they qualify the building as "historic" and worthy of preservation according to quantifiable characteristics. These characteristics are based on the Western ideals of aesthetics which govern US preservation policies, like those adopted by the National Register of Historic Places. But what about the intangible aspects that this building and property hold? Ones not directly connected to the style of architecture or the importance of academic and politically recognized design details?

While the building has had various owners throughout its lifespan, including a prominent Irish Catholic family named the MacMahons, several charities and mutual aid organizations, and a mutual aid hospital, the Tents have been the owners of the building since the 1940s, making them the longest occupant of the house. During their ownership, the Tents have held community events and rented the space to other organizations and churches. As a result, a far larger community than just Tents members hold a connection to this place. So my question is: what stories associated with this place are part of the collective memory and not in the material archives of both the members of the Tents themselves, as well as the larger community?

Figure 2.1 The United Order of Tents Eastern District #3 Headquarters.

Photograph taken by author 2021.

As membership to the Tents declined in the late twentieth century, those who attend meetings have been primarily elders within the organization. The once-coveted aspect of secrecy, which protected them from the outside world, is now a force of demise and erasure. More recently, they realize they need to recreate themselves to entice new members to carry on their legacy.

Urbanization and erasure

Many policies, such as the National Housing Act of 1934, provided loans for homes within approved security areas which were indicated by a colour-coding system on government-issued maps. Areas highlighted in red were deemed Grade D and were known as red-lined neighbourhoods. These red-lined areas were generally determined not by the housing stock, or economic components of an area, but rather by the demographics, and lines were laid along colour lines. These policies, along with restrictive covenants and local urban planning policies, have included the displacement of working- and middle-class communities of colour, specifically Black communities, throughout the United States. These intentionally discriminatory housing policies drove communities to the periphery of the urban landscape, including areas of Brooklyn like Bedford Stuyvesant. These neighbourhoods were largely forgotten throughout the twentieth century, and buildings built in the mid to late-nineteenth century were also left untouched, for new development was not encouraged and modification was rare. Now, however, these structures exist in communities that have been deemed to have "character" that is coveted by developers, and thus whole neighbourhoods have become the object of gentrification. Bedford Stuyvesant is one of these places and the community is at present fighting to preserve its tangible and intangible heritage through this process of change.

As the Tents begin to preserve the materiality of their nineteenth-century structure in a twenty-first century, rapidly gentrifying neighbourhood, I wonder can somatic explorations of urban space be harnessed to not only better understand the history of the organization and the neighbourhood, but also impart activism to preserve the organization, landscape, and empower the community moving forward? Although COVID-19 put a pause on this research due to my institution's restrictions on conducting research during the pandemic, through the following brief example I hope to highlight some of the aspects I'm exploring.

The power of social media

As I have written about in other publications (Britt 2023), December 26, 2020, became a turning point for the Tents' secrecy and preservation efforts of both their tangible and intangible heritage. A Facebook post on the Bedford Stuyvesant Brooklyn community page asked about the status of the house located at 87 MacDonough Street, for the writer had many fond memories there as a child. This posting solicited many comments. As of 2021,189 comments were made, and after a cursory subjective categorization of comments, I found over 70 of them directly related to inquiries about Tents' history, memories of community members with a relationship to the physical house and space, or comments regarding its preservation for the "community" (Britt 2023). In addition to the comments reflecting on the physical structure of the building, its history, and legacy, about 50 comments focused on the property as real estate, including a post that showed the property listed as currently for sale for $9.75 million on the Zillow real estate app (Britt 2023). While the Zillow ad was determined to be fake, created as part of the Great Gotham Challenge, which is essentially an online scavenger hunt focused on team building through learning about history and culture, the seemingly "for sale" status prompted much response from the community, primarily in support to save and preserve the building as the Tents' headquarters. This posting led the Tents to realize the secrecy that once guarded and supported their organization was now a detriment to their legacy and home. Through events both online and in-person, the members are beginning to emerge from secrecy and share their organizational and site history, invoking a real community dialogue about heritage (Britt 2023).

The Tents and Friends of the Tents put together a public event to bring some of the histories of this organization to the larger public. The event took place in March 2021 in celebration of Women's history month and was hosted by the local library. While many community members were expected to join, the unexpected tweet before the event by the founder of the Langston League, a "multi-consultant curriculum firm that specializes in teaching educators how to create culturally responsive and sustaining instructional material, for all students" (http://www.langstonleague.com/), highlighting the Tents organization, its history and the upcoming event, went viral. Registration for the event went from 40 to 450 almost overnight. The thirst for knowledge of this heritage by the public was evident. By the weekend of the event, over 650 people were registered and on the day of, close to 200 connected through Zoom and stayed with the panel of speakers from the Tents, Friends of Tents, and community representatives for over an hour and a half. Thanks to the work of undergraduate student Julia Leedy, an intern with the Tents through Brooklyn College, the Tents have a website where people could follow up, and membership requests and additional inquiries on how to help started to come in (Britt 2023).

Conclusion: AfroFuture abolitionist heritage

During the Spring 2021 semester, students from my Urban Archaeology at Brooklyn College course conducted short research projects on aspects of Bedford Stuyvesant, exploring places of social and ritual movements, and they created an ArcGIS StoryMap for each project. While we conducted a group interview with one Tents member, the students mainly explored primary source documents and maps and learned to use the platform to build their stories. Going forward, to build on my research and incorporate student participation into the project, I intend to continue individual class projects exploring places of Bedford Stuyvesant experienced through the community, with the involvement of both long-time residents and newly placed ones, to explore the complex entanglements of place-making in urban settings.

Past and present historic preservation initiatives and success stories from communities of colour within the borough and the city at large need to be researched and compared. Additionally, in both my research agenda and student-led projects, the incorporation of more ethnographic methods within surveys, and additional ethnographic interviews with more Tents members, former juvenile Tents members, as well as community members, would enhance the phenomenological knowledge of the neighbourhood. Additionally, I would like to incorporate movement analysis exploring how individuals and groups experience places within the community somatically, and even highlight some of their experiences in StoryMaps as well. With experimental modes of inquiry, I hope to unravel not repeated reflections about the important historical places within the community, including the Tent's Headquarters, but rather multiple modes of thematic reflections that indicate the meaning place holds within the memories of the residents that live here.

Since the first Facebook post that lured the Tents out of secrecy to hold community events, the Tents have held other successful events, including another online panel in collaboration with the local library in celebration of Women's History Month this year. At this event, the founder of the Langston League eloquently captured the somatics of place. As she told her story of what brought her to the Tents, the word "familiar" was echoed again and again. As she narrated her physical journey with a friend walking to witness the Tents home for the first time, she stated the "feeling grew as [she] got closer to the house …" and [she] "knew immediately in that moment that was the ancestors that were walking us there" (United Order of Tents Eastern District 3 Website 2022). Through her comments, it is evident that the building physically held a resonance and wonder that she connected to. The Tents' mission of community service and sisterhood of which she now was a direct part drew her in and captured her.

Annette Lane Harrison Richter, the great-great-granddaughter of Annetta M. Lane, one of the co-founders of the Tents, expressed the following story to me via phone, but also published it recently in 2019 with E-Flux Journal, an art publication:

> I have a flashback to slavery almost every day of my life. In some incidents, it doesn't have to be anything unpleasant but just something that brings to mind slavery. It must've been in the early 1970s, I was on liaison with the federal agency where I was working at the time, and that day was a beautiful sunny warm day. I walked from my apartment house in downtown Washington, DC, over to the FBI on official business, and when I left the Bureau I was walking past the White House and all of a sudden I felt a presence next to me. I had never experienced anything like that before. I felt this presence and I thought it was Annetta. And I thought about how she would never believe that a descendant of hers worked for a federal agency of the United States, and in a capacity that was tasked with making decisions on whether or not applicants could work for that federal agency or employees could continue working for it. At the time I was in security—the Office of Security—which was my career. And I was running background investigations. And it just occurred to me that Annetta wouldn't believe this. Here I am walking

past the White House, on my way to the Office of Personnel Management and from there I was going to the Department of State, on the liaison that I ran two or three times a week. And I thought it would just be beyond her comprehension.

These illustrations of an embodiment of memory are something I continue to witness, from a student's response during a field trip to the Tent's home as being able "to feel the ancestors", to responses from visitors at other African American sites across New York City, including Weeksville Heritage Center, 227 Duffield Place, Flatbush African Burial Ground, and Van Cortlandt Historic House Museum, places linked to enslavement and trauma but also liberation and freedom within the African diaspora. In one of the cases shown above, that somatic connection through the built environment led to direct action— membership into the Tents organization to ensure its legacy. It begs the question: could embodied heritage provide communities with ways to organize on a variety of social justice issues? Such as an abolitionist heritage? Possibly— but more work needs to be done.

Many people think of historic preservation and its power to raise property values and aesthetical aspects of a neighbourhood. I see historic preservation's power in the stories and the memories of the people who lived, worked, and experienced these spaces to preserve collective memory and in many instances revive and restore stories that are not always highlighted in the history books. It gives voice to those stories and homage to the lives that have come before. In this instance, preservation of 87 MacDonough Street—home to the Tents since the 1940s—provides a powerful symbol of Black Women's role in this community, of its role in supporting the needs of the community, and it's continuing the advocacy and activism of its foremothers for social justice. I am still exploring how best to understand these experiences I am witnessing, whether through sensory archaeology, phenomenology, epigenetics, or memory studies— particularly Blood memory. With research restrictions recently lifted, additional work through ethnographic research and participant-led narrative walks through the built environment, I hope to gain additional testimonies of the Tents' experience, and thus build a more thorough comprehension of their lived experiences.

Acknowledgements

I would like to thank the Professional Staff Congress, The Tow Faculty Research Grant, and Laundromat Project's Create and Connect program for funding portions of this research. The research would not be possible without the support of many, but especially Dr. Robyn Spencer, Safiya Bendele, and so many of students from CUNY and elsewhere including Scott Ferrara, Madison Aubey, and Julia Leedy for their work on various portions of the research. This research wouldn't be possible without the sisters of the Tents and their openness for me to work with them as a Friend of the Tents. With that, an extra big thank you needs to be given to Mrs. Essie Gregory, the President of the Executive Committee of the Tents, whom I have worked the most closely with and who has become a dear friend as well. Any errors are my own.

Bibliography

Allen, Michael. 2016. "What Historic Preservation Can Learn from Ferguson". In *Bending the Future*, edited by Max Page and Marla Miller, 44-48. Amherst: University of Massachusetts Press.

Atalay, Sonya. 2012. *Community-Based Archaeology: Research with, by, and for Indigenous and Local Communities*. Berkeley: University of California Press.

Archaeology in the Community. n.d. *Archaeology in the Community* website. Accessed 29 July, 2022. https://www.archaeologyincommunity.com/.

Baldwin, James. 1965. "White Man's Guilt". *Ebony*, 47-48. Accessed 3 November, 2023. https://books.google.com/books?id=N94DAAAAMBAJ&pg=PA47&lpg=PA47&dq=white+man%27s+guilt+baldwin+ebony&source=bl&ots=dBzu4nHOjr&sig=bklAZymGXQthZgjIJ5Sfa5h_9zg&hl=en&sa=X&ved=0ahUKEwjHk-ak6s3OAhUK6iYKHc5JDusQ6AEIOTAE#v=onepage&q=white%20man's%20guilt%20baldwin%20ebony&f=false.

Boston University Center for Antiracist Research. n.d. *Boston University Center for Antiracist Research* website. Accessed 30 July, 2022. https://www.bu.edu/antiracism-center/antiracism-research/research-policy-teams/.

Britt, Kelly M. 2023. "Right to the City: Community-Based Urban Archaeology as Abolitionist Heritage". In *Advocacy and Archaeology*, edited by Kelly M. Britt and Diane F. George. New York, NY: Berghahn Books.

Britt, Kelly M., and Diane F. George, eds. 2023. *Advocacy and Archaeology: Urban Intersections*. New York, NY: Berghahn Books.

Britt, Kelly M. and Essie Gregory. 2019. "Clubhouse Excavation: The United Order of Tents". *Dilettante Army*. http://www.dilettantearmy.com/articles/united-order-of-tents.

Carney, Megan. 2021. "How Migrant Farmers Practice Archival Activism". *Sapiens*. June 9, 2021. Accessed 29 July, 2022. https://www.sapiens.org/culture/archival-activism/.

Dei, George J. Sefa and Gurpreet Singh Johal, eds. 2005. *Critical Issues in Anti-Racist Research Methodologies*. New York: Peter Lang Verlag.

Ferris, Kelly. 2018. "Somatics: A Buzzword Defined". ISMETA Blog. January 31, 2018. Accessed 9 December, 2019. https://ismeta.org/somatics-buzzword-defined.

Finn, Andrew. 2011. "Archival Activism: Independent and Community-led Archives, Radical Public History and the Heritage Professions". *InterActions: UCLA Journal of Education and Information Studies*, 7 (2). Accessed 29 July, 2022. http://dx.doi.org/10.5070/D472000699.

Flewellen, Ayana, Justin Dunnavant, Alicia Odewale, Alexandra Jones, Tsione Wolde-Michael, Zoë Crossland, and Maria Franklin. 2021. "The Future of

Archaeology Is Antiracist": Archaeology in the Time of Black Lives Matter". *American Antiquity* 86: 1-20. Accessed 30 July, 2022. doi:10.1017/aaq.2021.18.

Greenblatt, Stephen. 1990. "Resonance and Wonder". In *Exhibiting Cultures: The Poetics and Politics of Museum Display*, edited by Ivan Karp and Steven D. Levine, 42-56. Washington, DC: Smithsonian Institution Press.

Griffin, Farah Jasmine. 2013. *Harlem Nocturne: Women Artists and Progressive Politics During World War II*. New York: Civitas Books.

Hosking, Nada. 2018. "Placemaking: The Heart of Heritage Conservation". *Global Heritage Fund* April 24, 2018. Accessed 29 July, 2022. https://global heritagefund.org/2018/04/24/placemaking-heart-heritage-conservation/.

Jacobs, Steven Darryl. 2018. "A History and Analysis of the Evolution of Action and Participatory Action Research". *Canadian Journal of Action Research* 19 (3): 34-52.

Kirshenblatt-Gimblett, Barbara. 1998. *Destination: Culture: Tourism, Museums, and Heritage*. Berkeley: University of California Press.

Lester, K. 2015. "Environments for self-learning". In *Moving consciously: Somatic transformations through dance, yoga, and touch*, edited by S. Fraleigh, 93–108. Chicago: University of Illinois Press.

Mbembe, Achille. 2015. "Decolonizing Knowledge and the Question of the Archive. Africa is a Country", contributed by Angela Okune, *Platform for Experimental Collaborative Ethnography, Platform for Experimental Collaborative Ethnography*, last modified 14 August 2018. Accessed 7 November, 2023. https://worldpece.org/content/mbembe-achille-2015-"decolonizing-knowledge-and-question-archive"-africa-country.

Rizvi, Uzma. 2016. "Decolonization as Care". *Slow Reader: A Resource for Design Thinking and Practice*, edited by Carolyn F. Strauss and Ana Paula Pais. A SlowLab Collaboration with Valiz, 85-95. Amsterdam: Valiz Publishers.

———. 2020. "Community-Based and Participatory Praxis as Decolonizing Archaeological Methods and the Betrayal of New Research". In *Archaeologies of the Heart*, edited by Kisha Supernant, Jane Eva Baxter, Natasha Lyons, and Sonia Atalay, 83-96. Cham, Switzerland: Springer Nature Switzerland. Accessed 30 July, 2022. https://doi:10.1007/978-3-030-36350-5_6.

———. 2022. "Community Engagement in Archaeology and Heritage in Pakistan". *Journal of Community Archaeology Heritage* 9 (1): 1–8. Accessed 30 July, 2022. https://doi:10.1080/20518196.2021.2008443.

Shackel, Paul A. 2001. "Public Memory and the Search for Power in American Historical Archaeology". *American Anthropologist* 103 (3): 655–70.

Smith, L. 2006. *Uses of Heritage*. London: Routledge.

———. 2020. "Uses of Heritage". In *Encyclopedia of Global Archaeology*, edited by C. Smith, 10969-10975. Cham, Switzerland: Springer Nature.

Supernant, Kisha, Jane Eva Baxter, Natasha Lyons, and Sonia Atalay, eds. 2020. *Archaeologies of the Heart*. Cham, Switzerland: Springer Nature. Accessed 30 July, 2022. https://doi:10.1007/978-3-030-36350-5_6.

Tilley, Christopher. 2010. *Interpreting Landscapes: Geologies, Topographies, Identities; Explorations in Landscape Phenomenology 3* (1st ed.). New York: Routledge.

Trouillot, Michel-Rolph. 1995. *Silencing the Past: Power and Production of History.* Boston, MA: Beacon Press.

Tuck, Eve and K. Wayne Yang. 2012. "Decolonization is Not a Metaphor". *Decolonization: Indigeneity, Education & Society* 1 (1): 1-40.

United Order of Tents. n.d. *History of the United Order of Tents J.R. Giddings and Jolliffe Union.*

University of Minnesota Libraries. 2022. "Conducting Research Through an Anti-Racist Lens". *University of Minnesota Libraries* website. Accessed 30 July, 2022. https://libguides.umn.edu/antiracismlens.

Van Dyke, Ruth M. 2014. "Phenomenology in Archaeology". In *Encyclopedia of Global Archaeology,* edited by Claire Smith, 5909-5916. New York: Springer. Accessed 18 November, 2023. https://doi.org/10.1007/978-1-4419-0465-2_295.

Vukliš, Vladan and Anne J. Gilliland. 2016. "Archival Activism: Emerging Forms, Local Applications". *Archives in the Service of People – People in the Service of Archives,* edited by B. Filej, 14-25. Maribor, SI: Alma Mater Europea.

Yako, Louis. 2021. "Decolonizing Knowledge Production: A Practical Guide". *Counterpunch.* April 9, 2021. Accessed 30 July, 2022. https://www.counter punch.org/2021/04/09/decolonizing-knowledge-production-a-practical-guide/.

Zinn, Howard. 1977. "The Secrecy, Archives, and the Public Interest". *The Midwestern Archivist* 2 (2): 14- 26.

Chapter 3

Archaeology at the frontlines of rising sea levels: heritage as social action for repairing the world/ *Tikkun Ha-Olam*

Uzi Baram

New College Public Archaeology Lab at New College of Florida; Marie Selby Botanical Gardens, in Sarasota, Florida, United States

Abstract

Archaeologists are recognizing the pressing challenge of rising sea levels on coastal sites and providing insights from the ancients and elders to meet the challenges of climate change. That makes archaeology in the Anthropocene an action word. The ethical underpinnings for archaeology as heritage are explored through the concept of *Tikkun Ha-Olam*. The focus is Florida, which is on the frontline for the rising sea levels as a low-lying peninsula with a rapidly growing population of now more than twenty million people. Through the insights from Florida's first peoples, colonial consequences, long-buried histories of freedom-seeking peoples, and twentieth-century memories, archaeology is building up understandings of the past that can connect residents to place. Since climate change is not an event, archaeology can focus attention on the processes of change and the ethics of healing the world can encourage the present to be prepared for the new coastal zones.

Keywords: Anthropocene, climate change, Florida, heritage, public archaeology

***

Preface: Researching heritage, being inspired by heritage

Our world faces many challenges, and in response, activist anthropologists are attempting to address their concerns and open avenues for action. In my case, from the start my undergraduate and graduate training focused on research to address anthropological, and specifically, archaeological issues and questions to make the world better. Yet my personal identity seemed uninteresting and not relevant during my studies. Then, after many years of anthropological and archaeological practice, I started to acknowledge my ethnic and religious background as a professional. However, I was hesitant about publicly acknowledging my heritage and its importance to my professional endeavours. The question is why: what stimulated this change in perspective? The answer came through my response to local environmental challenges and ongoing community involvement around them.

Teaching at a small liberal arts college on the Florida Gulf Coast, my research program focused on the history of the region through community-based partnerships, the politics of historic preservation, and historical archaeology of nineteenth-century communities of Seminoles, Anglo-Americans, Cuban fisher folk, and maroons. As I expanded my collaboration and partnerships with descendants and local community members in pursuit of the past, more of my own heritage values came to the fore while my efforts remained purely academic. This shift occurred when a hurricane threatened my home, college, and the local landscapes. Shifting my research to meet the crisis, I delved into literature for the preservation of coastal cultural heritage and struggled to master the nuances of climate change science communication. I was familiar with the long-standing debates on politics in archaeology, archaeology as politics, and the moral mission of studying the past, but now the impetus for investigation was different from what I had had in the past. I had experienced hurricanes in the US northeast and in Florida. The 2017 Hurricane Irma was different, part of the more intense and more frequent storms predicted for the Anthropocene and now our unfortunate reality. The warnings that Sarasota, my home since the late 1990s, was in danger of devastation resonated with me. I had to shelter my elderly parents and three teenagers, which was especially challenging since their mother (my then spouse) abandoned our home a couple of weeks before. We got through the storm, the house stood, and in the end, we were all physically safe. Since then, the region has faced more hurricanes with, for example, Hurricane Ian in 2022, causing hundreds of deaths and substantial destruction to property, emphasizing the tremendous challenge of the more intensive weather patterns to individuals and communities. Climate and environmental concerns that were part of my research, community engagement, and courses as an anthropologist expanded from the academic to the social and personal. As many other archaeologists (some of whom are cited below) have done, I began to be explicit on issues of social justice for and in my work.

In such efforts, heritage plays a recursive role in offering insights from the past and opportunities for community resilience. As David Lowenthal (1996) long ago noticed, heritage links us to ancestors, connects us to neighbours, and provides comfort in unsettled times. As I used heritage as a framework for researching climate change, heritage became an avenue for expressing lessons from the past and personal insights for my research endeavours.

My personal commitment to improving the world is not directly connected to the many published approaches to activism for academics and scholars. I had felt for some time like an outsider in academia due to my Jewish heritage, working class origins, having immigrated to the USA a young child, and general personal unease in the unstated norms and social expectations of being a professor at a small college. This unease carried into my academic discipline (even though I earned the rank of Professor of Anthropology). Importantly, the shift in my outlook and involvement came from my efforts at public outreach and engagement; community members facilitated my integration of the professional and the personal into my academic and communal undertakings. With a long-term, community-based, archaeological program facilitating multiple annual public presentations, I was asked, several times, particularly by African Americans, why was I so committed to local archaeological research on an early nineteenth-century maroon community? The project had very little funding and there was very little evidence of settlement when the research team began. Nonetheless, I spent more than a dozen years of my career dedicated to identifying and representing the remains of a community of formerly enslaved Africans who escaped to the remote swamps and hammocks of the Florida Gulf Coast, as well as locating their descendants. Because some of the public presentations were in churches, when I was asked about my commitment to the project the answer became easier to articulate: the story of freedom is the story of my own people's Jewish history and heritage. Just like my ancestors, the maroons were exiles, having left enslavement for a new land and freedom. I felt emancipated by those questions: I could invoke my family's traditions and my Jewish practices in expressing the reasons for my commitment. Plus, since the location for my archaeological research is 10 miles from my campus and located on the shores of a lovely river, I, with community members, gave tours, held discussions, and explored possibilities often. As discussed below, this dynamic became my impetus for action based on the Jewish concept of תיקון עולם *Tikkun Ha-Olam*, the responsibility of each person for repairing/healing the broken/fragmented aspects of our world.

As I pursued my research, I read an ever-increasing number of explicit presentations in publications establishing political and social goals for archaeology, studies illustrating the idealism and commitments of a large portion of the archaeological community. However, the Jewish concept of Tikkun Ha-Olam was not included in those published discussions of archaeology for social justice or as social action. Nonetheless, these traditions prove exceptionally useful for illuminating the reasons for pursuing, presenting, and promoting archaeology in the present.

The approach used for this chapter aligns with the community-based approaches that Fryer and Raczek (2020) advocate for an engaged feminist heritage praxis, especially for grounding arguments and actions in social goals. Similarly, the concept of healing the world can be associated with postcolonial approaches using archaeology as therapy, as noted in the words of Schaepe et al. (2018, 503): "We aim to show how archaeology's acknowledged capacity to transport participants, figuratively speaking, to different times, places, and social settings can reveal continuities and connections across centuries, territories, and cultural legacies, and, in so doing, contribute to health and well-being within descendant communities". Several archaeologists have been animated by such healing approaches, including Rachael Kiddey (2017) in *Homeless Heritage: Collaborative Social Archaeology as Therapeutic Practice*, and the studies in *Archaeology, Heritage, and Wellbeing: Authentic, Powerful, and Therapeutic Engagement with the Past* (Everill and Burnell 2022). Those strands of archaeology as therapeutic practice and feminist heritage praxis propel my increasing formulation of heritage research and action based on the concept of Tikkun Ha-Olam, one's personal responsibility for repairing the world.

The challenge of rising sea levels and how archaeology can inform responses

Rising sea levels are not an event but a long-term process of environmental change. As Amitav Ghosh (2016) in *The Great Derangement: Climate Change and the Unthinkable* lays out, climate change is a problem of the imagination. On the Florida Gulf Coast, as in so many other low-lying coastal regions, the process of recognition of the current environmental crisis is ongoing in an uneven manner. Archaeological sites in particular are under threat from rising sea levels, yet they offer potential avenues to address transformations of the Anthropocene, the useful label for the new weather patterns and environmental dynamics of our era. Coastal sites are under threat of inundation, with professional debates over preservation, documentation, and excavations dominating discussions as to what appropriate actions to take. When the past is made useful in the present, it is heritage. The knowledge that past archaeological findings provide has the potential to contribute toward scholarly, informed social action that can inspire individuals and communities to rearrange their interests and efforts toward acknowledging the material and social transformations of the Anthropocene. This redirection of action offers hope for future generations.

Drawing on the anthropological insights from Eric Wolf (1982) and James C. Scott (2009), as well as Amitav Ghosh (2016), a well-known novelist who began his career as an anthropologist, and Michel-Rolph Trouillot (1995), who created the familiar concept of the 'unthinkable' in anthropology and who explicated the power of silencing to make aspects of the past unthinkable, archaeologists are offering perspectives from the long history of humanity, especially those of alternative social communities that increase the well of conclusions for how to address contemporary social concerns and imagine potential futures. This chapter examines climate change and the role of archaeology in addressing it. This topic can be introduced through a well-known meme often quoted by archaeologists:

> Climate change?
>
> Ask an archaeologist.
>
> We have thousands of years of experience.

The play on words in this meme works to illuminate the long perspective on human history, including previous climate change periods, and serves to humorously state that archaeological findings hold much information about how to view and address climate change.

Archaeology as a keyword

Archaeology is an action word, broadly speaking, and evidence is everywhere. For example, popular cultural portrayals of archaeology, prominently shown in the movies, such as the 1981 film *Raiders of the Lost Ark*, sustain the nineteenth-century image of the archaeological explorer who uncovers lost civilizations. The film situates archaeology as `discovery', which has been problematic since colonial and imperial times, simultaneously presenting a compelling though unethical image of the discipline. Archaeology as offering materials, like mummies for Western schoolchildren to learn about the past, is another contested aspect of popularized archaeology. Those types of images, for political, radical, and critical scholars, continue to present archaeology as a colonialist and imperialist endeavour. But the majority of twenty-first-century archaeologists do not follow the popular imagery nor the colonial traditions, even if the field continues to benefit from the adventurous, popular entry point. With the commitment of the World Archaeological Congress, expansion of Indigenous archaeology in the USA (e.g. Backhouse et al. 2017), and other dynamics, contemporary archaeologists are making positive social contributions to communities. The action of archaeology is breaking free of the field's colonial roots.

Jeremy Sabloff (2016) offers *Archaeology Matters: Action Archaeology in the Modern World* to show relevance for contemporary concerns. Sabloff (2016, 29) posits that with the current environmental challenges, the long-standing discourse in Americanist archaeology over relevance to current populations and issues has taken new turns. Archaeology as the storehouse of knowledge of the spatial past has much to offer to contemporary climate debates (e.g. Van de Noort 2011). Van de Noort (2013) chose the Florida Gulf Coast as a case study (along with the North Sea on the European continental shelf, the Sundarbans at the Bay of Bengal, and the Iraqi marshlands) to illustrate such challenges and argues that archaeology can contribute to community resilience. Archaeological research can "produce descriptions and interpretations of components of society that have come into the present from some point in the past" (Rockman and Hritz 2019, 8296). Rockman and Hritz (2019, 8297) go on to state: "The work to bring the full range and depth of human experience, including experiences that can be seen as adaptive and those now understood to have been maladaptive, into the modern global response to climate change has not yet been done". There is much to be accomplished.

Focusing on climate change as a danger to the planet, as part of earth science or biology class, is meaningful, but for social change to occur, climate change cannot be taught abstractly as a scientific phenomenon that is happening. Climate change happens to people, and the field of archaeology provides opportunities to highlight past, present, and future dynamics overdetermined by climate change. Archaeologists, as witnesses to material and social change (see Hausner et al. 2018), are, and should be recognized as being, on the frontlines of the response to climate change.

What kind of social action? (When the task is overwhelming)

Scholarly literature demonstrates the long-term intersections of archaeology and environmental concerns, from observations on the contemporary to recovering past ecologies and theories on the relationships among climate and human history. Scholars are expected to master that literature and have their debates and discussions inform understandings for research designs, archaeological evidence, and anthropological conclusions, but they cannot expect the same of the interested public. The challenge for heritage as social action is for archaeologists to continually renew the ways and means they use to disseminate their insights, and to find new means to communicate effectively. This will help the public to recognize climate change and work productively toward potential equitable futures. This is the challenge for heritage as social action.

Heritage as social action, with archaeology as an action word, incorporates the tangible and intangible from historic places, and offers opportunities for community resilience, as well as meaningful plans for commemorations as the Anthropocene advances—a productive avenue for recognizing the past to face the challenges of a future of continuing sea level rise. For example, in the aftermath of Hurricane Katrina, Dawdy (2006, 724) presented how race and poverty in New Orleans became exposed by the flooding. Multiple axes of cultural assumptions and historical erasures became visible in the aftermath of the sudden, devastating hurricane and flooding. Rising sea levels added another layer of complexity, as the sudden weather event intersected with climate-driven landscape transformations, impacting coastal archaeological sites. The sites in areas such as this are impacted by the changing frontlines of expanding coastal zones, and archaeologists can, and should, actively adapt to focus on the inequities of implications for peoples and places.

But what do archaeologists mean when they claim social justice? Even with the expansion of articles and books about social activism, social justice, and peace, there is little exploration of those terms or their goals. The terms are invoked as obviously positive, and academics usually consider themselves as well-meaning and good people, so it therefore follows that social justice becomes a personalized stance: of course, the projects are socially meaningful—I am a good person, therefore, I am doing good work. Yet there is a need for expanding the ontology for more substantial and productive efforts. One of the greatest limitations of the current discourse is the search for an assessment of the projects—did they change the world in a meaningful manner?

To face the enormity of the climate change that is coming, a different metric is needed, and I offer insights from Tikkun Ha-Olam. The concept of Tikkun Ha-Olam comes from the Mishnah, part of the Talmud, the code of Jewish law. The usual translation (transliterated from the Hebrew as *Tikkun Olam*) is to repair the world, and the concept is understood as a responsibility for healing the earth, its peoples, and the ecology. Implicit in Tikkun Ha-Olam is an imperative for each person to gather fragments together and to make the world a better place. As an imperative, the concept insists the effort to repair the world is our collective and individual obligation to the planet, nature, and mankind. As Rabbi Jonathan Sacks (1948-2020), former Chief Rabbi of the United Kingdom, explained in numerous speeches (e.g. 2012), Judaism is a future-oriented faith, with a sense of responsibility to future generations. Applying the concept further, to fulfil that ethical responsibility, archaeologists in particular can take the remains of societies from the past, and the knowledge gained from them, and offer humanity lessons through their materiality, understood as belongings and not simply artefacts.

Engaging with the climate crisis is challenging; knowing that pain and the threat of survival has started for some coastal communities already, and that more storms and erosion are coming, can be overwhelming. Archaeological efforts, whether implicitly or explicitly, have focused on traumas to archaeological sites and historic structures as well as homes and roads facilitated by the Anthropocene climate changes, and these efforts have dovetailed with increasing discussions of social activism in archaeology. Starting with Barbara Little (2009) asking "What Can Archaeology Do for Justice, Peace, Community, and the Earth?", archaeologists have been offering answers. Most leave the intellectual underpinnings of their social activism implicit in publications, typically stating witnessing injustice and especially racism in the USA as the impetus for their archaeological research (i.e. Ferguson 2004; Barton 2021) rather than the ontological source of their beliefs in social justice, equity, and transformative representations of the past. One of the few exceptions is Leone (2010) who invokes Catholic tradition via Leo XIII's *On Capital and Labor*, while Baram (2019) turns to Jewish Rabbinic teachings on tradition which state, 'It is not upon you to finish the task, nor are you free to desist from it' *Pirkei Avot* 2:21 (a tractate of the Mishnah on ethics).

I offer Tikkun Ha-Olam here because it is not enough that someone believes they are good or are hopeful that archaeology changes the world. There must be a metric for the development of relationships, meaning, and impact. This seems a useful framework for social justice for archaeological projects and moves us beyond reading the literature that invokes social justice in archaeology. That literature is frustrating because it is aimed at other scholars and because the foundations are too limited for successfully confronting the challenges of climate change.

On the frontlines of rising sea levels are also the structural challenges of political economic inequalities and a need for restorative justice. These include recognition of the Indigenous presence and the continuing legacies of racial separations. Recognizing that transformation toward equity is not a simple step but a long-term process of change means that just having one's consciousness raised is not enough. Archaeology, as both a collective profession and a set of knowledge on humanity, can contribute to historicizing what seems recent but is part of an evolving story of human society. My inspiration comes from Tikkun Ha-Olam, and my aim is to encourage archaeologists to establish a goal of disseminating information about the past in a manner that inspires communities to acknowledge the challenges of the present, and by doing so, to act for a more equitable future, as recognized through relationships, meaning, and impact.

Artefacts as belongings, archaeological sites as heritage locales

Reaching into the Jewish tradition of Tikkun Ha-Olam inspires a recognition of the ontology of archaeology. To move beyond the historical limitations of archaeology means decolonizing, even undisciplining, archaeology (Schneider and Hayes 2020) to open up assumptions about the past and future. One step is to rethink the disciplinary terminology. Dawdy (2006, 719) demonstrated that potential with opening up taphonomy from its focus on the creation of the archaeological record toward the "complexity, the mix of the accidental and manipulation, the silences and erasures, the constraining structures, and the sudden ruptures that all go into the creation of history and the 'ethnographic present.'" In her research, Dawdy (2006, 720) focused on describing the immediate post-Katrina period in New Orleans, highlighting the "special role that trash and dirt play in disaster recovery". Katrina was a devastating hurricane, and such storm events are disasters. The greater frequency and intensity of hurricanes in the twenty-first century is but one component of the Anthropocene. Another component is rising sea levels, which facilitate disasters and also long-term transformations of our present landscapes. A study of rising sea levels foretells of our potential coastal future, connecting to Dawdy's (2006, 724) point that: "Few seem willing to concede that nature has won part of the battle, nor are they willing to redraw the map to allow for a greater interdependence between city and swamp".

One current shift within archaeology has been the recognition of sites as heritage locales and artefacts as belongings. In Florida, some signage still claims the temporal identity of mounds and sacred places as prehistoric, instead of situating the very old as ancient rather than pre-history (see, for instance, Austin 2021); ancient can be meaningful, particularly as lessons learned. To place the challenge fully in front of communities, new understandings are needed to demonstrate that locales that survived centuries are now in danger of inundation.

Anderson et al. (2017) starkly laid out the impact of rising sea levels for archaeological sites, historic buildings, and cultural landscapes in a scientific report, and the number of impacted sites for the coasts of the southeastern United States is overwhelming. Numbering in the tens of thousands, the potential loss of the material record encourages initiatives like the Florida Public Archaeology Network's Heritage Monitoring Scouts (Dawson et al. 2020), an initiative that utilizes citizen science to document observable impacted sites. Florida, with its 8,436 miles/13,576 kilometres of Atlantic Ocean and Gulf of Mexico coastline, counting tidal inlets, (see Wikipedia entry for List of U.S. states and territories by coastline and topography) faces rising sea levels that are a threat nearly everywhere on the peninsula.

The retreat from the coastal zone

I begin public presentations on climate change with the line: *We used to go to the beach*. That statement may become a memory for Floridians. Rising sea levels mean the coastal zone is expanding and barrier islands that have beaches are being erased. Some governments have beach renourishment projects; for instance, the City of Sarasota spent $12.6 million between July and December of 2020 to move approximately 680,000 cubic yards of sand to the beach along with two protection groins (consisting of 5,000 tons of armour stone). Elsewhere the loss of beach sand is part of the acceleration of change on the coast. Already houses in the Florida Keys are being abandoned. Miami Beach is facing regular flooding. After two years, parts of the panhandle have not recovered from the October 2018 Hurricane Michael, followed by Hurricane Sally in September 2020, a storm which flooded Pensacola. Nuisance flooding and more frequent and intense hurricanes are no longer predictions but regular occurrences, and evidence for the increasing inundations is everywhere. In response, archaeologists working on coastal middens and historic sites are holding discussions, planning, and organizing workshops. They are excavating and 3D photo-documenting significant places and are moving forward to record the Florida that was. An analysis of places like Castillo de San Marcos and Egmont Key demonstrates the challenges and opportunities of being on the frontlines of rising sea levels.

Castillo de San Marcos

Figure 3.1 Castillo San Marcos, St. Augustine. July 2009.

Photograph taken by author.

Castillo de San Marcos sits on the western shore of Matanzas Bay in the city of St. Augustine, one the oldest colonial cities on the Atlantic coast of Florida. Construction of Castillo de San Marco began in 1672 using a sedimentary rock known as coquina. The massive structure became Fort Mark under British rule (1763-1783) and Castillo de San Marcos during the Second Spanish Period

(1783-1821). The United States Government renamed the military complex as Fort Marion. The fort became a historic monument in 1924 with the original Spanish name. Managed by the National Park Service, the historic site is a popular tourist attraction. However, flooding is now a current concern as water levels in Matanzas Bay are changing. As a large, important, and iconic structure of Spanish Colonial architecture, tremendous financial and intellectual resources are going into its preservation as the sea levels rise.

Egmont Key

Egmont Key, on the Gulf of Mexico coast of Florida, is a small island at the mouth of Tampa Bay. The Indigenous presence goes back centuries. While the first archival record about Egmont Key is from 1757, the written record notes the key was first occupied by the Spanish, followed by the English. With increasing shipping from Tampa Bay, the USA completed a lighthouse on the key in 1848. During what the US government calls the 'Third Seminole War' (1855-58), Egmont Key was a prison camp for Seminoles, who were sent to the island as a holding place before being deported to Indian Territory (now Oklahoma). The legacy of those prisoners, particularly Polly Parker (Emateloye), a Seminole who escaped to join her people, is expressed in an online publication *Egmont Key –a Seminole Story* (Mueller and Boge 2020). The island's heritage continues its military legacy with the Civil War and Spanish-American War. The island became a state park in 1989, with a ferry service for day trips. Since 2013, the Seminole Tribe of Florida has discussed the preservation of this small (about 300 acres) and rapidly eroding place. To ensure community engagement, the Seminole Tribe of Florida's Tribal Historic Preservation Office leads guided tours of the island for tribal members to see the island before the tides wash their history away. Archaeologists are ensuring, through 3D photo-documentation, a virtual record remains.

These two Florida coastal historic sites illustrate the challenge of rising sea levels and there are efforts underway, particularly 3D photo-documentation of the sites, to document their presence and history. While in the early twentieth-century Americans were reasonably confident that the country's major cities were safe from environmental destruction, as even Miami after Hurricane Andrew in 1992 eventually recovered, that assumption shifted with Hurricane Katrina for New Orleans in 2005 (see Dawdy 2006), Superstorm Sandy for New York City in 2012, and Hurricane Harvey for Houston in 2017. Certainly, what a dualist Cartesian worldview sees as nature separate from culture falls apart as the outside comes flooding in. Shannon Lee Dawdy (2006) describes that ideological crisis well through stories of snakes in people's kitchens after New Orleans was inundated by floodwaters during Hurricane Katrina. The intensity and damage from that crisis alone can lead to a gloom and doom vision for climate change, but there are alternative perspectives. By connecting the relatively recent recognition of archaeology as potentially contributing to social justice (Little 2009, Atalay et al. 2015) through climate crisis response, some possibilities emerge to suggest how present communities can imagine their coastal futures.

Figure 3.2 Egmont Key, at the mouth of Tampa Bay. December 2018.

Photograph taken by author.

For example, archaeology has disciplinary traditions that are useful in the Anthropocene: the focus on the long-term, the respect for the cultural landscape with its material and intangible attributes, and a dynamic framework for situating the past for the present. Most importantly for places facing the loss of their cultural landscape, archaeology contributes to a sense of belonging even for diasporic peoples as climate refugees will become.

Furthermore, archaeology provides knowledge about local heritage. Archaeology as heritage work starts with the recognition of the increasing significance of heritage in Anthropocene social lives (see Lowenthal 1996), the roles of international and national governmentality in authorized heritage discourse (Smith 2006), the opportunity for heritage as social action (Harrison 2010), and the relevance and application of heritage in contemporary life (Yu et al. 2018). When heritage is more than social memory, when it is harnessed to address the crises before us, new senses of belonging can come forward. For the places being inundated, heritage is necessary since what was will be gone, and survivors will need a sense of community to rebuild their lives.

The Seminole Tribe of Florida ensures the memory of Egmont Key and the US National Park Service strives to preserve Castillo de San Marcos. However, not all coastal material heritage inspires and generates those levels of support. In fact, there are too many heritage locales on the Florida coast for such major initiatives. For smaller, less-known heritage locales, there are different strategies and concerns.

For a manageable examination of the threat in Florida, and the potential for action, I joined a group of faculty members at New College of Florida for an integrated heritage approach to a roughly 25-mile/approximately 50-kilometre stretch of the southwest Florida coast, organized as Sarasota and Manatee counties. This region is known professionally for its archaeological sites, but its past has not received widespread public recognition and the region has no major ancient monuments, no charismatic sites, to symbolize the threat. Yet much history will be lost as the waters rise in the area.

Figure 3.3 Map of the five heritage preservation projects.

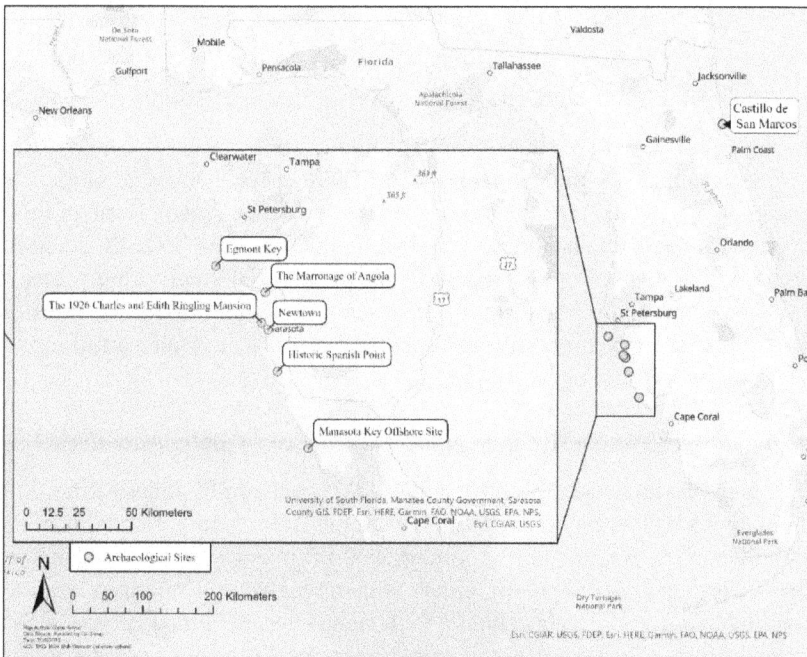

Map created by Glenn Kolyer 2023, printed with permission.

The following five heritage preservation projects on the Florida Gulf Coast, a stretch between Tampa Bay and Charlotte Harbor, offer insight into the social dynamics involved in the preservation and protection of heritage from climate change, and how such programs are positive social actions. With archaeological sites and historic locales at the frontlines of rising sea levels, concise case studies such as these on the Gulf Coast of Florida can provide valuable insights and illustrate how efforts to protect heritage can be viewed as social actions to prepare more secure futures for the generations to come. The climate crisis is a threat multiplier—for marginalized communities, for under-recognized heritage locales, and for emotionally exhausted, post-democratic societies. Gulf Coast Florida preservation efforts therefore offer unique examples of opportunities for meeting the challenges of the Anthropocene.

The following examples of archaeological sites from the region are wide-ranging:

- *Manasota Key Offshore Site* (8So7030), an Archaic period cemetery
- *Historic Spanish Point* (8So2) three sites that range from the Archaic through Manasota archaeological period (roughly 6000 BP to 800 BP)
- *The Marronage of Angola* (8Ma103) from the early nineteenth century
- *Newtown*: An early twentieth-century African American community
- *The 1926 Charles and Edith Ringling Mansion* (National Registry #82001039), now College Hall for New College of Florida

The point of identifying these examples, all from only twenty-five miles of the Florida coastline, is to highlight the tremendous challenges identified by Anderson et al. (2017) for the southeast USA as sea levels rise. None of these sites are labelled as 'outstanding universal significance' (the UNESCO standard for World Heritage), but all are significant in their potential to inform us of possible futures, are meaningful for descendants, are part of the cultural landscape for contemporary residents and visitors, and all contribute to regional heritage and beyond.

Manasota Key Offshore Site: state support to preserve an underwater site.

During the last Ice Age, the coasts of Florida extended fifty miles further into the Gulf of Mexico than their present locations. The ancient inhabitants of the land during the Archaic period (about 9000 BP to 2500 BP) faced rising sea levels. The history of this long epoch is complicated and nuanced, with an important source of insights coming from cemeteries. In Florida, archaeologists have recovered one of the adaptations for those ancient peoples to the expanding coastal zone: underwater burials in ponds (Wentz and Gifford 2007).

The success of that adaptation is clear with the Manasota Key Offshore Site, now under 21 feet of water in the Gulf of Mexico and a quarter mile/about half a kilometre off Manasota Key (a barrier island off the coast of Florida) in southern Sarasota County. The site was discovered when a fossil hunter noticed human remains on the Gulf bottom, and subsequently, in 2016, the State Underwater Archaeologist began investigations. It was determined that the remains were from a pond cemetery dating to the Archaic period eight thousand years ago when the pond was on a nine-foot rise. The findings were that the sea had preserved the buried to the present. Archaeologists further inferred that Archaic period people observed the rising sea levels and chose pond burials for a world of contracting land.

Research and dissemination of insights from that finding came together due to the diligence of the Florida Secretary of State, Ken Detzner, whose responsibilities include the Bureau of Archaeological Research. He facilitated the support from the Gulf Coast Community Foundation, which is headquartered in the town of Venice, near Manasota Key. The political and financial connections that developed were fortuitous for the archaeological project. The combination of the Secretary of State, who took a personal interest in the project, and the Gulf Coast Community Foundation, inspired the unified involvement of residents from Manasota Key, the Seminole Tribe of Florida, the state's underwater archaeologists, the Florida Public Archaeology Network, and other stakeholders from across the region. Notably, similar to Egmont Key, the collaboration with the Seminole Tribe of Florida facilitated defining the meaning of the heritage locale and contributed to the Gulf Coast Community Foundation's goal of "enhancing our unique places".[1]

After several seasons of excavations, the insights from this project and its findings are being readied for publication. However, for the Archaic-period cemetery, any attempt to secure buoys and mark the site of the cemetery failed when a hurricane passed through the Gulf of Mexico. Unlike terrestrial sites, where putting soil over the location would help with preservation, the ocean currents prevent such solutions for a graveyard resting on the Gulf bottom. Local community members are keeping an eye on the location but, ultimately, no conservation is possible, and the 8000-year-old archaeological site will fade to the salt waters. Importantly, significant relationships were expanded between the government, the local community, and the Seminole Tribe of Florida, building new understandings of, and respect for, cultural differences.

Historic Spanish Point: academic support for three historic sites within a museum.

On grounds that are today Marie Selby Botanical Gardens' Historic Spanish Point campus, located on the shores of Little Sarasota Bay, are extensive ancient remains. The late Archaic period shell ring (4500-3750 B.P) is one site within a wide-spread US Southeast coastal phenomenon (Russo 2002), created when the shoreline stabilized. Near the shell ring is material evidence of the people who postdate the ones who built the shell ring: two shell midden ridges and a Manasota-period (2500-1300 BP) burial mound. Unfortunately, this complex of archaeological sites is threatened by rising sea levels.

Historic Spanish Point gets its name from Anglo-American settlers who learned of the location on Little Sarasota Bay from a Cuban, otherwise called Spanish, fisherman. Cuba-based fisherfolk set up fishing ranchos on the Florida Gulf Coast from the 1740s through the 1840s, and it is from an unnamed fisherman that the point is credited as Spanish Point. Anglo-American settlement began in 1867 and shortly thereafter the Webb family took an interest in the mounds on their property. The next owner, Bertha Palmer (famous in Sarasota as a socialite, businesswoman, and philanthropist) preserved the mounds as she organized her home and gardens on the property. In 1980, the Palmer heirs donated the land to be a museum, along with a range of historic and more recent architecture. In 2020, that museum merged with Marie Selby Botanical Gardens, based in the city of Sarasota.

Figure 3.4 Historic Spanish Point, Sarasota County. September 2017.

Photograph taken by author.

For thousands of years, the evidence suggests, the coastal zone around the museum was consistent—the plants and animals might have shifted but the shoreline was stable. But the coastal region now faces inundation. The Botanical Garden's grounds are a living museum, the permanence of which is now challenged by the rising seas. To investigate this issue, faculty from Florida Gulf Coast University are studying a shell ridge from the Manasota period (2500-1300 BP), and the Marie Selby Botanical Gardens scientists are working with New College of Florida faculty to address the environmental challenges facing the plants and monuments. The coastal museum is illustrating to the public the transformation of the Anthropocene. Significant decisions must be made whether to preserve the architecture—ancient and more recent. The New College faculty-led research proposal encourages visitors to come, not for disaster tourism, or as voyeurism of coming tragedy, but to witness change and, similar to how museums edify visitors, so they can document and learn from the transformations visible against the ancient mounds.

The Marronage of Angola: building community action and respect through archaeology.

Four rivers empty into Tampa Bay, and the southernmost one is the Manatee River. Historically it was called the Oyster River, due to its extensive oyster beds. A historical archaeology project has located material evidence of an early nineteenth-century marronage on the south side of the river. To accommodate anticipated rising river water levels, 2019 plans to transform the park where excavations took place require lagoons and other water features.

Figure 3.5 Angola Excavations, Bradenton. January 2020.

Photograph taken by author.

The marronage, known as Angola, was built by self-emancipated and free people of African heritage, known after the mid-nineteenth century as Black Seminoles. Starting in the 1770s, a community of freedom-seeking people developed near the Manatee Mineral Spring. The south side of the Manatee River, similar to earlier marronage by the Apalachicola and Suwannee rivers, has a natural barrier against aggression from the north, protection as maroons moved southward to avoid slave raids and the US military. The community grew to more than seven hundred, but Angola was destroyed in 1821 just as Spain transferred Florida to the United States. The havens of freedom across the Florida Gulf Coast, the southern route of the Underground Railroad, are significant chapters in the struggle against slavery but nearly forgotten until the twenty-first century. Continuing analysis of recently excavated material evidence for the marronage are promising insights into the courage and determination of the peoples of Angola.

The approach to finding this marronage was led by a community scholar who organized an interdisciplinary research team committed to public engagement. Starting in 2005, public presentations on the little-known history for those who found a haven of freedom in today's Bradenton, Florida, facilitated public interest. A combination of excavations done in the sunshine (a term for public archaeology coined by Milanich 1991), community organizing (Baram 2011), and support from a local non-profit historic preservation organization, engendered local and regional community support for the history of Black freedom. This combined effort is archaeology as an action word, and the image of archaeology as well as the practice of archaeological research resonated and built-up local community support. Ethnographic research laid the foundation for robust engagement with the descendant community, those whose ancestors fled to Andros Island in the Bahamas and continue to reside there. Archaeological success came with analysis of test excavations, announced in 2014; a Back to Angola festival in July 2018, planned as an annual event before the COVID-19 pandemic; and transnational excitement over material details of the saga of the freedom-seeking people's history being revealed by archaeology (Baram 2021).

When the City of Bradenton, through its public-private partnership *Realize Bradenton*, announced turning the area by the spring into the eastern terminal of its Riverwalk (a linear entertainment district along the Manatee River), stakeholders united to express concern over what would happen to the archaeological record by the spring, now known as the Manatee Mineral Spring Park. The wellspring of community support, the result of increased recognition of the significance of the early nineteenth-century history pre-dating the founding of the village that became Bradenton, led to city funding of major excavations of the marronage site.

The excavations revealed that the water table was indeed rising at a significant rate. Previous excavations, volunteer efforts on single weekends over three years, built on previous archaeological testing of the area. There were no reports of reaching the water table in the 2005 excavations, which went down to sterile subsoil. And the 2008 and 2013 excavations were able to go into sterile sand, although the 2009 excavation unit filled with water after a brief rainstorm. In 2020, however, the excavations grappled with ground water at nearly every area. Since the main excavations were 150 meters south from the riverbank, the change seems related to the rising water table, a reminder that rising sea levels are coastal and subterranean.

The increased community support, activism and interest will ensure that exhibits and displays on or near the site of the marronage along the increasingly popular Riverwalk will facilitate public audiences for the history and heritage of the significant African American community. Lagoons purposely built for the park will regulate rising water for decades to come and will ensure the riverbank will be safe for decades, and the story of the marronage will continue to be told where freedom-seekers once lived and struggled for their liberty.

Newtown: local community engagement to empower citizens and promote African American heritage.

Legacies of racial segregation haunt Sarasota, Florida, as they do throughout the USA. In Sarasota, the African American community is based in Newtown, once simply the only neighbourhood where Blacks could live and now a geographically delineated northern part of the modern city. A heritage vitalization program begun in 2015 known as *Newtown Alive* has energized local interest in the twentieth-century Black past and offered heritage tourism opportunities to sustain the African American community (Baram 2019). But its location is chilling even in the warming trends of the Anthropocene.

Coastal racial formation (Hardy 2017) led the development of the immediate coastline of Sarasota to be white, and the nearby area that had been less desirable, marshy and relatively low-lying, to become the Black residential areas. While the coast faces storm surges, Newtown is located within a geographic basin with a bayou acting as an avenue for bay waters that can be pushed into the neighbourhood during storms. In the half-decade of heritage revitalization of Newtown, a heritage trail, countless programs, and a museum have developed programs offering remembrances of twentieth-century Black determination and dignity. But nearly all of Newtown could be inundated, as was New Orleans' Ninth Ward in the 2005 aftermath of Hurricane Katrina, if a storm pushes the bay into the bayou and into the community. Importantly, historic sites of importance to the heritage of this African American community, those which have not yet been investigated by archaeologists, may be lost. This example is a reminder that climate change is a crisis multiplier for racialized communities, and political organizing is needed to improve infrastructure to protect culturally important, yet extremely vulnerable places. As has been demonstrated in Newtown already, change can be energized by heritage campaigns. Archaeology in this case is social action, as a tool to highlight material significance and expand historical memory of the struggles against twentieth-century racism, and to build capital for ongoing preservation efforts. Such heritage efforts are going through community-based partnerships.

The Charles and Edith Ringling Mansion: a seawall for a college landmark.

In 1926 Charles and Edith Ringling used their wealth, generated from the Ringling Brothers Circus, to purchase land on Sarasota Bay and have a mansion constructed next to John and Mable Ringling's mansion. The Ringlings' estates set the tone for Sarasota, a neo-Mediterranean vision that still is part of the cultural landscape a century later. Charles died nine months after moving into the home, but Edith stayed until her death in 1953; in many ways, it was her home, even if the National Registry of Historic Places names the building the Charles Ringling Mansion. In 1962 the mansion became College Hall for the newly created New College (now New College of Florida).

The mansion, along with another built directly to its south for the Ringling's daughter and her family, is protected by a sea wall, first built with the original house. Rising sea levels over the twentieth century plus the effects of erosion led New College to rebuild the seawall in 2012, replicating the historic balustrade with contemporary materials. The new seawall is higher than the initial one, and the restoration created a lagoon to its north, to mediate the high tides. The mansion suffered some damage by Hurricane Irma in 2017 but has been repaired, and continuing maintenance makes the historic mansion a centrepiece for the liberal arts college. The uneven pace of climate change means ongoing threats to the structure will come from rising sea levels, rising groundwater, and heavier rainfalls – challenges in every direction for the mansion.

College Hall offers a counterexample to the other locations. The answer to the challenge of rising sea levels came from the expenditure of state funds, done in such a way that the landscape looks historic, as if nothing has changed since the Ringlings built their home in 1926. Continuing the approach seen in the New College of Florida Climate Action Plan, prepared in 2010, the goal is to modify the campus community's contribution to climate change rather than address the transformations that will change the relationship to the coastal zone as the seas continue to rise.

Figure 3.6 View of Sarasota Bay from College Hall, New College of Florida, Sarasota. January 2021.

Photograph taken by author.

Five histories in less than twenty-five miles

These five places on Florida's Gulf Coast, representing thousands of years of coastal history, offer the range of challenges and opportunities—past and present—for confronting sea level rise during the Anthropocene. Current projections indicate the land on which this coastal material heritage rests will be lost in the coming decades. If we are passive, some of these places will be missed, some erased from memory, and new landscapes will develop as the coastal zones move inland. With archaeology as action, the effort insists on their significance even as the crises multiply. For the above case studies, there are different community interests, different histories, and different goals. These are only a fraction of the archaeological and historical sites at the frontlines of rising sea levels around Florida. The climate emergency is leading to many approaches, with communications among scholars, heritage professionals, and others coming through different media and discussions. The goal is to bring the fragments and disparate cases together, to heal the divides, and to find and implement useful solutions.

For most of the diverse examples, research into their heritage is building up relationships among stakeholders, community members, and larger audiences of citizens and visitors. By stressing the meaning of the past as integration of cultural and environmental heritage and change, the local offers an avenue to the global concerns. An assessment of the impact of these examples and their amalgamation as regional heritage is still in the future.

Archaeological insights from the ancient mounds of Florida's first peoples, from the long-buried and nearly silenced histories of freedom-seeking peoples, and from the shadows of the twentieth-century history of segregation, expose complicated histories of resilience. More importantly, sites such as these from the Florida Gulf Coast, a tiny fraction of the coastlines documented by Anderson et al. (2017) for the US Southeast, provide only a minuscule number of solutions to the global challenge of facing climate change, yet they can provide some understandings of the past that connect residents to place and thereby focus attention on cultural landscapes as non-static components of our quotidian lives. These sites encourage present populations to be prepared for and to respond to the transformations of coastal zones, vistas, communities, towns, and cities in the near and distant future.

Archaeology is a keyword, heritage is social action

As Dawson et al. (2020, 8283) proclaim: "Unlike public archaeology programs in the twentieth century that had time on their sides, archaeologists can no longer afford gradual or independent development of approaches—we must build our local solutions on others' successes". And that building requires clarity to disseminate accurate information and dynamic actionable approaches to preserving what we can of coastal heritage. By advocating for archaeology as a keyword, heritage experts and enthusiasts alike can clarify a realm that is filled with confusion.

Archaeology offers a foundation of generalized public support based on decades of popularized representations. Archaeology offers a long tradition of representations, with lessons learned and new approaches bubbling up. And archaeologists act, from planning and consulting with descendants and local communities, to implementing excavations and/or laboratory research. Archaeological endeavours are heritage as social action.

From the case studies briefly presented in this chapter, the far-sighted decisions of Archaic-period peoples to bury their deceased in freshwater ponds, the mounds and networks of ancestral Native Floridians, the use of rivers for liberty by maroons, and the joy of heritage for an African American community, all point to heritage as social action, and as a well of conclusions, to borrow Henry Glassie's (1995) definition of tradition, from which to foresee our new coastal futures. Archaeology, a keyword for heritage during the Anthropocene, therefore plays a significant role in extending the view of the present past the gloom and doom of today, and toward places and memories of hope for the future.

Conclusion: The past as a key to the future

The Florida that was—expansive beaches, cool winters, and coastal settlements—may soon be gone. Egmont Key will return to the waters. Castillo San Marcos may still stand, preserved through massive effort and cost as a national monument. Many will never know of the histories at Historic Spanish Point, the Manatee River, or the New College campus. There are many choices to be made for preserving information from coastal sites, and unfortunately, some places will be lost. But if the present does not act, does not recognize that the cultural landscape will be transformed by rising sea levels, future populations will be shocked by the unexpected changes and the results may be harnessed to blame minority groups. By preparing the public for the transformations wrought by climate change, by using the knowledge from a century and a half of archaeology, professionals can share that landscapes have historically changed, and we can memorialize and potentially protect what matters to many, while preparing for the potential new social realities of the Anthropocene. The past can be a key to our positive futures.

Meeting the challenges for coastal heritage is not an event; this chapter is part of a process that recognizes that the sea levels will be rising for generations, and decisions and actions for preserving and remembering material coastal heritage in this generation will not be the formula for the next generations. As residents and researchers of archaeological and historic sites on the Florida Gulf Coast grapple with rising sea levels—one of the locations where the climate crisis is increasingly acute—projects are ongoing and the results are in process. Archaeology is a lens for realizing the dynamics of change over time, and the discipline will surely be challenged and changed by the Anthropocene climate and its coastal zone transformations.

Acknowledgements

Many thanks to Susan Shay and Kelly M. Britt for the invitation to the World Archaeological Congress session and this book and their editing and support for this chapter. The external reviewer extended their suggestions. As I state in the chapter, my engagement with climate change accelerated with Hurricane Irma passing over my home in 2017, followed by hosting the 2018 Tidally United, a summit held in Sarasota as a joint project of the Florida Public Archaeology Network and the New College Public Archaeology Lab. My campus colleagues in biology have expanded my heritage framework, Marie Selby Botanical Gardens and De Soto National Memorial gracefully welcomed us to their coastal properties, and a January 2021 pilot project benefited from a dozen enthusiastic undergraduates. I think about my now teenagers and the challenges they will face if they stay in Sarasota, Florida, as I work through the role of archaeology on the frontlines of rising sea levels.

Notes

[1] See https://www.gulfcoastcf.org/our-initiatives/arts-and-culture/manasota-key-offshore-archaeological-site, Accessed April 2021.

Bibliography

Anderson, David G., Thaddeus G. Bissett, Stephen J. Yerka, Joshua J. Wells, Eric C. Kansa, Sarah W. Kansa, Kelsey Noack Myers, R. Carl DeMuth, Devin A. White. 2017. "Sea-level rise and archaeological site destruction: An example from the southeastern United States using DINAA (Digital Index of North American Archaeology)". *PLoS ONE* 12 (11). Accessed 2017. e0188142. https://doi.org/10.1371/journal.pone.0188142.

Atalay, Sonya, Lee Rains Clauss, Randall H. McGuire, and John R. Welch, eds. 2015. *Transforming Archaeology: Activist Practices and Prospects.* Walnut Creek: Left Coast Press.

Austin, Robert. 2021. "Fact and Fiction: Public Interpretation and the Pinellas Point Mound". *Central Gulf Coast Archaeological Society Bulletin* 9 (2): 2-9.

Backhouse, Paul N., Brent R. Weisman, and Mary Beth Rosebrough, eds. 2017. *We Come for Good: Archaeology and Tribal Historic Preservation at the Seminole Tribe of Florida.* Gainesville: University Press of Florida.

Baram, Uzi. 2011. "Community Organizing in Public Archaeology: Coalitions for the Preservation of a Hidden History in Florida". *Present Pasts* 3 (1): 12-18.

———. 2019. "Gentrification and Nostalgia: Archaeology of Memory for the Segregated Past in a Coastal Florida City". *International Journal of Heritage Studies* 25 (7): 722-735.

———. 2021. "On the Trail of Early Nineteenth-century Freedom-Seeking People Across Gulf Coast Florida: Archaeological Clues to a Robust Heritage Hidden in Plain Sight". *Journal of Florida Studies* 9 (1): 1-20.

Barton, Christopher P., ed. 2021. *Trowels in the Trenches: Archaeology as Social Activism.* Gainesville: University Press of Florida.

Dawson, Tom, Joanna Hambly, Alice Kelley, William Lees, and Sarah Miller. 2020. "Coastal Heritage, Global Climate Change, Public Engagement, and Citizen Science". PNAS 117 (15): 8280–8286. Accessed 2020. www.pnas.org/cgi/doi/10.1073/pnas.1912246117.

Dawdy, Shannon Lee. 2006. "The Taphonomy of Disaster and the (Re)Formation of New Orleans". *American Anthropologist* 108 (4): 719-730.

Everill, Paul and Karen Burnell, eds. 2022. *Archaeology, Heritage, and Wellbeing: Authentic, Powerful, and Therapeutic Engagement with the Past.* New York: Routledge.

Ferguson, Leland. 2004. *Uncommon Ground: Archaeology and Early African America, 1650-1800.* Washington, DC: Smithsonian Institution Press.

Fryer, Tiffany C. and Teresa P. Raczek. 2020. "Introduction: Toward an Engaged Feminist Heritage Praxis". *Engendering Heritage: Contemporary Feminist Approaches to Archaeological Heritage Practice*. Archaeological Papers of the American Anthropological Association 31: 7-25.

Glassie, Henry. 1995. "Tradition". *Journal of American Folklore* 108 (430): 395-412.

Ghosh, Amitav. 2016. *The Great Derangement: Climate Change and the Unthinkable*. Chicago: University of Chicago Press.

Hardy, R. Dean, Richard A. Milligan, and Nik Heynen. 2017. "Racial Coastal Formation: The Environmental Injustices of Colorblind Adaptation Planning for Sea-level Rise". *Geoforum* 87: 62-72.

Harrison, Rodney. 2010. "Heritage as Social Action". In *Understanding Heritage in Practice*, edited by Susie West, 240–276. Manchester, NH: Manchester University Press.

Hausner, Mark, Whitney Battle-Baptiste, Koji Lau-Ozawa, Barbara L. Voss, Reinhard Bernbeck, Susan Pollock, Randall H. McGuire, Uzma Z. Rizvi, Christopher Hernandez, and Sonya Atalay. 2018. "Vital Topics Forum: Archaeology as Bearing Witness". *American Anthropologist* 120 (3): 535-548.

Kiddey, Rachael. 2017. *Homeless Heritage: Collaborative Social Archaeology as Therapeutic Practice*. New York: Oxford University Press.

Leone, Mark P. 2010. *Critical Historical Archaeology*. Walnut Creek: Left Coast Press.

Little, Barbara. 2009. "Forum: What can Archaeology do for Justice, Peace, Community and the Earth?" *Historical Archaeology* 43 (4): 115-119.

Lowenthal, David. 1996. *Possessed by the Past: The Heritage Crusade and the Spoils of History*. New York: The Free Press.

Milanich, Jerald T. 1991. "Archaeology in the Sunshine: Grass Roots Education through the Media and Public Involvement". In *Protecting the Past*, edited by G. Smith and J. Ehrenhard, 109-116. Boca Raton: CRC Press.

Mueller, Bradley and Alyssa Boge. 2020. *Egmont Key - A Seminole Story*. Clewiston: The Seminole Tribe of Florida, Tribal Historic Preservation Office.

Rockman, Marcy and Carrie Hritz. 2019. "Expanding Use of Archaeology in Climate Change Response by Changing Its Social Environment". *PNAS* 117 (15): 8295–8302. Accessed 2019. https://doi.org/10.1073/pnas.1914213117.

Russo, Michael. 2002. *Archaic Shell Rings of the Southeast*. Tallahassee: U.S. Southeast Archeological Center, National Park Service.

Sabloff, Jeremy. 2016. *Archaeology Matters: Action Archaeology in the Modern World*. New York: Routledge.

Sacks, Jonathan. 2012. *Future Tense: Jews, Judaism, and Israel in the Twenty-first Century*. New York: Schocken.

Schaepe, David, Bill Angelbeck, David Snook, and John Welch. 2018. "Archaeology as Therapy: Connecting Belongings, Knowledge, Time, Place, and Well-Being". *Current Anthropology* 58 (4): 502-533.

Schneider, Tsim D. and Katherine Hayes. 2020. "Epistemic Colonialism: Is it Possible to Decolonize Archaeology?" *The American Indian Quarterly* 44 (2): 127-148. Accessed 2020. https://doi.org/10.5250/amerindiquar.44.2.0127.

Scott, James C. 2009. *The Art of Not Being Governed: An Anarchist History of Upland Southeast Asia*. New Haven: Yale University Press.

Smith, Laurajane. 2006. *Uses of Heritage*. New York: Routledge.

Trouillot, Michel-Rolph. 1995. *Silencing the Past: Power and the Production of History*. Boston: Beacon Press.

Van de Noort, Robert. 2011. "Conceptualising Climate Change Archaeology". *Antiquity* 85 (329): 1039-1048. Accessed 2012. doi:10.1017/S0003598X00068472.

———. 2013. *Climate Change Archaeology: Building Resilience from Research in the World's Coastal Wetlands*. New York: Oxford University Press.

Wentz, Rachel and John Gifford. 2007. "Florida's Deep Past: The Bioarchaeology of Little Salt Spring (8SO18) and its Place Among Mortuary Ponds of the Archaic". *Southeastern Archaeology* 26 (2): 330-337.

Wolf, Eric R. 1982. *Europe and the People without History*. Berkeley: University of California Press.

Yu, Pei-Lin, Chen Shen, George S. Smith, eds. 2018. *Relevance and Application of Cultural Heritage in Contemporary Society*. New York: Routledge.

Activating indigenous heritage

Chapter 4

Mobilizing indigenous heritage in cultural keystone places for climate change action

Tanja Hoffmann

Heritage for Global Challenges, University of York, United Kingdom

Natasha Lyons

Simon Fraser University, British Columbia, Canada; Ursus Heritage Consulting

Roma Leon

Katzie knowledge holder, Katzie First Nation, British Columbia, Canada

Abstract

Here we engage directly with the role of heritage in the "future-making potential of ontological pluralism" where "different forms of heritage practices enact different realities and hence work to assemble different futures" (Harrison 2015, 24). We focus on the ongoing experience of the q̓íc̓əy̓ (Katzie First Nation) and their work to regain decision-making authority over a cultural keystone place in the heart of their traditional territory. The authors recount how efforts to re-enact Indigenous law provide an opportunity to manifest different futures in service of meaningful climate change action. We argue that, despite cause for optimism given the emerging willingness on the part of state agents to embrace their commitments to Indigenous peoples, including to Indigenous knowledge, and Indigenous law, significant political and policy barriers remain, many of which reinforce colonial power structures and the nature: culture dualism foundational to western ontologies.

Keywords: Biodiversity, Canada, conservation, climate change, cultural keystone place, heritage, Indigenous, Indigenous law, Katzie First Nation, policy, reconciliation, sovereignty, UNDRIP

***

Introduction

This chapter is an outcome of many conversations between the authors over a decade-long collaboration aimed at finding ways to reinstate Katzie First Nation decision-making authority in Katzie territory, and most recently a focus on θéθqəɬ (the Widgeon Valley)—a Katzie cultural keystone place. Cultural keystone places occur within Indigenous cultural landscapes where there is particularly high biodiversity, cultural importance, and intensive use (Cuerrier et al. 2015, 428). For Roma Leon, a Katzie knowledge holder, the importance of the Widgeon Valley to the past, present, and future of her people cannot be overstated. The Widgeon Valley, lauded by western conservationists and recreational users for its biodiversity and natural beauty, is the last remnant of an expansive wetland ecosystem that once existed at the heart of Katzie territory and Katzie lifeways. Roma has worked for over two decades to reacquaint herself and her community with the ongoing legacies of Ancestral presences in the Widgeon Valley. Roma and other Katzie people actively mobilize Katzie sovereignty by accessing, harvesting, and managing their relationships with Widgeon and all who dwell within it according to protocols and teachings foundational to Katzie law. In doing so they enact their own lifeworld—one that exists beyond, and often in spite of, the boundaries of municipal, provincial, and federal jurisdiction layered upon the Valley. Tanja Hoffmann and Natasha Lyons are accomplice scholars (Powell and Kelly 2017) working to wield the tools of western science in support of Katzie sovereignty efforts. Natasha is a palaeoethnobotanist keen to understand how past and ongoing Katzie/plant partnerships speak to the deep-time relationship that exists between Katzie people and Katzie territory. Tanja works in heritage and resource management policy negotiation looking for ways to leverage state commitments to Indigenous peoples to manifest the future that Katzie envisions.

Through the lens offered by Katzie in their fight to regain decision-making authority over the Widgeon Valley, we gaze at a much broader landscape. We join a growing number of Indigenous and accomplice scholars who argue that Indigenous sovereignty, specifically the reestablishment of Indigenous law, advances twin social and environmental justice initiatives foundational to effective climate-change action. Simultaneously, the re-instatement of Indigenous Law opens avenues for ontological plurality, where protocols and teachings emerging from deeply-relational ways of being can provide the wider non-Indigenous populace an opportunity to make different choices and in doing so, enliven different futures. This declaration hinges on two key points. The first concerns the nature of many Indigenous ontologies, one hallmark of which is the notion that human beings exist 'as relationship' rather than 'in relationship with' the places in which we dwell (Wilson 2020). Moreover, many of these deeply-relational Indigenous ontologies presume pervasive non-human agency and focus on "working out specific performative and ethical implications of agent ontologies on their own terms" (Rosiek, Snyder, and Pratt 2020, 336). At the heart of the presumption of non-human agency lies a commitment to reciprocal relations which run counterpoint to the nature:culture dualism foundational to western ontologies, among whose latest manifestation looks to define what 'services' the 'ecosystem' might offer the human species. The second key point is that the performative and ethical aspects of sustaining oneself or one's community *as relationship* are often relayed through Indigenous law, known among the peoples who practice it as 'caring for country' (Woodward et al. 2020; Rose 2016), *Naaknigewin* (Anishinabek Nation 2023), *Inuit Qaujimajatuqangit* (Karetak, Tester, and Tagalik 2017), and *tikanga Māori* (Mead 2016), among myriad other terms. Indigenous laws are enacted through protocols and teachings that instruct one in how to live *as relationship*. A growing body of scholarship shows how Indigenous ontologies and the laws and practices that flow from them have a vital role to play in climate change response (Etchart 2017). Indeed, having enacted these laws over millennia within deeply relational ontologies that promote living *as relationship*, it follows that Indigenous peoples have developed a more suitable theoretical and practical basis upon which to base innovative global climate change response. It is our argument here that as Katzie works to reinstate Indigenous law in their territory, they are among those Indigenous peoples that invigorate worlds that can manifest a markedly different future for us all.

Despite growing consensus around the lasting legacy and future potential of Indigenous peoples' contributions to climate action, including vital biodiversity preservation, nation-states have been slow to return meaningful control over lands and waters to Indigenous peoples. In this chapter we draw a through-line linking Indigenous sovereignty, Indigenous law, and broad social justice initiatives (as expressed in international, national, and regional policy, including those aimed at 'reconciliation') with cultural keystone places, thinking in a Canadian context. Canada is often cited as a world leader in Indigenous reconciliation, yet barriers forestall what many Indigenous leaders consider movement toward true reconciliation—namely the return of control over lands and waters to Indigenous peoples (Lightfoot 2016). We suggest that in an era where the Canadian government cites truth and reconciliation as a national priority (CBC 2022), the re-establishment of Indigenous law in cultural keystone places constitutes meaningful reconciliation at a local scale, and bold climate-change action at a global one.

In contemplating how Katzie works with state agents to re-establish Indigenous law as the primary driver of decision-making *as relationship* with the Widgeon Valley, our emphasis on negotiating with state actors who claim jurisdiction in Katzie territory should not be construed as acquiescence to the worldviews reinforced through state resource management planning. Unlike western resource management practices that enact and enforce a nature: culture dualism that sees humans as able to stand apart from and 'manage' environmental 'resources', Katzie worldviews do not entertain a hierarchy that imbues humans with decision-making authority over the territory. Rather, Katzie are guardians working to regain their right to exercise their responsibilities to their territory through re-instatement of Indigenous law. Nor should the emphasis on preserving cultural keystone places be mistaken as Katzie 'giving up' on regaining a territory-wide sovereignty. Rather, Katzie's efforts to have western resource managers follow protocols stemming from Indigenous law to guide human activity in Katzie territory, beginning with a part of the territory that is under direct threat, should be taken for what it is— as one vital step toward a future of Katzie's making.

This chapter proceeds as follows. We begin by introducing the reader to Katzie, Katzie territory, and θéθqəł (the Widgeon Valley), including the justification Katzie use to identify θéθqəł as a Katzie cultural keystone place. Discussion of the role of Indigenous peoples in climate-change response provides the context necessary to explore the global implications of local cultural keystone place designations. Next, we provide a brief summary of the jurisdictional overlap that exists on the ground in θéθqəł, tying these jurisdictions and their management priorities to broader national and global policy and political commitments to climate change and social justice. We reveal how, in the case of cultural keystone place designation and other Indigenous-led sovereignty initiatives, the on-the-ground actions of regulatory agents indicate the degree to which subaltern efforts to enact meaningful sovereignty are meeting resistance or finding purchase at a range of policy scales. Finally, we discuss the evidentiary basis (which includes many forms and expressions of heritage) and moral imperatives used by Indigenous peoples to entreat, provoke, and in some instances force, change in state policy and policy-makers actions. We argue that Indigenous sovereignty efforts that mobilize Indigenous law can be understood as one example of heritage's role in the "future-making potential of ontological pluralism" (Harrison 2015, 24). We conclude with some thoughts on the future of 'future making' revealing how our research plans involve exploring how ontological shifts demanded by the application of Indigenous law in Indigenous cultural keystone places like θéθqəł can enact different realities to inform broad-based behavioural change necessary for effective climate change action.

Katzie: A people of place

In earlier times this Fraser River resembled an enormous dish that stored up food for all mankind; for the Indians flocked here from every quarter to catch the fish that abounded in its water. What I shall now relate to you about this land is not a mere fairy-tale, but a true history of my people, as it was taught me in my childhood by three old men whom my mother hired to instruct me (Jenness 1955, 10).

Thus begins q̓ícə̓y̓ (Katzie) Elder Peter ('Old') Pierre's account of the origins of the peoples of the Fraser River. His stories, legends, and traditions describe, in the most eloquent terms, the genesis and significance of the interconnections between people and place. They detail how Katzie are descendants of θe'ɫəctən ("clothed with power"), a powerful leader that *ci'cəɫ sie'm* ("the Lord Who Dwells Above") placed at Pitt Lake (Suttles 1955, 10). They tell how the special leader *swa'n'əsət* (Swaneset), the "Supernatural Benefactor", and later χe'els (Khaals) "a being of marvellous power", shaped the physical and mythical landscape of the Fraser River, most particularly Pitt Lake and the Pitt Valley wetlands which lie at the centre of Katzie territory (Jenness 1955, 12). (Figure 4.1) The founding accounts of Katzie do not differentiate between the people and the natural world but rather relay the performative and ethical behaviours that sustain Katzie as people of place.

A journey through Katzie territory takes one through a beautiful and diverse landscape. The territory begins at the headwaters of *sq̓ʷá·nx̓íləɫ stá?ləw* ("River of Katzie"), whose glacial-fed upper reaches support valuable salmon spawning habitat and whose forests are home to grizzly bear, dear, and elk. At the centre of the territory are *sq̓ə́yc̓əya?ɫ x̌aca?* ("Lake of the Katzie" or Pitt Lake), and *sq̓ə́yc̓əya?ɫ státləw*. The sq̓ʷá·nx̓íləɫ stá?ləw (Fraser River) flows through the centre of Katzie territory and its banks are home to ancestral winter village sites where Katzie families have resided for millennia. The southernmost extent of Katzie territory includes the Nickomekl and Serpentine Rivers, along which Katzie travelled to trade with their saltwater neighbours (Suttles 1955, 11). Katzie are *hən' q̓əminəm'* (downriver dialect) speakers and count among their upstream and downstream neighbours other *halkomelem*-speaking peoples of the Salish Sea and the sq̓ʷá·nx̓íləɫ stá?ləw (Fraser River).

The non-Katzie reader will be most familiar with Katzie territory's placement in the colonial settler geography of Canada. Katzie's homelands are located in the lower Fraser River Valley, in the southeast of the province of British Columbia. Katzie territory encompasses portions of the municipalities of Pitt Meadows and Maple Ridge on the north side of the Fraser River, and Delta, Langley, and Surrey on the south side of the river. All are part of the 21 municipalities that make up the rapidly expanding metropolis of Metro

Vancouver. Much of the northern part of Katzie territory is included within the boundaries of the Garibaldi, Golden Ears, and Pinecone Burke Provincial Parks. Today, Katzie residential communities are located on three of their five Indian Reserves, whose total area measures less than 1 per cent of their traditional territory.

Figure 4.1 Map of Katzie First Nation Territory.

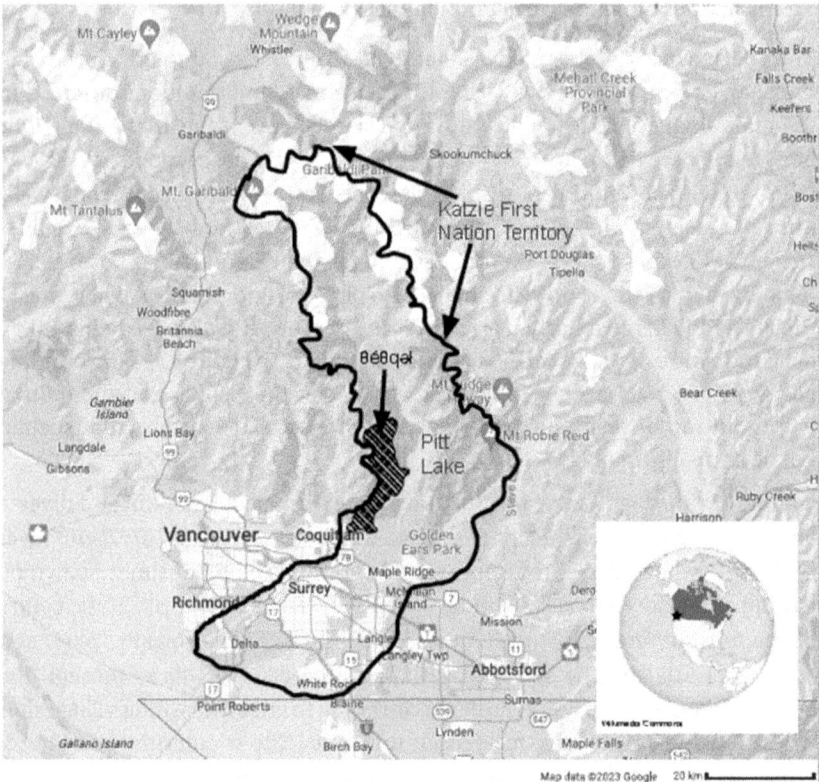

Image produced by Tanja Hoffman using Google Maps.

θéθqəł (Widgeon Valley) as a Katzie cultural keystone place

Katzie territory is renowned for the Pitt Valley wetlands located at the south end of Pitt Lake, one of the largest fresh-water tidally influenced lakes in the world. A patchwork of freshwater marsh, bog, and fen systems, the "Pitt Valley wetlands were one of the largest inland estuarine habitats in coastal British Columbia" (WSP 2010, 13) and were home to a diverse and abundant array of culturally significant animal, bird, fish, and plant resources (Spurgeon 2001). An extensive land reclamation and dyking program, initiated by Dutch farmers in 1891 and continuing through the 1950s, dramatically reduced the size and overall productivity of the wetlands (Collins 1975). Today θéθqəł (Widgeon Valley) is the last intact remnant of the much larger Pitt Polder wetland and currently constitutes the largest concentration (55.8 %) of highly protected wetland in the whole of the Fraser Lowland (McPhee and Ward 1992). Possessing exceptionally high species richness and density, the wetland is home to several federally and provincially recognized endangered faunal and floral species (Gebauer and Albert 2020).

Figure 4.2 The distinctive, arrow-shaped leaf of the semi-aquatic wapato (Sagittaria latifolia) plant.

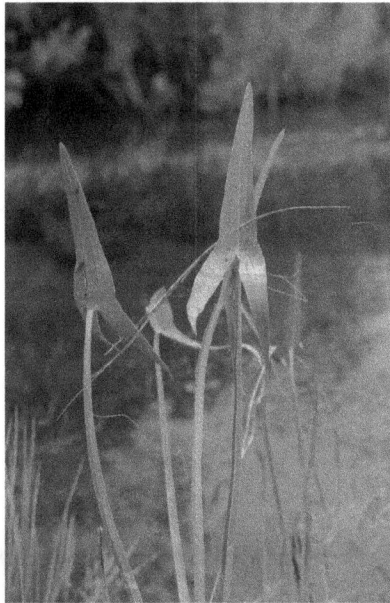

Photograph by Tanja Hoffmann.

θéθqəł exhibits the levels of biodiversity, cultural significance, and intensive use that qualify it as a cultural keystone place. Through it flow the last of the unaltered course of slow-moving waters of the tidally influenced sloughs gifted to Katzie by Swaneset. In these sloughs spawn now-endangered populations of sturgeon, *θe'ləctən's* children, and salmon relatives, who transform from their human to salmon form in order to visit and sustain their Katzie family through the spring, summer, and fall. Now-endangered Sandhill cranes, descendants of the Sandhill crane sisters, make their nests and rear their young in Widgeon Slough, reminders of a time when the cranes were so plentiful Katzie marked time according to their seasonal arrival. Bog cranberry and *wapato*, (Figure 4.2), two foods for which Katzie territory is renowned, and which once were so plentiful they were traded widely amongst Katzie's neighbours, still grow in small patches in θéθqəł, as does tule or hard stem bulrush, a prized resource that was used extensively in weaving mats for summer shelters. A prominent rock outcrop at the edge of the slough is an ancient village site that was an important location for the winter dance season, during which time Katzie acted as hosts to delegates from neighbouring relatives and distant communities. From this same vantage point, Katzie practised being 'good hosts' through traditional governance protocols that included inviting people to access cranberry bogs and wapato patches, the remnants of which still grow along the slough (Suttles 1955). Cultural keystone places are often marked by the presence of rock art (Turner 2020), and the pictographs found along Pitt Lake, several near an ancient village at the mouth of Widgeon Creek, adhere to this pattern. Lands and waters in the watershed are still known by their ancient place names.

Figure 4.3 Boundaries of θéθqəł (Widgeon Creek) Katzie Cultural Keystone Place.

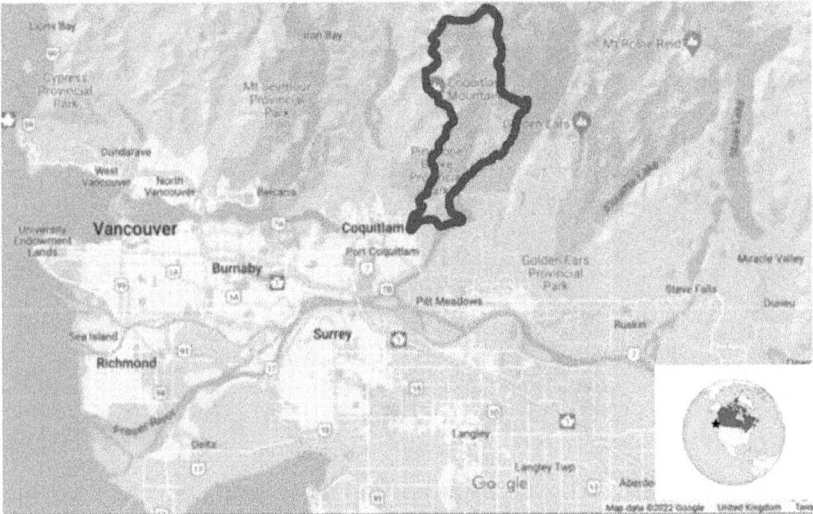

Image produced by Tanja Hoffman using Google Maps.

Katzie world views are built upon interrelationships, where expectation of, and respect for, the agency, or as Katzie call it 'vitality', of other-than-human beings informs one's own beliefs and behaviours. In contrast to colonial and settler perceptions of wetlands as dangerous places or wasted lands only useful if drained and therefore "reclaimed" (Collins 1975; Lyons et al. 2021), the wetland's foods, waters, and other-than-human relatives literally flow through Katzie—they *are* Katzie. Katzie heritage mobilization in contemporary contexts works to revitalize, in some cases reconstitute, and reapply the connections foundational to deeply relational ways of being now and for the future. As one of the remaining remnants of the world as Katzie know it, θə́θqəɫ is critical to this future-making enterprise.

Enacting worlds:
Implications of non-Katzie jurisdiction in the Widgeon Valley

In Canada, the driver of federal and provincial commitments to seek reconciliation rests in part on constitutionally entrenched fiduciary responsibilities. The extent and application of fiduciary commitments have been informed by outcomes of landmark court decisions (Haddock and McNeil 2022), the Royal Commission on Aboriginal Peoples (Dussault and Erasmus 2006), and more recently the results of the Truth and Reconciliation Commission on Indian Residential Schools (TRC and Canada 2015), and the National Inquiry into the Missing and Murdered Indigenous Women and Girls report (2019). Canada's efforts to reconcile with First Nations, Inuit, and Métis also reflects global recognition of Indigenous rights, including those expressed in the United Nations Declaration on the Rights of Indigenous Peoples (UNDRIP). In the province of British Columbia, municipal governments do not have fiduciary responsibility, though increasing calls from the voting public for meaningful reconciliation are motivating local governments to take more proactive stances when it comes to Indigenous peoples' role in municipal planning and decision-making.

Actions taken by all levels of Canadian government reflect, on the surface at least, considerable advances by a liberal democracy toward reconciliation with Indigenous peoples. However, Canada, Lightfoot (2010, 84) argues, exhibits a form of counter-intuitive behaviour in international relations called 'over-compliance' which occurs when "a state's legal or policy 'behaviour' exceeds its treaty or international normative '*commitments*'". Over-compliance in state-centred reconciliation efforts actually represents a resistance to Indigenous reconciliation as opposed to progress toward it (Lightfoot 2010). For Katzie and many other First Nations, Inuit, and Métis peoples, meaningful enactment of even the most basic principles of the outwardly laudable federal, provincial, and municipal commitments to reconciliation has proven to be a slow, arduous, and often seemingly impossible task (Wilson-Raybould 2019). Katzie's latest effort at sovereignty in the form of a bid to manage θə́θqəɫ as a cultural keystone place is the latest in a long list of attempts to move all levels of government beyond rhetoric toward meaningful reconciliation action.

θə́θqəɫ is a jurisdictional microcosm, representative of the overlapping multi-scale Indigenous rights and state governance discourses transpiring in many regions of Canada and indeed in post-colonial nations around the world. Currently divided into parcels of private and state-owned land of varying size, parts of θə́θqəɫ are managed respectively as a: Federal National Wildlife Area, Provincial Protected Area, Provincial Crown Land, Class A Provincial Park

(Pinecone Burke Provincial Park), and a municipal park. Directives for state engagement with Indigenous interests in θéθqəɫ range from those imparted by international-level policies of UNDRIP and IUCN, to fiduciary obligations on the part of the Crown, legislated Provincial commitments to UNDRIP, and finally municipal-level commitments to reconciliation. Regulatory agencies with presence in the Widgeon Valley include the Canadian Wildlife Service, who are the federal agency responsible for the selection and management of Canada's National Wildlife Areas and are members of the IUCN; the Department of Fisheries and Oceans, who are mandated to protect oceans, freshwater and aquatic species from negative impacts of humans and invasive species (DFO 2023); and British Columbia Parks, who are responsible for managing the Class A Pinecone Burke Provincial Park that encompasses the inland reaches of θéθqəɫ. Most of the fee simple properties in θéθqəɫ are owned by the Nature Trust of British Columbia and Ducks Unlimited Canada, both of whom are charities that maintain their own conservation ethic and commitments to Indigenous peoples.

Among the most complicating factors slowing the re-establishment of Katzie decision-making authority over θéθqəɫ are western policy manifestations of nature:culture dualism. In θéθqəɫ this dualism manifests in the priorities of various regulatory agencies. Some regulatory bodies prioritize conservation; others attempt to balance ecological protection with public demands for nature-based recreation. Their respective policies and management plans reflect dimensions of broader debates where, at its most extreme, competing ideologies of 'nature-tourism' are pitted against those of 'fortress conservation'. Recent manifestations of the former view wilderness as the essential backdrop for meaningful human:nature interaction promoting human mental and physical well-being, while the latter regards complete removal of human involvement as fundamental to wilderness conservation and 'rewilding' (Domínguez and Luoma 2020; Hoffmann et al. 2021). All of these initiatives take as their central assumption the enlightenment spectator/subject where humans stand apart from, and to some extent can assert control over, the natural world.

Lands and waters set aside as parks or protected areas are often the centre stage upon which the nature:culture dualism performs, and the Widgeon Valley is no exception. Historically, park designation almost always spelled the marginalization, and in some cases wholesale removal, of Indigenous peoples from all or part of their traditional lands and waters. In a Canadian provincial and territorial parks context, Indigenous sovereignty initiatives and the concurrent ontological shifts such initiatives demand, are reconfiguring both the existence and purpose of parks and protected areas (Youdelis et al. 2020). Interestingly, for reasons manifestly different than those that motivate fortress conservationists, Indigenous authorities increasingly demand that parks allow Indigenous access whilst simultaneously restricting public entry to areas of high eco-cultural value (Smith and Bulkan 2023). These restrictions create tensions for park planners who are mandated to ensure public access to wilderness areas. Yet it is this very access that is of considerable concern to Indigenous peoples who view the one-way relationship that typifies the transactional nature of non-Indigenous interactions with nature as an extension of western dualisms. Here, the natural world is commodified as "wilderness", lauded for the "services" it provides to humans (Youdelis et al. 2020). Before discussing how Katzie challenges to western conservation and recreation demands influence the actions of regulatory bodies, we first detail the extent and implications of specific state policy commitments in θéθqəɬ. In describing the extent and tenor of regulatory body commitments to state priorities in each area, we emphasise how those policies reinforce western ontologies, but also highlight instances where management goals could possibly enable Katzie priorities.

Federal interests in θéθqəɬ / Widgeon Valley

In 1973 Environment and Climate Change Canada signed a 99-year lease with The Nature Trust of British Columbia establishing 125 hectares of Widgeon Valley as a National Wildlife Area to be managed under the *Canada Wildlife Act* (Canada 2021). The Widgeon Valley National Wildlife Area is the largest undyked freshwater marsh in southwestern British Columbia. The area was set aside for the specific purpose of maintaining a wetland for the benefit of migratory birds and other wildlife, and the WVNWA management plan cites the fact that the area may harbour no fewer than 54 species of conservation concern, 21 of which are considered species at risk. The area is also designated under the IUCN management category 1a "Strict Nature Reserve" whose primary objective is to:

> To conserve regionally, nationally or globally outstanding ecosystems, species (occurrences or aggregations) and/or geodiversity features: these attributes will have been formed mostly or entirely by non-human forces and will be degraded or destroyed when subjected to all but very light human impact (IUCN 2021).

The IUCN sets out some exceptions to human use of Category 1a areas, including ceremonial activities that are in keeping with the biodiversity conservation priorities of the designated area.

The 2019 Widgeon Creek Management Plan sets out two primary management goals. The first is to conserve or enhance high-quality habitat for waterbirds, and the second to do the same for *Species at Risk Act* (SARA) listed species

(Canada 2019). These goals are accomplished through a joint scheme of baseline information gathering, active intervention (e.g. removal of invasive species, active control of shrubland succession), and monitoring. Several of these management objectives align with ancient Katzie management practice that sustained wetland habitats throughout Katzie territory for millennia. The Canada Wildlife Service lists the major threats and challenges to the Wildlife Area as those related to "excessive recreational access", citing casual picnicking or camping by canoers and kayakers as among those activities most potentially destructive to sensitive Widgeon Valley habitats. Excessive recreational access is also of paramount concern to many Katzie who see that individuals unschooled in Indigenous law, specifically the protocols and teachings about how to be a 'good guest' in Katzie territory, often mistreat and disrespect Widgeon and all who live there.

Provincial interests in θéθqəł / Widgeon Valley

The majority of the upland portions of the Widgeon Valley fall within the boundaries of the Pinecone Burke Provincial Park. Pinecone Burke Park is designated as a Class A Park. According to the British Columbia Parks Service, Class A parks are areas of Crown land set aside for the "inspiration, use and enjoyment of the public". Development is limited to that required to sustain recreational use of the park. Activities with historic connection to the park are permitted, but commercial resource extraction is prohibited (BC Parks 2021).

In a contemporary manifestation of Indigenous territorial marginalization, in the early 1990s, the Provincial Government of British Columbia announced their intention to designate a significant portion of Katzie territory (then held as Crown lands) as a Class A Provincial Park. Once designated, the lands would no longer be available as Treaty settlement lands. Unable to reverse the Province's decision and in an attempt to protect the future interests of Katzie people, in 1995 Katzie First Nation and the Province of British Columbia negotiated a Memorandum of Understanding (MOU) for the newly designated Pinecone Burke Provincial Park (KFN BC Parks 1995). The MOU dictates how "the Province and Katzie agreed to work cooperatively together with respect to the planning and management of the park, including how the aboriginal rights and interests of Katzie may be exercised within the park". The BC Parks website notes the following with regard to cultural heritage, "Pinecone Burke Park includes part of the traditional territory of the Katzie First Nation, and borders a Katzie Indian Reserve. The area within the park was used extensively for its plant, fish and wildlife resources". With regard to conservation, BC Parks (BritishColumbia 2021) notes:

> Pinecone Burke Park protects the western shore of Pitt Lake, the largest
> fresh water tidal lake in North America. It is a wilderness area protecting

old-growth forests, numerous alpine lakes, rugged terrain and remnant icefields. Widgeon Slough is the largest freshwater marsh in southwestern BC and Widgeon Lake is largest hanging lake in Greater Vancouver's north shore mountains. All five species of Pacific salmon, cutthroat trout, steelhead trout, and migratory Dolly Varden char can be found in the park. Pinecone Burke Park provides habitat for black-tailed deer, mountain goats, black bears and grizzly bears. Six sensitive or vulnerable species occur in the park, including the tailed frog, great blue heron, Vaux's swift, Huttons' vireo, shrew mole, and the Pacific jumping mouse. The park also contains nationally recognized wetlands in the Widgeon Valley.

Katzie are actively participating in the latest round of park management planning in hopes of increasing levels of cooperation and to address Katzie needs and interests within the Park. At the time of writing, BC Parks had yet to release the draft management plan for public comment.

Municipal Interests in θéθqəɫ / Widgeon Valley

Metro Vancouver, which maintains property and interests in the Widgeon Valley, is a federation of 21 municipalities, a single Treaty nation (Tsawwassen First Nation), and an electoral area, working collaboratively to provide regional solutions in key areas including air quality, climate change response, solid waste management, and regional parks access (MetroVancouver 2021). The fiduciary duty held by the Federal and Provincial governments of Canada does not transfer directly to municipal governments, and only impacts them when municipal plans trigger one or more provincial or federal legislated processes such as an environmental impact assessment. Thus, the degree of commitment toward Indigenous reconciliation expressed by municipalities is often tied to the demands of their respective constituencies, or more often, by Indigenous peoples' deliberate triggering of provincial and federal approval processes that work to ensure Indigenous rights are considered and accommodated within municipal planning—no matter how cumbersome those processes may be.

Metro Vancouver has planning authority over 621 hectares currently designated as the Widgeon Marsh Regional Park, two thirds of which is classified as critical wetland habitat. In 1992 Metro Vancouver entered into partnership with landowners the Nature Trust of BC and Ducks Unlimited to manage the regional park. According to the Widgeon Marsh Regional Park Planning document, the park aims to protect and enhance park habitat while providing opportunities for the public to experience the park's ecology and landscape. The park management plan notes that, in addition to conservation and public access and education objectives, it also aims to "protect traditional and cultural resources … in collaboration with First Nations" (MetroVancouver 2019, 14), acknowledging that the park has one of the few wild patches of wapato, a plant critical to Katzie culture and foodways, remaining in the region (MetroVancouver 2019, 17). Section 6.3 (MetroVancouver 2019, 34) of the current plan suggests Metro Vancouver will "work with First Nations to protect and enhance wapato (*Sagittaria latifolia*) within the park". Finally, the plan suggests Metro Vancouver explore "opportunities for Cultural Planning and Co-operation Agreements with First Nations" (MetroVancouver 2019, 17). Metro Vancouver's original plans include provision of facilities to support up to 150,000 park visitors annually.

Barriers to managing θéθqəł as an eco-cultural landscape

These varying scales of policy content and applications through management planning reflect how state decision-makers both conceive of and operationalise their understanding of mandated priorities. From an Indigenous Katzie perspective, the policy-driven decision-making in the Widgeon Valley exemplifies the assumptions that inform a western nature:culture dualism. In the Widgeon Valley, western ontologies are reflected in policy approaches in two fundamental ways. First, governing bodies assume that their individual resource management priorities can be enacted successfully within their respective, arbitrarily defined properties. This view is often not shared by on-the-ground managers who, having been to Widgeon, understand it to be a vitally interconnected whole. Nonetheless, institutionally mandated boundaries and their attendant management regimes create artificial divisions in what in actuality are highly integrated eco-cultural landscapes. Second, it is clear that policy reflects a growing acknowledgement of Indigenous rights at varying scales of governance, but it is equally clear that barriers to meaningful reconciliation remain. These include a prioritization of scientific data gathering, and restrictions on the range and type of activities permitted in protected areas, such as the restrictions on human activities imposed by IUCN management category 1a, or Metro Vancouver's suggestion that traditional plant gathering is acceptable within their parks but hunting is not. Such constraints continue to privilege western conservation and recreational priorities over those of Indigenous peoples. First Nations, including the Katzie First Nation, are looking to push beyond discourses of acknowledgement to insist that governments demonstrate commitments to meaningful acts of reconciliation, which include prioritization of Indigenous access and use. In the case of θéθqəł, this includes ensuring that all actions taken within θéθqəł are done so in accordance with the teachings and protocols that stem from Katzie's particular form of Indigenous law.

Indigenous law as heritage: Indigenous ontologies at work.

Restoration of Indigenous sovereignty over Indigenous territories is a slow, often incremental process. In areas where Indigenous peoples have successfully re-established decision-making authority, they use Indigenous law to prioritise management protocols and regimes that foreground Indigenous cultural, social, environmental, and economic values (Finegan 2018). There are examples of successful Indigenous initiatives, variously titled Self-Governance Land Management Regimes, Indigenous Protected Areas, or Park Reserves among others, currently operationalised throughout Canada (Fligg and Robinson 2020) and in other countries including Australia and New Zealand (Artelle et al. 2018). Reflecting the diversity of Indigenous peoples, the exact nature of protocols and teachings reflected in Indigenous law and its applications differ between and among Indigenous peoples (Turner 2020).

The categorization of Indigenous law as a globally relevant form of 'intangible heritage' is legitimized in the eyes of the western world through international forms of recognition, including the growing list of globally important forms of Intangible cultural heritage associated with the 2003 UNESCO Convention for the Safeguarding of Intangible Cultural Heritage. Expressions of Indigenous law currently featured on the UNESCO list include: "Ancestral system of knowledge of the four indigenous peoples, Arhuaco, Kankuamo, Kogui and Wiwa of the Sierra Nevada de Santa Marta" (Colombia), the "Gada system, an indigenous democratic socio-political system of the Oromo" (Ethiopia), and the "Manden Charter, proclaimed in Kurukan Fuga" (Mali).

Indigenous law is the foundation upon which many other intangible heritages are based and sustained. Indigenous legal scholar John Borrows defines five types of Indigenous law. These include: customary law, which are "those practices developed through repetitive patterns of social interaction that are accepted as binding on those who participate in them"; sacred law, which are those laws that stem from the Creator and include creation stories and ancient teachings; natural law, which is based on observations of the physical world that "attempt to develop rules for regulation and conflict resolution from a study of the world's behaviour"; and deliberative law, which stems from processes of deliberation, council, persuasion, and discussion (Borrows 2010, 34). A fifth and final source of Indigenous law is positivistic law, which engages with power and ideology, but must be balanced through the application of the other forms of law since overreliance on positivistic law is apt to lead to corruption and misuse of power (Borrows 2010, 59). It stands to reason that many other forms of intangible heritage (whether featured or not on the UNESCO list), including forms of sustainable cultivation and harvest, ceremonies that promote multi-generational knowledge exchange, and artistic traditions that convey deeply relational connection to place, reference foundational aspects of one or more of these categories of Indigenous law.

The (re)application of any or all of these categories of Indigenous law holds considerable potential for the ontological re-working of management priorities for western state regulatory agencies. For example, the Secwepemc of what is now the south-central interior of British Columbia, Canada, used their Indigenous *stsquey* (law) embedded in an epic story of a place called Pipsell to detail "Secwepemc Indigenous law about 'caretakership' of the land and the reciprocal accountability of its sentient beings and about the preciousness and interconnectedness of water, land, and air as embodied in the water cycle" to inform an Indigenous designed and led environmental assessment of a proposed mining development (Ignace and Ignace 2020, 133). Importantly, the story of Pipsell relates the consequences should anyone violate the laws of reciprocal accountability. In this case, Indigenous law was used to frame an environmental impact assessment, the results of which were used to successfully block the construction of a mine. As importantly, the story and the laws embedded within it were used to introduce state agencies to new ways of thinking about a different world of relations (Ignace and Ignace 2020).

As in the case of Pipsell, communication and application of Indigenous law reshaped both the research process and the outcomes of government action. More generally there are increasing indications that Indigenous laws, many of which mobilize cultural values of relation, reciprocity, respect, and guardianship, will be important in determining the direction of Indigenous and non-Indigenous futures (Artelle et al. 2018). Examples of Indigenous law applications exist in other countries including Australia, New Zealand, and in South America and Africa (Rist et al. 2019; Murray and Burrows 2017). In these and other areas of the world, Indigenous and non-Indigenous scholars and resource managers have demonstrated that "When Indigenous nations become sovereign partners in environmental management, the power structures and worldviews that underlie decision-making can be productively challenged … creating new solutions to pressing environmental issues" (Muller, Hemming, and Rigney 2019, 399).

The application of Indigenous law is equally vital to ensuring that settlers and visitors to Indigenous territories are afforded the opportunity to reconsider their own relationships with, and demands of, the world around them now and for future generations. Ontological reconfiguration achieved through state and public engagement with Indigenous law could have a profound impact on how non-Indigenous peoples behave in and relate to eco-cultural landscapes in a future defined by climate change (Anker 2021). Opportunities for public exposure to Indigenous law are ripe in an era where increasing numbers of people are seeking mental and physical well-being through outdoor pursuits.

While designation of θéθqəł as a Katzie cultural keystone place would permanently secure a culturally safe place for Katzie traditions to continue, in the future Katzie foresee providing Katzie-led initiatives that expose the public to Katzie's world and the protocols for being a 'good guest' within it. Such initiatives simultaneously promote innovative means to address western park and resource management priorities that look to balance vital biodiversity conservation with growing demand for public access to natural places. For Katzie, nowhere is this potential more apparent than in opportunities to reconcile the competing conservation and recreation priorities of the government stakeholders who claim jurisdictional authority over portions of θéθqəł. Below we consider how the mobilization of Indigenous sovereignty is facilitating resolution of these tensions in other First Nation/government agreements, before considering how Katzie law can work to address recreation pressures while advancing social and environmental justice priorities in θéθqəł.

Indigenous peoples' efforts to regain sovereignty within the Canadian nation-state takes many forms. Recent designations include "Indigenous Protected Areas" (IPAs) and earlier conservation reserves. Both of the examples discussed below can be categorized as forms of co-management. The Haida example shows how long term, step-wise movement toward centring Indigenous law can become a reality for more recently designated areas such as that achieved by the Thaidene Nëné. On Haida Gwaii, whose homeland is the group of islands situated off the Northwest Coast of what is now known as Canada, the "Gwaii Haanas National Park Reserve, National Marine Conservation Area Reserve, and Haida Heritage Site" is the first to provide interconnected ecosystem management planning from "mountain top to sea floor". The wholistic approach taken in Haida Gwaii confronts western principles of resource management where forests and oceans are typically managed by separate departments whose siloed approaches to their own departmental priorities rarely extend from sea to shore and vice versa. The "Gwaii Haanas Gina 'Waadluxan KilGuhlGa Land-Sea-People Management Plan (hereafter Gwaii Haanas Plan) … provides a blueprint for responsible and respectful stewardship that will ensure the continuity of Haida culture and protect the natural heritage of Gwaii Haanas for future generations" (HaidaNation 2018). The Council of Haida Nation and the Government of Canada "view the Gwaii Haanas as an example of reconciliation in action, offering lessons from more than 25 years of experience". Of particular relevance is the fact that the management Gwaii Haanas Plan's guiding principles "are based on ethics and values from Haida law" (2018, 7). The plan acknowledges the impacts of current legal contexts suggesting that the plan will be reviewed when legal issues of rights and title are resolved (2018, 13). The document acknowledges both the commitment required for meaningful government-to-government collaboration, and the tensions that arise when values collide. Nonetheless, the management plan establishes precedent for collaborative management and planning across multiple regulatory jurisdictions.

Recently established Indigenous Protected Areas (IPA), such as Thaidene Nëné near the Dene community of Łutsel K'e in the Northwest Territories, seek to rebalance Parks Canada's relationship with Indigenous peoples. Thaidene Nëné, a 26,525 square kilometre area of lakes, old-growth forest and abundant wildlife, is one of the planet's only remaining intact, unimpeded watersheds. In addition to re-establishing permanent access to traditional lands, the IPA provides for long-lasting economic and social opportunity. The community of Łutsel K'e purchased a high-end fishing lodge, and the park is further supported by a $30 million trust fund (established by a $15 Federal fund matched by Nature United) that will generate dividends of $1 million per year to support guardians, training, planning, research partnerships and youth camps. The park is governed collaboratively by the Łutsel K'e, Parks Canada, and the Northwest Territories government. The community likens their co-management relationship to the effort it takes to properly tan a moose hide, comparing the long-term goals to the poles or *"Dení dhëdh chené"* of the tanning frame, and short term objectives to the ropes or *"Bet'á ʔenélką ʔetth'é"* that hold the hide in place. With the correct tools and respectful approach and an awareness of when to adjust the tension and sharpen the tools, "we will work under a consensus process with the Parties as we move forward to co-govern Thaidene Nëné" (LKDFN 2021). Among the long term goals is the desire to incorporate Dene laws into the management plan by 2025 (LKDFN 2021).

Owing to the fact that θéθqəł is located within close proximity to a densely populated and rapidly expanding urban centre, there is some urgency to the Katzie cultural keystone place designation that sees Katzie law take the lead in informing future management directives. The pressure on θéθqəł and other near-urban wilderness areas is increasing as city dwellers seek consumptive (e.g. hunting, fishing) and non-consumptive (e.g. wildlife viewing, hiking) opportunities in increasing numbers, particularly in parks and protected areas within easy reach of urban centres. Over-tourism in parks and protected areas has resulted in many peri-urban natural areas being "loved to death" (Taff et al. 2019; Smith and Bulkan 2023). In response, western managers have instituted planning or willingness-to-pay mechanisms designed to restrict or discourage public access to parks. These include the introduction of park permit systems or raising park entrance fees. However, such mechanisms have met with limited success. Restricting access can effectively reduce direct, short-term impacts, but it does little to educate the public about how to be a 'good guest' when visiting eco-cultural landscapes. As exhibited in the Haida "Gwaii Haanas National Park Reserve, National Marine Conservation Area Reserve, and Haida

Heritage Site" and by future plans for the Thaidene Nëné, if acting in alignment with and in adherence to Indigenous law, humans need not cordon off the natural world (Artelle et al. 2018). By using government policy commitments to reconciliation to leverage co-management, or in some cases exclusive management agreements, Indigenous peoples are mobilizing intangible heritage in the form of Indigenous law to realign management of parks or protected areas to reflect Indigenous ontologies and by extension, Indigenous priorities. We argue that the outcomes of co-management structures guided by Indigenous law will accrue significant cumulative benefits, and it is to these that we now turn.

θéθqəl: A cultural keystone place for global climate action

Having established the mechanisms that Indigenous peoples are using to regain sovereignty and decision-making authority in their territories, and the role of Indigenous law in the management of those areas, we turn now to the implications of Indigenous-controlled areas for climate change action. There are three compelling arguments linking the designation of Indigenous-controlled areas, including cultural keystone places, to effective global climate change action. The first speaks to the critical link connecting Indigenous resource management practices to biodiversity conservation; the second, to the broad impact of innovative approaches to localized climate change mitigation and response; and the third, to meaningful enactment of social justice imperatives expressed through state commitments to reconciliation.

Climate scientists and policy-makers readily acknowledge biodiversity preservation as fundamental to climate change mitigation (Díaz et al. 2019; Mittermeier et al. 2011). Evidence correlating the world's remaining biodiversity with the presence of Indigenous peoples is mounting (Garnett et al. 2018; Corrigan et al. 2018), as is the evidence suggesting a causal link between Indigenous management and long-term biodiversity enhancement and maintenance (Armstrong 2017; Brondízio et al. 2021; Lepofsky et al. 2017). Recognizing the correlation between biodiversity preservation and Indigenous presence, an emerging climate-change discourse proposes the reconstitution of Indigenous resource management practices as a promising new dimension of climate change response (Artelle et al. 2019; Mittermeier et al. 2011; Schmidt and Peterson 2009; Schuster et al. 2019). Taken cumulatively, localized biodiversity and enhancement practices of Indigenous peoples, including those of the Katzie, have global implications. Evidence suggests that the biodiversity observed in Katzie territory is the direct outcome of the relationship, sustained over millennia, between Katzie and their lands and waters (Hoffmann et al., 2016; Lyons et al., 2018). θéθqəl is the last remaining relatively unencumbered or impacted portion of a cultural landscape defined by what was once one of the Lower Fraser River Valley's largest wetland mosaic systems. Remnant patches of this larger wetland constitute a portion of the world's highly valued remaining areas of terrestrial and aquatic biodiversity. Indeed, the long-term maintenance and increase of biodiversity in the Widgeon Valley that is of global benefit may very well depend upon the reapplication of Katzie law and the protocols and teachings that stem from it.

While biodiversity preservation can work to forestall and mitigate climate change impacts, Indigenous management of cultural keystone places can also contribute to climate change response. Climate change has been described as the existential crisis of our time (Wagner and Weitzman 2016). Whilst looking to slow the impacts of climate change, global leaders are also looking toward the strategies employed by Indigenous peoples to seek solutions for how human society might adapt to changing environmental baseline conditions that could cause profound shifts in status quo socio-economic conditions (Makondo and Thomas 2018; Shukla et al. 2019; Wuebbles et al. 2017). Cultural practices guided by ancient forms of Indigenous law ground reciprocal interactions between people and place over very long time periods, including those characterised by significant social and environmental change (Borrows 2019). Adaptive responses recorded in millennia of oral histories and captured in archaeological sites provide some insight into how wider society might look to respond to environmental change (Rockman and Hritz 2020). With respect to anticipated impact of climate-induced water level rise on the lower mainland of British Columbia, Figure 4.4 illustrates land predicted to be below the annual flood conditions by 2050 (Climate Central 2023). Threats to sensitive wetland habitats from rising sea levels include replacement of freshwater species via incursion of brackish or saltwater-adapted species, and subsequent migration of freshwater wetlands into unencumbered inland reaches of waterways (Neubauer and Craft 2009). Temperature rises that correlate with rising water levels are predicted to impact sensitive bog habitats, fundamental changes which could result in the extirpation of eco-culturally significant plant species such as bog cranberry.

Katzie are wetland peoples. Having successfully managed to sustain themselves within wetland environs for millennia, broader society has much to learn from Katzie in the face of anticipated impacts of predicted climate-induced sea level and temperature rise, including those that threaten food security. Katzie resource management knowledge concerning wetland plant foods like wapato, for example, could be vital to the reintroduction of sustainable yields of edible plants as one component of a local food security program. Additionally, archaeological evidence suggests that Katzie successfully managed the complex hydrological regimes of one of the world's only freshwater tidal lakes, having both shaped and been culturally shaped by living in this particularly dynamic wetland environ (Hoffmann et al. 2016). Ancient practices of landscape engineering could form the basis of practical response to management of water incursion in developed areas (Duncan et al. 2021; Krause et al. 2021).

Figure 4.4 Climate Central predicted annual flood by 2050 in Katzie Territory.

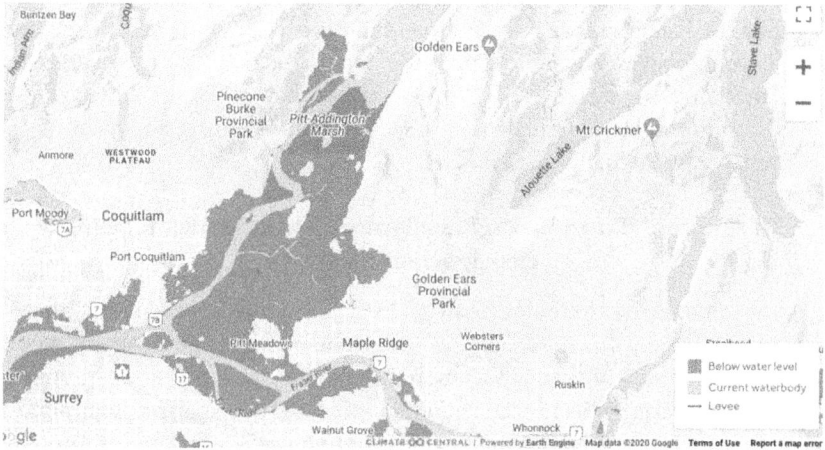

Reproduced with permission of Climate Central.

Canada is among a growing number of countries committed to social justice initiatives that include repairing relations with Indigenous peoples (TRC and Canada 2015). Canada has acknowledged the harm to Indigenous peoples from decades of colonial practice intended to extinguish Indigenous cultures, and to actively destroy the languages, practices, and places upon which those cultures depend (Dussault and Erasmus 1996; TRC and Canada 2015). Canadian national, provincial, and municipal governments have made legal and policy commitments seeking to establish meaningful reconciliation with Indigenous peoples. Despite the very public and seemingly earnest nature of these commitments, for many First Nations, Inuit, and Métis peoples of Canada, these commitments have yet to manifest as meaningful action—most remain as unfulfilled promises (CBC 2022). Reintroduction of Indigenous management regimes requires return of decision-making control over traditional lands to Indigenous peoples. Indeed, the return of traditional lands is frequently cited as a fundamental to decolonization, and by extension, meaningful reconciliation with Indigenous peoples (Corntassel 2012; Alfred and Corntassel 2005; Tuck and Yang 2012; Claxton and Price 2020).

Owing to the twin pressures of urban expansion and the public's seemingly insatiable appetite for access to 'nature', Katzie are rapidly losing areas of their territory that are suitable for the maintenance of traditional ceremonial and sustenance practices. The designation of θéθqəl as a Katzie cultural keystone place would permanently secure a culturally suitable place for Katzie traditions to continue as guided by the teachings and protocols that flow from Katzie law. As envisioned by Katzie, the establishment of θéθqəł as a Katzie cultural keystone place would provide both a concrete example of Canada's commitment to reconciliation and a global exemplar for the implementation of the core principles of the United Nations Declaration on the Rights of Indigenous Peoples, to which Canada is a signatory and British Columbia has passed into law. It would provide a place for Katzie to re-gain a modicum of real sovereignty, and in doing so, reactivate Indigenous laws that underpin Katzie's deep relationship to place to the benefit of Katzie, but also the residents of Metro Vancouver, and arguably all Canadians.

The future of "future making": Indigenous law as heritage for climate change action at θéθqəł

Having initiated the cultural keystone place designation process, Katzie remain optimistic, hoping that the willingness shown by individual government agents to work together with Katzie for the benefit of θéθqəł will yield institutional change that will provide innovative solutions to what in the past seemed almost insurmountable barriers to creating a future of Katzie's making. Paramount among these changes is Katzie's call that management of θéθqəł should adhere first and foremost to Katzie customary protocols and teachings, some of which will, in the short term at least, necessitate restricting plans that facilitate a dramatic increase in public access to the Valley.

The future success of Katzie's bid to assert decision-making authority over θéθqəł is a litmus test reflecting the degree to which Canadian government promises will manifest as meaningful on-the-ground practice. By many measures, Canada is a global leader in Indigenous relations, but there remains much work to be done to heal past, and some would argue, ongoing state attempts at cultural genocide. Stretching toward a future that embraces ontological pluralism requires the government to look to re-configure western management planning in service to Indigenous priorities that, in turn, enliven Indigenous law.

Government willingness for bold action is dependent, at least in part, upon that of the voting citizenry, and here, too, Indigenous peoples are changing hearts and minds. Katzie are one of hundreds of Indigenous communities in Canada, and thousands around the world, fighting for their inherent rights, title, and recognition. A recent nation-wide survey found that in Canada there is a "growing awareness of the mistreatment of Indigenous Peoples" coupled with a willingness to identify Canadian government policies, and not Indigenous peoples themselves, as the main obstacle to achieving equitable futures (Environics 2021, 1). Reflecting positive precedent for meaningful reconciliation, there are agreements in several Canadian provinces, including

British Columbia, that provide for Indigenous-led management or meaningful co-management of National Wildlife Areas, parks, and other Indigenous lands and waters claimed by the state. Some of these agreements have been in place for several years and have met with considerable success. Through these examples, the reinstitution of Indigenous law has been shown to have ongoing and future applications that are of benefit not only Indigenous peoples, but arguably the planet as a whole (Artelle et al. 2019; UNEP 2022). Indeed, on a global scale, the restitution of Indigenous law constitutes one of the most powerful ways to unlock the 'future-making potential of ontological pluralism' since it flows from deeply relational ontologies that look to establish the performative and ethical bases of living *as relationship* (Smith 2016; Artelle et al. 2018). These laws manifest in many ways, and those include the stimulation and maintenance of critical areas of biodiversity that are key to ongoing and future management of climate change impacts. In closing, we argue that re-establishment of Katzie law in the cultural keystone place called θéθqəɫ has the potential to challenge the public imaginary such that the broader citizenry might embrace protocols and teachings that create a future where we all learn to live *as relationship*.

Bibliography

Anishinabek Nation. 2023. Anishinabek Governance. https://www.anishinabek. ca/governance/anishinaabe-chi-naaknigewin/.

Alfred, Taiaiake, and Jeff Corntassel. 2005. "Being Indigenous: Resurgences against contemporary colonialism". *Government and opposition* 40 (4): 597-614.

Anker, Kirsten. 2021. "Indigenous Law: What non-indigenous people can learn from indigenous legal thought". In *Routledge Handbook of Law and Society*, 37-42. Routledge.

Armstrong, Chelsey Geralda. 2017. "Historical ecology of cultural landscapes in the Pacific Northwest". Simon Fraser University, Department of Archaeology, PhD Thesis.

Artelle, Kyle A., Janet Stephenson, Corey Bragg, Jessie A. Housty, William G. Housty, Merata Kawharu, and Nancy J. Turner. 2018. "Values-led management: the guidance of place-based values in environmental relationships of the past, present, and future". *Ecology and Society* 23 (3): 35.

Artelle, Kyle A., Melanie Zurba, Jonaki Bhattacharyya, Diana E. Chan, Kelly Brown, Jess Housty, and Faisal Moola. 2019. "Supporting resurgent Indigenous-led governance: A nascent mechanism for just and effective conservation". *Biological Conservation* 240: 108284.

Borrows, John. 2010. *Canada's indigenous constitution*. Toronto: University of Toronto Press.

———. 2019. "2. Earth-Bound: Indigenous Resurgence and Environmental Reconciliation". In *Resurgence and Reconciliation*, 49-82. Toronto: University of Toronto Press.

British Columbia. 2021. "Pinecone Burke Provincial Park". Accessed 17 May, 2021. https://bcparks.ca/explore/parkpgs/pinecone/.

Brondízio, Eduardo S., Yildiz Aumeeruddy-Thomas, Peter Bates, Joji Carino, Álvaro Fernández-Llamazares, Maurizio Farhan Ferrari, Kathleen Galvin, Victoria Reyes-García, Pamela McElwee, and Zsolt Molnár. 2021. "Locally based, regionally manifested, and globally relevant: indigenous and local knowledge, values, and practices for nature". *Annual Review of Environment and Resources* 46: 481-509.

Canada. 2019. *Widgeon Valley Wildlife Area Management Plan.* (Gatineau, Quebec). Accessed 10 November, 2023. http://publications.gc.ca/site/eng/9. 867636/publication.html.

———. 2021. "Widgeon Valley National Wildlife Area". National Wildlife Areas. Government of Canada. Accessed 18 May, 2021. https://www.canada.ca/en/ environment-climate-change/services/national-wildlife-areas/locations/ widgeon-valley.html.

CBC. 2022. "Beyond 94: Truth and Reconciliation in Canada". CBC News. Accessed 28 February, 2022. https://newsinteractives.cbc.ca/longform-single/beyond-94?&cta=1.

Claxton, Nicholas Xemt̸oltw, and John Price. 2020. "Whose land is it? Rethinking sovereignty in British Columbia". *BC Studies* (204): 115-236.

Climate Central. 2023. "Predicted Sea Level Rise for Fraser Valley British Columbia, 2050". http://sealevel.climatecentral.org/.

Collins, John Eric. 1975. "The reclamation of Pitt Meadows". Simon Fraser University, Department of History. Master's Thesis.

Corntassel, Jeff. 2012. "Re-envisioning resurgence: Indigenous pathways to decolonization and sustainable self-determination". *Decolonization, Indigeneity, Education & Society* 1 (1): 86-101.

Corrigan, Colleen, Heather Bingham, Yichuan Shi, Edward Lewis, Alienor Chauvenet, and Naomi Kingston. 2018. "Quantifying the contribution to biodiversity conservation of protected areas governed by indigenous peoples and local communities". *Biological Conservation* 227: 403-412.

Cuerrier, Alain, Nancy J. Turner, Thiago C. Gomes, Ann Garibaldi, and Ashleigh Downing. 2015. "Cultural keystone places: conservation and restoration in cultural landscapes". *Journal of Ethnobiology* 35 (3): 427-448.

DFO. 2023. "Mandate and Role". Department of Fisheries and Oceans Canada. Accessed 10 August, 2023. https://www.dfo-mpo.gc.ca/about-notre-sujet/ mandate-mandat-eng.htm.

Díaz, Sandra Myrna, Josef Settele, Eduardo Brondízio, Hien Ngo, Maximilien Guèze, John Agard, Almut Arneth, Patricia Balvanera, Kate Brauman, and Stuart Butchart, Kai M.A. Chan, Lucas Alejandro Garibaldi, Kazuhito Ichii, Jianguo Liu, Suneetha Subramanian, Guy Midgley, Patricia Miloslavich, Zsolt Molnár, David Obura, Alexander Pfaff, Stephen Polasky, Andy Purvis, Jona Razzaque, Reyers, Belinda; Rinku Roy Chowdhury, Yunne-Jai Shin, Ingrid Visseren-Hamakers, Katherine Willis, Cynthia Zayas. 2019. "The global assessment report on biodiversity and ecosystem services: Summary for policy makers". *Intergovernmental Science-Policy Platform on Biodiversity and Ecosystem Services*. Accessed 10 November, 2023. https://ri.conicet.gov. ar/handle/11336/116171.

Domínguez, Lara, and Colin Luoma. 2020. "Decolonising conservation policy: How colonial land and conservation ideologies persist and perpetuate indigenous injustices at the expense of the environment". *Land* 9 (3): 65.

Duncan, Neil A., Nicholas J.D. Loughlin, John H. Walker, Emma P. Hocking, and Bronwen S. Whitney. 2021. "Pre-Columbian fire management and control of climate-driven floodwaters over 3,500 years in southwestern Amazonia". *Proceedings of the National Academy of Sciences* 118 (40), e2022206118. Accessed 10 November, 2023. https://doi.org/10.1073/pnas.2022206118.

Dussault, René, and Georges Erasmus. 1996. "Report of the royal commission on aboriginal peoples". *Looking Forward Looking Back.* Ottawa, Canada: Canada Communication Group.

Environics. 2021. *Canadian Public Opinion about Indigenous Peoples and Reconciliation.* Environics Institute. Accessed 10 November, 2023. https://www.environicsinstitute.org/docs/default-source/default-document-library/fc2021-indigenous-peoples-final-sept-29d44baa3c6d8147c787937fa72130c28b.pdf?sfvrsn=c6caed70_0.

Etchart, Linda. 2017. "The role of indigenous peoples in combating climate change". *Palgrave Communications* 3 (1): 1-4.

Finegan, Chance. 2018. "Reflection, acknowledgement, and justice: A framework for Indigenous-Protected Area Reconciliation". *International Indigenous Policy Journal* 9 (3).

Fligg, Robert A., and Derek T. Robinson. 2020. "Reviewing First Nation land management regimes in Canada and exploring their relationship to community well-being". *Land Use Policy* 90: 104245.

Garnett, Stephen T., Neil D. Burgess, John E. Fa, Álvaro Fernández-Llamazares, Zsolt Molnár, Cathy J. Robinson, James E.M. Watson, Kerstin K. Zander, Beau Austin, and Eduardo S. Brondizio. 2018. "A spatial overview of the global importance of Indigenous lands for conservation". *Nature Sustainability* 1 (7): 369-374.

Gebauer, Martin, and Courtney Albert. 2020. "Desktop Assessment of Species at Risk Occurrence at the Widgeon Valley National Wildlife Area, British Columbia". Report Prepared for Environment and Climate Change Canada. https://www.researchgate.net/publication/345691862_Desktop_Assessment_of_Species_at_Risk_Occurrence_at_the_Widgeon_Valley_National.

Haddock, Leslie, and Kent McNeil. 2022. *Bibliography on Indigenous Rights in Canada, 1995-2022.* Osgoode Hall Law School of York University. Toronto, Canada: Osgoode Digital Commons. Accessed 10 November, 2023. https://digitalcommons.osgoode.yorku.ca/cgi/viewcontent.cgi?article=1358&context=all_papers.

Haida Nation. 2018. *Gwaii Haanas Gina 'Waadluxan KilGuhlGa Land-Sea-People Management Plan 2018.* (Council of Haida Nation and Government of Canada). Accessed 10 November, 2023. https://www.pc.gc.ca/en/pn-np/bc/gwaiihaanas/info/consultations/gestion-management-2018.

Harrison, Rodney. 2015. "Beyond 'natural' and 'cultural' heritage: Toward an ontological politics of heritage in the age of Anthropocene". *Heritage & Society* 8 (1): 24-42.

Hoffmann, Tanja, Natasha Lyons, Roma Leon, Mike Leon, and Michael Blake. 2021. "Integrated Plant Management Research in Action: Indigenous

Challenges to Settler Memory". Royal Anthropological Institute Anthropology and Conservation Virtual Conference, Online, October 25 to 29, 2021.

Hoffmann, Tanja, Natasha Lyons, Debbie Miller, Alejandra Diaz, Amy Homan, Stephanie Huddlestan, and Roma Leon. 2016. "Engineered feature used to enhance gardening at a 3800-year-old site on the Pacific Northwest Coast". *Science Advances* 2 (12): e1601282.

Ignace, Marianne, and Chief Ronald E. Ignace. 2020. "A Place Called Pípsell: An Indigenous Cultural Keystone Place, Mining, and Secwépemc Law". *Plants, People, and Places: The Roles of Ethnobotany and Ethnoecology in Indigenous Peoples' Land Rights in Canada and Beyond*: 131-50.

IUCN. 2021. "Protected Area Category Ia: Strict Nature Reserve". Accessed 18 May, 2021. https://www.iucn.org/theme/protected-areas/about/protected-areas-categories/category-ia-strict-nature-reserve.

Jenness, Diamond. 1955. *The faith of a coast Salish Indian.* Vol. 3: British Columbia Provincial Museum.

Karetak, Joe, Frank Tester, and Shirley Tagalik. 2017. *Inuit Qaujimajatuqangit: What Inuit have always known to be true.* Halifax Canada: Fernwood Publishing.

Katzie First Nation and BC Parks. 1995. Pinecone Burke Provincial Park Memorandum of Understanding. Copy on file with Katzie First Nation Referrals Department.

Krause, Samantha, Timothy P. Beach, Sheryl Luzzadder-Beach, Duncan Cook, Steven R. Bozarth, Fred Valdez Jr, and Thomas H. Guderjan. 2021. "Tropical wetland persistence through the Anthropocene: Multiproxy reconstruction of environmental change in a Maya agroecosystem". *Anthropocene* 34: 100284.

Lepofsky, Dana, Chelsey Geralda Armstrong, Spencer Greening, Julia Jackley, Jennifer Carpenter, Brenda Guernsey, Darcy Mathews, and Nancy J. Turner. 2017. "Historical ecology of cultural keystone places of the Northwest Coast". *American Anthropologist* 119 (3): 448-463.

Lightfoot, Sheryl. 2016. *Global indigenous politics: A subtle revolution.* London: Routledge.

Lightfoot, Sheryl R. 2010. "Emerging international indigenous rights norms and 'over-compliance' in New Zealand and Canada". *Political Science* 62 (1): 84-104.

LKDFN. 2021. *2020-2025 Strategic Plan Thaidene Nëné.* Łutsël K'e Dene First Nation. Accessed 10 November, 2023. http://www.landoftheancestors.ca/uploads/1/3/0/0/130087934/thaidene_nene_strategic_plan_2020-2025.pdf.

Lyons, Natasha, Tanja Hoffmann, Debbie Miller, Stephanie Huddlestan, Roma Leon, and Kelly Squires. 2018. "Katzie & the Wapato: An archaeological love story". *Archaeologies* 14 (1): 7-29.

Lyons, Natasha, Tanja Hoffmann, Debbie Miller, Andrew Martindale, Kenneth M Ames, and Michael Blake. 2021. "Were the Ancient Coast Salish Farmers? A Story of Origins". *American Antiquity* 86 (3): 1-22.

Makondo, Cuthbert Casey, and David S.G. Thomas. 2018. "Climate change adaptation: Linking indigenous knowledge with western science for effective adaptation". *Environmental science & policy* 88: 83-91.

McPhee, Michael, and Peggy Ward. 1992. *Wetlands of the Fraser Lowland: Ownership, management and protection status. Technical Report Series,* Canadian Wildlife Service. Pacific and Yukon Region 1994. Environment Canada, no. 200. Accessed 10 November, 2023. https://publications.gc.ca/collections/collection_2015/ec/CW69-5-200-eng.pdf.

Mead, Hirini Moko. 2016. *Tikanga Maori (revised edition): Living by Maori values.* United Kingdom: Huia Publishers.

MetroVancouver. 2019. *Widgeon Marsh Regional Park Management Plan.* Accessed 10 November, 2023. https://metrovancouver.org/services/regional-parks/Documents/widgeon-marsh-regional-park-management-plan.pdf.

———. 2021. "Metro Vancouver". https://metrovancouver.org/.

Mittermeier, Russell A., Will R. Turner, Frank W. Larsen, Thomas M. Brooks, and Claude Gascon. 2011. "Global biodiversity conservation: the critical role of hotspots". In *Biodiversity Hotspots: Distribution and Protection of Conservation Priority Areas,* edited by Frank E. Zachos and Jan Christian Habel,3-22. Heidelburg: Springer Berlin.

Muller, Samantha, Steve Hemming, and Daryle Rigney. 2019. "Indigenous sovereignties: relational ontologies and environmental management". *Geographical Research* 57 (4): 399-410.

Murray, Grant, and Danielle Burrows. 2017. "Understanding power in Indigenous Protected Areas: the case of the Tla-o-qui-aht Tribal Parks". *Human Ecology* 45 (6): 763-772.

National Inquiry into Missing Murdered Indigenous Women, and Girls. 2019. *Reclaiming power and place: The final report of the national inquiry into missing and murdered indigenous women and girls.* National Inquiry into Missing and Murdered Indigenous Women and Girls. Accessed 10 November, 2023. https://www.mmiwg-ffada.ca/final-report/.

Neubauer, Scott C., and Christopher B. Craft. 2009. "Global change and tidal freshwater wetlands: scenarios and impacts". *Tidal freshwater wetlands,* edited by A. Barendregt, D.F. Whigham, A.H. Baldwin, 253-266. Kerkwerve, The Netherlands: Backhuys.

Powell, Jessica, and Amber Kelly. 2017. "Accomplices in the academy in the age of Black Lives Matter". *Journal of Critical Thought and Praxis* 6 (2).

Rist, Phil, Whitney Rassip, Djalinda Yunupingu, Jonathan Wearne, Jackie Gould, Melanie Dulfer-Hyams, Ellie Bock, and Dermot Smyth. 2019. "Indigenous protected areas in Sea Country: Indigenous driven collaborative marine protected areas in Australia". *Aquatic Conservation: Marine and Freshwater Ecosystems* 29: 138-151.

Rockman, Marcy, and Carrie Hritz. 2020. "Expanding use of archaeology in climate change response by changing its social environment". *Proceedings of the National Academy of Sciences* 117 (15): 8295-8302.

Rose, Deborah Bird. 2016. "Country and the Gift". In *Humanities for the Environment: Integrating knowledge, forging new constellations of practice,* edited by Joni Adamson and Michael Davis, 47-59. London: Routledge.

Rosiek, Jerry Lee, Jimmy Snyder, and Scott L. Pratt. 2020. "The new materialisms and Indigenous theories of non-human agency: Making the case for respectful anti-colonial engagement". *Qualitative Inquiry* 26 (3-4): 331-346.

Schmidt, Paige M., and Markus J. Peterson. 2009. "Biodiversity conservation and indigenous land management in the era of self-determination". *Conservation Biology* 23 (6): 1458-1466.

Schuster, Richard, Ryan R. Germain, Joseph R. Bennett, Nicholas J. Reo, and Peter Arcese. 2019. "Vertebrate biodiversity on indigenous-managed lands in Australia, Brazil, and Canada equals that in protected areas". *Environmental Science & Policy* 101: 1-6.

Shukla, P.R., J. Skea, E. Calvo Buendia, V. Masson-Delmotte, H.O. Pörtner, D.C. Roberts, P. Zhai, Raphael Slade, Sarah Connors, and Renée Van Diemen. 2019. "IPCC, 2019: Climate Change and Land: an IPCC special report on climate change, desertification, land degradation, sustainable land management, food security, and greenhouse gas fluxes in terrestrial ecosystems". Accessed 30 October, 2023. www.ipcc.ch.

Smith, Heather A. 2016. "Disrupting the global discourse of climate change: the case of indigenous voices". In *The Social Construction of Climate Change: The Case of Indigenous Voices*, edited by Mary E. Pettenger, 221-240. London: Routledge.

Smith, Tonya, and Janette Bulkan. 2023. "'LOVED TO DEATH': Conflicts between Indigenous Food Sovereignty, Settler Recreation, and Ontologies of Land in the Governance of Lílwat tmicw". *BC Studies* (216): 13-170.

Spurgeon, Terrence. 2001. "Wapato (Sagitaria latifolia) In Katzie Traditional Territory, Pitt Meadows, British Columbia". Simon Fraser University, Department of Archaeology, Master's Thesis.

Suttles, Wayne. 1955. "Katzie ethnographic notes. Anthropology in British Columbia, memoir no. 2". *British Columbia Provincial Museum, Victoria.*

Taff, B. Derrick, Vicki Peel, William L. Rice, Gary Lacey, Bing Pan, Celine Klemm, Peter B. Newman, Brett Hutchins, and Zachary D. Miller. 2019. "Healthy parks healthy people: Evaluating and improving park service efforts to promote tourists' health and well-being introduction". Travel and Tourism Research Association: Advancing Tourism Research Globally. 27. University of Massachusetts Amherst ScholarWorks @UMASS Amherst. Accessed 30 October, 2023. https://scholarworks.umass.edu/ttra/2019/research_papers/27.

Truth and Reconciliation Commission of Canada (TRC). 2015. *Canada's Residential Schools: The Final Report of the Truth and Reconciliation Commission of Canada.* Vol. 1. McGill-Queen's Press-MQUP.

Tuck, Eve and K. Wayne Yang. 2012. "Decolonization is Not a Metaphor". *Decolonization: Indigeneity, Education & Society* 1(1): 1-40.

Turner, Nancy J. 2020. *Plants, People, and Places: The Roles of Ethnobotany and Ethnoecology in Indigenous Peoples' Land Rights in Canada and Beyond.* Vol. 96. McGill-Queen's Press-MQUP.

UNEP. 2022. *Spreading like Wildfire: The Rising Threat of Extraordinary Landscape Fires.* United Nations Environmental Programme (Nairobi: United Nations Environmental Programme).

Wagner, Gernot, and Martin L. Weitzman. 2016. *Climate Shock: The Economic Consequences of a Hotter Planet.* Princeton, NJ: Princeton University Press.

Wilson, Shawn. 2020. *Research is ceremony: Indigenous Research Methods.* Nova Scotia: Fernwood publishing.

Wilson-Raybould, Jody. 2019. *From where I stand: Rebuilding Indigenous Nations for a stronger Canada.* Vancouver: UBC Press, Purich Books.

Woodward, Emma, Rosemary Hill, Pia Harkness, and Ricky Archer. 2020. "Our Knowledge Our Way in caring for Country: Indigenous-led approaches to strengthening and sharing our knowledge for land and sea management. Best Practice Guidelines from Australian Experiences". https://repository.ocean bestpractices.org/handle/11329/1633.

WSP. 2010. *A Wetland Action Plan for British Columbia.* (Wetland Stewardship Partnership). https://bcwetlandsca.files.wordpress.com/2016/11/bcwetland actionplan_wsp_2010.pdf.

Wuebbles, Donald J.; Fahey, David W.; Hibbard, Kathy A.; Arnold, Jeff R.; DeAngelo, Benjamin; Doherty, Sarah; Easterling, David R.; Edmonds, James; Edmonds, Timothy; Hall, Timolthy; Hayhoe, Katharine; Huffman, Forest M.; Horton, Radley; Huntzinger, Deborah; Jewett, Libby; Knutson, Thomas; Kopp, Robert E.; Kossin, James P.; Kunkel, Kenneth E.; LeGrande, Allegra N.; Leung, L. Ruby; Maslowski, Wieslaw; Mears, Carl; Perlwitz, Judith; Romanou, Anastasia; Sanderson, Benjamin M.; Sweet, William V.; Taoylor, Patrick C.; Trapp, Robert J.; Vose, Russell S.; Waliser, Duane E.; Wehner, Michael F.; West, Tristram O.; Alley, Richard; Armstrong, C. Taylor; Bruno, John; Busch, Shallin; Champion, Sarah; Durre, Imke; Gledhill, Dwight; Goldstein, Justin; Huang, Boyin; Krishnan, Hari; Levin, Lisa; Muller-Karger, Frank; Rhoades, Alan; Stevens, Laura; Sun, Liqiang; Takle, Eugene; Ullrich, Paul; Wahl, Eugene; and Walsh, John. 2017. "Climate Science Special Report: Fourth National Climate Assessment (NCA4), Volume I". Agronomy Reports. 8. Accessed 30 October, 2023. https://lib.dr.iastate.edu/agron_reports/8.

Youdelis, Megan, Roberta Nakoochee, Colin O'Neil, Elizabeth Lunstrum, and Robin Roth. 2020. "'Wilderness' revisited: Is Canadian park management moving beyond the 'wilderness ethic?'" *The Canadian Geographer/Le Géographe canadien* 64 (2): 232-249.

Chapter 5

Challenging the authorized past: heritage, identity and empowerment in Hawai'i

Susan Shay

Heritage Research Centre, University of Cambridge, United Kingdom

Abstract

Courtrooms provide Indigenous peoples opportunities to challenge authorized versions of the past to achieve greater forms of political recognition, land control and sovereignty. The Indigenous sovereignty sought is often based on cultural, spiritual and religious land and resource rights, as well as on traditional and customary practices and ways of living. However, Indigenous legal challenges have inherent difficulties, for Native peoples have to overcome social, educational, cultural, political and epistemological challenges to build, support, and defend their legal narratives. Their efforts are also complicated by historic trauma, discrimination and dislocation from ancestral lands. Through an examination of how Indigenous heritage was used in the construction of legal narratives for contemporary Native Hawaiian land claim lawsuits, this chapter will demonstrate that not only are the legal outcomes of court cases important for Indigenous empowerment, but equally significant are Indigenous legal representation and involvement in court narrative investigation, construction, presentation and defence.

Keywords: cultural, empowerment, Hawai'i, Hawaiian, heritage, identity, Indigenous, land claims, lawsuits, Native Hawaiian, rights, sovereignty, traditional

***

Introduction

In addition to my academic research, I am an experienced registered architect and have been involved in historic preservation and disaster recovery projects. In working with communities to rebuild or restore local resources, I have found that when the need arises to make collective decisions on how to allocate funding, the sites, buildings, and monuments selected and prioritized by communities often are not those chosen by funding bodies, including government agencies. When this occurs, the community may battle for the right to decide what is the most important to them. These fights are highly emotional, with a passion stemming from shared narratives associated with the sites. If the argument cannot be successfully arbitrated, it may well end up in the courts, and it is in this very public forum that community members have to present their cultural narratives and defend their decision-making processes. My interest is in the impact the fight to protect important cultural resources has on heritage and identity. The Native Hawaiian legal battles to restore control over ancestral land epitomize the complexity of the issues involved.

I have been investigating Native Hawaiian land battles for control or return of ancestral lands since 2008. I was fortunate to be an Affiliated Scholar at the East West Center and the University of Hawai'i in Honolulu, and the scholars there greatly influenced and aided in my investigations. Importantly, the research for this chapter was guided by Native Hawaiian leaders, elders, academics, and community members. I was honoured by their willingness to explain the heritage values and cultural practices discussed in the court narratives, and I sincerely thank them for their assistance in this project and for kindly and generously sharing their wisdom.

Heritage is a social and cultural process of meaning making (Harrison 2010; Lowenthal 1996; Sørensen and Carman 2009). As a social process, heritage is inherently and dynamically political (Smith 2006), reacting to changes in social, economic, and political forces to remain relevant, while also determining who has the power to interpret the past. In doing so, heritage does not attempt to explore and explain the past, according to historian David Lowenthal (1996), but instead to clarify pasts so as to infuse them with present purposes. It is not enough to only inherit the past, explains Lowenthal, "but it must constantly be reanimated and assigned meanings to be made relevant to our lives" (Lowenthal 1996, xi).

This issue of the relevance of the past to contemporary life is at the heart of Indigenous[1] land claim court conflicts in Hawai'i. In their efforts to regain control over ancestral lands, Native Hawaiians, the Indigenous people of the US Hawaiian Islands, must demonstrate in court that the past has meaning in the present, and that ancient practices have been continuously exercised and actively performed in order to justify legal protection. This chapter investigates the impact that Indigenous legal narrative construction within lawsuits using heritage for the return and control of traditional lands has had on the contemporary Native Hawaiian community. Specifically, it will discuss how a modern identity essential to efforts for Indigenous self-determination can emerge through involvement in the legal process.

Heritage and Indigenous identity

Worldwide, Indigenous peoples are using their heritage to regain control over their futures. They are struggling to overcome historical injustices wrought by colonialization, marginalization, and cultural appropriation. Repeatedly subjected to discriminatory policies, they suffer from generational trauma, poverty, and high rates of incarceration, with low levels of educational achievement. In their battles for cultural survival as unique communities, they struggle for recognition and greater forms of sovereignty. Importantly, they are fighting to regain control over their traditional lands in order to restore and maintain their fundamental cultural and religious relationships with ancestral sites. These cultural sites are the basis for their heritage, and an intrinsic and essential part of their lifeways and worldviews. Critically, the relationship to traditional, ancestral lands underpins their spiritual values and social connections. To Indigenous Native Hawaiians, the relationship with land is familial and so profound that it exists at the core of their society, satisfying and providing a sense of belonging to the earth and to the community (Daes 2011). The restoration of Native Hawaiian traditional and cultural relationships to ancestral lands is therefore vital to their continuation as a unique people. In this they are not alone, for the realization of the critical nature of their people's relationship to land has inspired movements for Indigenous nationalism and self-determination throughout the globe, encouraging Native community members worldwide to engage similarly in activism for rights to access or control land.

One common response from many Indigenous communities to loss of land and sovereignty is to bring land claim cases based on heritage into the courts in an effort to achieve increased levels of self-determination. Such legal challenges have the potential to bring about substantial improvements in the lives of Indigenous people. Significantly, they may also have more subtle and less scrutinized repercussions, such as the illumination of new forms of living culture, the reification of other elements of heritage, and the development of contemporary forms of Indigenous identity.

To achieve their goals, Indigenous court participants must overcome significant obstacles. The obstacles include those that are not only legal, but also cultural, historic, linguistic, social, economic, and political. The participants must deal with legal systems and a legal profession that is not knowledgeable about their heritage practices and beliefs, or their use of language or epistemology, and does not accept their forms of knowledge or expertise. They must learn to build legal case narratives using the strict procedural regulations required by the court, employing common legal language and terminology defined according to Western standards. They must seek representation that can comprehend complex Indigenous heritage values and beliefs and translate them into language that can be understood and interpreted through the formalized procedures of Western legal proceedings. They must enter into the contentious and expensive legal system armed with the resources and fortitude to withstand attacks, and they must build political capital for their positions within their community, the legal profession, and outside the courtroom to support their cause. Critically, according to law professor and Indigenous scholar James Youngblood Henderson, they must overcome the "existing colonial ideology of contrived superiority of European law, and the humanity and psychology of cultural and racial inferiority of Aboriginal people. They must revitalize the justice system, decolonize the judicial precedents, and renew respect for ecological and human diversity" (2002, 2).

To frame and clarify the complex legal and cultural issues involved in the following Indigenous land claim case studies, it is important to first supply essential background information on the differences between Indigenous and Western understandings, and to define the important legal terms, concepts, and courtroom procedures that are relevant and underlying Indigenous narrative construction and court presentation. Since the case studies explore Native Hawaiian efforts for land control in the state of Hawai'i, cultural, legal, and historical information on Hawai'i and the Native Hawaiian loss of land and sovereignty will also follow.

The courtroom as a tool for Indigenous empowerment

Since the 1980s scholars have been reconsidering the role of law in society, reflecting on its function as more than just an authoritative mechanism that maintains and controls social order. Many scholars now view law as a government institution that operates to construct identity while mirroring, reproducing, supporting or challenging cultural norms (Bederman 2010; Butler 1990, 1993, 2012; Cover 1983; Fraser 2000). These norms have their basis in communal narratives and practices that help to define and determine acceptable behaviour in society.

Like heritage, cultural norms are not static, but shift in response to changes in external power structures (Foucault 1977, 1980). Recent theoretical research (Butler 2012; Butler and Athanasiou 2013; Fraser 2000) suggests that repetitive challenges to authorized power within official public spheres, such as courtrooms, can impact the balance of power by correcting imbalances and forcing social changes that might not occur otherwise. For Indigenous peoples, these types of challenges to social norms are attempts to rectify historic injustices by confronting interpretations of the past. As will be explained later in this chapter, narrative in the courtroom plays a vital role in this process.

Reclaiming the past for Indigenous empowerment

Regaining control over land is essential for Indigenous empowerment, as it restores traditional relationships and recovers agency. For Indigenous peoples, renewed control over land is tied to critical rights, including those of self-definition, language, traditional practice, and resource management. With the self-confidence gained, Indigenous people can challenge political hierarchies, the legacies of settler-colonial intrusions. Indigenous land claims are therefore much more than legal arguments over land ownership; they are also an attempt to regain authority over disruption in historic processes and the resultant loss of lifeways, traditions, culture, and customs. It has therefore become increasingly more important for Indigenous peoples to regain control over the past through the courts as a way to restore their traditional, spiritual, and cultural relationships to ancestral lands, and thus maintain their unique identities. Significantly, recovering suppressed historical cultural material in the pursuit of cultural justice may uncover and encourage "the rediscovered sense of collective selfhood" necessary for minority empowerment (Niezen 2009, xiv).

Heritage and authenticity: Indigenous vs Western conceptualizations

To base a legal claim on heritage, Indigenous peoples must present tangible evidence to the court. This is a problem, since Western and Indigenous conceptualizations of heritage are fundamentally different. Western heritage creation begins with the capturing of personal ephemeral memories associated with artefacts, sites, and places, and commemorated and reinforced through practices and symbols, such as memorials, monuments, and landmarks. The resultant stories, images, and concepts connote, but do not construct, reality. Instead, they provide a sense of things, such as an emotional relationship to an ancestral past or a spiritual tie to specific places, beliefs, and traditions. Some memories are included, while others more painful are repressed or ignored. What emerges in this process as memory is not provable by historic record, but instead contains selective portions of events that have relevance and importance to the originator or narrator of the story. Events remembered in this way give meaning to the past and are adopted as reality.

Native American scholar Margaret Kovach (2009) distinguishes Indigenous heritage from non-Indigenous heritage. She claims that Indigenous heritage is more inclusive, formed from personal memories, as well as integrating ancestral memories passed down through oral legend and myth. It includes concepts unfamiliar to Western knowledge systems including metaphysical sources, empirical observations, and revelations from dreams and visions (Kovach 2009, 56). The inclusion of such concepts into legal processes in respectful and inclusive ways is thought by Indigenous scholars to be part of a continuing cultural renaissance to decolonize minds both within Indigenous communities as well as outside (Kovach 2009, 2). As they are retold, Indigenous narratives are re-interpreted to reflect contemporary perceptions of the world and to maintain relevance to temporal and political conditions. However, exposing these responsive collective narratives publicly makes them susceptible to charges of inauthenticity.

Two critical difficulties arise in documenting Indigenous heritage narratives for the court. First, in traditional Indigenous contexts, 'truths' are embodied within intangible cultural knowledge. Such knowledge is often considered privileged information and may be known only to recognized and designated experts who selectively reveal them to insiders or relay them to outsiders (Boyer 1994, 48). In such circumstances, data needed for court presentation may be either hidden, protected, culturally complex, or religious and spiritual. Hawai'i exemplifies this situation. Due to the historic trauma of cultural appropriation and governmentally authorized assimilation, Native Hawaiian cultural practitioners[2] are protective and secretive of their cultural protocol. Access to traditional knowledge is highly restricted, and when shared, carefully curated. The second difficulty is that Native Hawaiian heritage is based on orally transmitted ancestral memory imbued with spiritual significance. Once documented, the challenge in the presentation of Native Hawaiian heritage within the court is fourfold: Indigenous intangible concepts are very difficult to translate into the language of the court, practices may not be understood by other court participants, contemporary traditions may not be recognized by an existing body of Western law, and witnesses may not be forthcoming within the framework of the court proceedings.

Underlying these difficulties is the fact that there are significant epistemological differences between Indigenous and non-Indigenous narratives, and not all narratives shared in Hawaiian courts are equally understood. Epistemological processes of thought, or ways of perceiving the world, frame our understandings of the world and of ourselves. The basis for the legal misunderstandings, therefore, may be differences in perception of the role of a person in society. From a Western, or Hegelian perspective, identity is individualistic, with each person, the 'self' distinct and in contrast to the 'other' and to the environment. Time is linear, with a distinct past and an imagined future. The Western self acts independently and is only responsible for personal actions (Geertz 1974, 31). Knowledge, land, and the environment exist as commodities separate from the individual and community, and to be sold, used, and manipulated for personal or financial gain. They are material goods with no spiritual relationship to the individual. This is a Western viewpoint based on an order to the universe with the Biblical hierarchy of man dominating over other creatures and the environment.

Alternatively, Native Hawaiian worldviews place community members within a familial network comprised of kin, community, and environment (McGregor 2007). Personal identity is integral with community identity, located in the physical environment, tied to particular places, based on genealogical connections, and supported by ancestors as guides for appropriate behaviour (Benham 2007). Within the Native Hawaiian community, members strive to assume social and cultural responsibility for the maintenance and well-being of both the network and the physical environment. This sense of responsibility is a primary principle of Indigenous culture underpinning individual identity and actions.

It therefore follows that in the courtroom an Indigenous individual speaks on behalf of the community, not as a single individual. In Hawai'i, this cultural responsibility restricts the number of individuals who are willing to testify as individual witnesses. Instead, a representative of the community is designated to speak on behalf of their collective interests. Not only does this limit potential witnesses, but it is time-consuming for the community to designate a speaker, and such decision-making may exceed the length of a hearing or trial.

The legal framework for indigenous land claims: Narrative

A lawsuit is based on an argument that cannot be solved any other way. Arguments are presented as court narratives or stories. These are carefully worded statements prepared by skilled and trained lawyers, each word selected for its meaning and position. At the basis of the court narrative is the client's story, transformed by lawyers into statements that, in the words of noted Harvard law professor Alan Dershowitz, form a statement "written back to front to achieve the desired result, a positive ruling" (Dershowitz 1996, 101). In other words, a legal narrative is carefully and strategically constructed, with the client's narrative as its basis, with the objective of winning the case. Statements made in the narrative are backed up by evidence, which can be tangible or intangible, but must conform to the court's regulations on who and what is considered credible and acceptable. The court therefore requires scientifically proven historical 'data', including written or recorded accounts of the past, rather than heritage, which is based on collectively accepted 'truths' curated through complex social negotiations (Palmenfelt 2010, 72). In the legal claims to follow, Hawaiians were challenged to develop a process to transform their intangible 'truths' into evidential court, scientifically proven, historical "data" to support and substantiate their legal claims.

Narratives, or stories, are dynamic elements of communication and essential to human experience (Shenhav 2015). Narratives are dynamic in that they convey ideas from one person to another and are critical to framing culture and traditions. In this way, narratives provide a relationship to the world that places us within a community and helps to tell us who we are. Narratives, importantly, also structure our actions (Gearey 2010) to organize human experience (Bruner 1991, 21). Each person filters fragments of memory selectively, regroups, and transmits them to others. The structured story is then created using cultural conventions and language familiar to the author (Potter 1996). All recollections, including those with unresolved issues, are incorporated into memory as some form of narrative story.

When narratives are shared with others, and reinforced through repetition, they become what sociologist Maurice Halbwachs (1992) calls "collective memory". Events and narratives are temporally and geographically specific and are therefore transformed in the retelling to reflect contemporary perceptions of the world from a specific time and place. Community members' memories and experiences are "entangled", lashing community members together through mutual associations and values (Assmann 2008; Ricouer cited in Clark 2010). Together, this sharing of collective memories becomes "the building stones of narrated cultural heritage" (Palmenfelt 2010, 63), and thus the basis for personal and collective identity. Restoring a collective sense of belonging lost through colonization and forced assimilation is essential for building a Native Hawaiian movement for social and political empowerment. However, in order to restore a sense of belonging, Hawaiian heritage must first be recovered and shared, and communal values adopted.

Forms of narrative

There are multiple forms of narratives. Narratives can be defined as a spoken or written description of related events, the narrated part of a literary work, as distinct from dialogue; a form of art involved in telling stories, or a representation of a set of values or aims of a particular group (Oxford Dictionary 2017)[3]. The first definition of narrative as a spoken or written description of related events can be interpreted as either a narrative of scientifically proven data on historic events, or as is the case in Hawai'i, as heritage, the personal and communal accounts of the past. The second definition, narrative as an art form, can be considered the creative written and rhetorical medium employed to present a particular perspective on the contested subject. For this discussion I will call this form 'legal', as it sculpts portions of the other multiple contributing narratives into a specific shape, artistically translating them into a particular form, and strategically employing elements to build an aesthetic and convincing argument. In Hawai'i, this form of narrative in land claims uses Indigenous heritage to develop the direction of an overarching legal narrative, and to support legal claims of validity. The third definition of narrative may be interpreted as the dramatization of the combined final argument. It represents, rather than describes, employing rhetorical speech and body language, inference, and insinuation, with the objective of representing the narrative with emotional force, dramatizing the issues, and convincing the audience of the legitimacy of the argument in order to actuate a process. Following linguist John A. Austin (1975), an act such as this is performative, going beyond mere communication to construct or impact identity (Austin 1975, 6-11). The presentation of a court narrative is theatrical, and therefore performative.

Philosopher Judith Butler (1993) advances this concept one step further, suggesting that such participation in a "discursive practice" is also a "performative act", and that such actions, particularly in legal forums, may bring about the changes it actively represents and describes (Butler 1993: 6). Thus, Native Hawaiian participation and control of the legal narrative process contributes toward "produc[ing] the effects that it names" (Butler 1993, 13), which is a new, modern, Hawaiian identity. All three narrative forms, heritage, law, and the performance of speech, therefore have the potential to individually and collectively influence Native Hawaiian identity. These separate elements may explain how the process of building and defending versions of the past through legal narrative construction can impact heritage and identity.

Legal narrative, in particular, is a language practice intricately involved in the generation and maintenance of social power. Narrativity in the law legitimizes stories, generates legal power, and contains, anthropologist Justin Richland offers, "the legitimizing authority that undergirds that power" (Richland 2013, 218).

Narratives are therefore the basic building blocks for court brief presentations. Furthermore, credible narratives depend on evidence, which in the case of Indigenous land claims, requires procedures of investigation and definitions of cultural concepts and terms that may not be easily defined, nor familiar to the court. Building Indigenous legal narratives using heritage is therefore unusually difficult and complex as it requires community consensus in the choice of information, public identification of practice and belief, and codification and transformation of traditional knowledge into legal language and description. Once built, the narrative must also survive legal scrutiny and be defended in the courts. Importantly, in the process of building legal narratives, Indigenous claimants may discover previously undocumented and unrecognized values and practices. Such discoveries may reveal heritage previously lost, obscured, or discouraged due to historic discriminatory government policies. This information can enrich communities by revealing new forms of ancestral knowledge, culture, and tradition. Importantly, it can also be used to substantiate claims of traditional practice within the court.

Hawai'i, history, and the law

It has been a mere 238[4] years since Hawai'i transitioned from a pre-literate society to a modern American state. It has been an incredibly rapid transition from a subsistence society to a globalized state caught in the crossroads of international trade and finance. During this time, the Indigenous Native Hawaiian people, descendants of ancient Polynesian voyagers (Denoon 1997, 64) have struggled to survive, their numbers sharply decreasing due to colonization, disease, alienation from land, and rapid changes in social, economic, and political control. Despite the historical trauma, links to Hawaiian heritage have survived, notwithstanding efforts by successive governments to suppress them (Van Dyke 1998, viii).

Starting in the 1970s, a cultural renaissance began and inspired an interest in Native Hawaiian heritage practices. From this renaissance grew a new awareness of the value of land to Indigenous heritage and identity, as well as the importance of the restoration of land control to Native hands for Indigenous survival. "Awareness of history", Lowenthal (1990) asserts, "enhances communal and national identity, legitimizing a people in their own eyes. Identification with a national past often serves as an assurance of worth against subjugation or bolsters a new sovereignty" (Lowenthal 1990, 44). Indigenous involvement in lawsuits is an attempt to re-establish ownership and relevancy over the past, thereby asserting authority in the present, and influence over the future (Smith and Waterton 2009, 84). Such legal actions may result in a redistribution of power, and with this empowerment, new forms of Indigenous identity and perceptions of the value of culture and heritage may emerge.

Hawaiian culture and the law

In Hawai'i, there is a unique relationship between Indigenous culture and the law. According to the 2015 seminal legal document *Native Hawaiian Law: A Treatise*, both US national law and Hawai'i state law "acknowledge a special relationship between Native Hawaiians and their traditional land … and recognize a legal and political relationship between the federal and state governments and the Native Hawaiian people" (Mackenzie, Serrano and Sproat 2015, 23).

The two relationships are profoundly different, yet fundamentally bound together. The first relationship, between Native Hawaiians and their land, is based on the Native Hawaiian physical and spiritual connection with their environment, an affiliation that serves as the basis for their cultural heritage (McGregor 2007). Land, or *'āina* (that which feeds and nourishes) (Andrade 2008 cited in Chen 2012, 6), is considered a central component of their existence, part of "an interdependent, reciprocal relationship between the gods, the land and the people" (MacKenzie et.al. 2007, 37). Each person is linked to the next through genealogy and *'ohana* (family),[5] creating a web-like network traced through legends to particular islands (Kanahele 1986, 80). These social and environmental familial relationships are the basis for concepts of self and community identity (Fujikane and Okamura 2008, 79; Ito 1985, 301; McKubbin and Marsela 2009, 376). This affiliation also nurtures and sustains Native Hawaiian behaviour and self-perception (Linnekin and Poyer 1990, 86; Handy and Pukui 1950, 252).

Inherent in this relationship is a responsibility and cultural obligation for sustaining, maintaining, and caring for the health and wellbeing of the land through *mālama 'āina* (care of the land) (Chen 2012; Kanehele 1986; Sproat 2008) and *pono* (righteous behaviour) (Takagi 1999). This implies that the 'āina is alive (Van Dyke 2008), conscious, and imbued with *mana* (divine authority) (Blaisdell, Lake, and Chang 2005, 373; McKubbin and Marsella 2009) and must be treated not as real estate to be conquered or earthwork to be simply used. Thus, each Hawaiian is a steward, not an owner of the land. It is this traditional bond that informs all Native Hawaiian land-based lawsuits.

The second relationship, between the federal and state governments and the Native Hawaiian people, reflects a political recognition of historic socio-cultural and political change in Hawai'i and its impact on Hawaiian culture and law. As a result of that recognition, in Hawai'i Indigenous heritage has been thoroughly integrated into State legislation. For example, the Hawai'i State Constitution includes ancient Indigenous 'rights', or legally guaranteed powers in realization of interests,[6] to Native Hawaiian customary and traditional heritage practices. Nowhere else in the United States are laws of Indigenous custom and tradition so highly regarded and protected.

Accordingly, contemporary Native Hawaiian struggles for sovereignty through land claims are based on the assertion of the continuation of those legislated 'rights' for the return or control of land. However, the law does not define what contemporary 'rights' are, nor does it elaborate on what the State Constitution includes as modern practices "customarily and traditionally exercised for subsistence, cultural, and religious purposes".[7] Instead, the burden of proof is on Native Hawaiians to effectively present information to support the historic record of the traditional use of land, proof of their genealogical lineage to pre-contact Hawai'i, and evidence of the continued exercise of religious, cultural, or subsistence heritage practices.

The lack of clarification in the law may, in fact, be a strength for Native Hawaiians, as it creates a means of negotiation for a more empowered future. However, in a state where land historically has been the basis of political power (Cooper and Daws 1985, 2), and those who hold land generally occupy the high ground in politics (Perkins 2013, 4), Native Hawaiians must present their proof in the face of significant political, social, and economic opposition.

Native Hawaiian challenges to the law

The present struggle for Native Hawaiian land control is a resurgence of efforts dating back to 1839 when King Kamehameha III of the Indigenous Nation of Hawai'i, afraid that foreign economic and political forces were separating his people from their traditional lands, created legal protections for Native Hawaiian access rights for traditional practices. The rights the king sought to protect were based on the customs and practices of the Hawaiian people at that time. Today we call this 'customary law'. Customary law is a system of generally established patterns of practice, customs, and beliefs accepted as obligatory rules of behaviour. This type of law includes a form of customary social governance, as the regulations and procedures are recognized and accepted as part of the general social contract. Customary law guides social behaviour and evolves from and through community actions, or from the bottom up (Benson 1988). Customary law works in addition to legislated or authoritative law, which, in contrast, is created through legislation and has a formal legality. Authoritative law is interpreted through the courts and enforced through legal punitive measures. It "provides predictability through law" and ... "allows people to know in advance which actions will expose them to the risk of sanction [and punishment] by the government apparatus" (Tamanaha 2012, 240). An understanding of these two types of law is critical to the following discussion.

In Hawai'i, the king's hope was that by ensuring rights to access land, cultural practices would continue, Native Hawaiian identity and heritage would be protected, and the unique culture of the Hawaiian Islands would survive. The king's efforts were successful in that every government, from kingdom to republic, republic to US territory, and US territory to US state, has recognized the unique relationship between the Hawaiian people and the Hawaiian Islands by incorporating the nineteenth-century law protecting Native Hawaiian traditional and customary rights into every version of state governance. Until statehood, the law was not substantially interpreted nor expanded, leaving past values, concerns, and perceptions from bygone eras as justification for contemporary land use practices.

However, during the last fifty years, the law protecting ongoing Native Hawaiian traditional and customary practices has been challenged in Hawai'i through a series of significant land claim lawsuits. Efforts have been made to reconcile ancient and modern systems of land use, and ultimately, judicial recognition of ongoing Native Hawaiian traditional and customary rights has been confirmed. In the process, Native Hawaiian heritage has been investigated, documented, and explored to determine the scope of ongoing practices; the relevancy of ancient practices to a modern population; and to define the extent, mode, and obligation of state legal protection. Increasingly Native Hawaiians have become directly involved in the process of case development and have participated in all aspects of the judicial process. In turn, the greater society in Hawai'i has reacted politically and socially. Judicial rulings on constitutional and statutory provisions have impacted the economic, political, and social capital of the Native Hawaiian population and have fostered and nurtured a new Indigenous identity.

The process of change is evident through an analysis of three significant Indigenous land claim lawsuits in the state of Hawai'i concerning what are called in state law "Traditional and Cultural Rights". Land claims such as these are employed in struggles for Indigenous sovereignty to reassert control over ancestral land, protect places of traditional and cultural value, safeguard spiritual and religious practices, regain jurisdiction over a contested past (Lowenthal and Gathercole 1990), and provide for a sustainable economic and political future for a marginalized population. Significantly, engagement in the land claim process has the potential to foster Indigenous community involvement and encourage political action, thereby stimulating a new Indigenous nationalist identity.

Regaining Indigenous control of Native Hawaiian heritage in Hawai'i is a highly political issue in the state. Native Hawaiian heritage has been appropriated by the state for tourism and therefore has great economic value to the government. Native Hawaiian heritage, from traditional practice to values and symbols, has become the narrative of the state, challenging ownership of fundamental components of Indigenous identity. In fact, it has become such an important component of state identity that the Native Hawaiian heritage narrative has been adopted and incorporated into state law. The official State narrative is of ancient and enduring Hawaiian values of *aloha* (peace), *mālama* (respect), and *pono* (righteousness), along with the traditional and customary practices of *hula* (dance), ritual chant, music, surfing, and *luau* (celebration). Elements of the Indigenous heritage narrative are also evident throughout all representations of state government. Lawsuits for Indigenous land control based on heritage values and traditional practices are therefore also power struggles for the restoration of authority over appropriated heritage and Native Hawaiian identity.

Indigenous empowerment through narrative construction

To explore the case studies, a research methodology was employed that combined an examination of legal records, including delving into the language of the narratives and the accompanying testimony, with legal narrative analysis, used to analyse the strategy and language. The intent was to uncover the intrinsic cultural meanings within briefs, evidence, submissions, and presentations; to determine how assertions of heritage value were substantiated; to uncover the shared cultural meanings in specific behaviours (Walliman 2006); and to analyse the use of heritage for cultural and political empowerment (Van Dijk 2001). Extensive interviews were conducted with a wide range of members of the Native Hawaiian community for insight into the intrinsic meaning of the language employed and the cultural values revealed. The case studies will discuss how historic narrative construction using heritage impacted Native Hawaiian identity and aided in achieving greater forms of sovereignty.

Throughout case examination, information on culture and meaning-making collected through ethnographic interviews, observation, and participation, informed and supported my findings and conclusions. Books on Native Hawaiian culture and history, such as *Nā Kua'āina: Living Hawaiian Culture* (McGregor 2007); *A Nation Rising: Hawaiian Movements for Life, Land and Sovereignty* (Goodyear-Ka'opua, Hussey and Wright 2014); and *Ku Kanaka: Stand Tall: The Search for Hawaiian Values* (Kanahele 1986) were used to analyse the meaning and intent of the wording employed while looking at perspective, purpose, and choice of words. The use of Hawaiian words was documented to explore the integration of Hawaiian culture into non-Native society. Clarifications were requested from previously contacted experts in culture and law to better understand cooperative arrangements between groups united for common objectives. Scholarly journals were also accessed to explain issues of regulation and precedent. The journals were crucial for an understanding of process and interpretation.

For the purposes of the following discussions, the three cases first will be identified by the full case name, and then abbreviated. Kalipi v Hawaiian Trust Company will be referred to as *Kalipi*, Pele Defense Fund v Paty will be referred to as *Pele*, and Public Access Shoreline Hawai'i v Hawai'i County Planning Commission will be referred to as *PASH*. Furthermore, the plaintiff in the Kalipi case will be referred to by his full name, William Kalipi, and the organization Pele Defense Fund will be referred to as PDF.

The cases are sequential, each case building on the previous, and the rulings expand on one body of law in Hawai'i, the Customary and Traditional Rights of Native Hawaiians. Since each case emerged through and within specific political and social environments, each case analysis will first identify the socio-political environment in which the case was initiated. Second, it will discuss the narrative that was constructed and defended by the Native Hawaiian plaintiffs, and last, it will explore the impact of the case narrative development and presentation on Native Hawaiian identity, heritage, and sovereignty.

The first case: Kalipi v Hawaiian Trust Company (Kalipi)

From a legal perspective, the grand narrative of modern-day Native Hawaiian land claims began with *Kalipi*. The case materialized in a period of great change, with dramatic increases in State population. With the new arrivals from the mainland came an increased awareness of American social and economic disparities, and a new willingness to rectify them. Political power was beginning to shift, creating greater opportunities for minority and marginalized voices. The discourse of Native empowerment and sovereignty had become the basis for Native Hawaiian land claim activism in the state. In the courts, *Kalipi* was the first significant Native Hawaiian case post-statehood in the Hawai'i Supreme Court to challenge the continued existence of eighteenth-century laws protecting Native Hawaiian traditional rights.[8] The legal case argument was whether laws passed in the eighteenth century protecting and preserving traditional access rights and practices remained viable and if so, how they should be interpreted in the legal context of the twentieth century.

The case began in 1975, as William Kalipi, an impoverished subsistence farmer on a tiny *kuleana* (traditionally inherited) parcel of land, discovered his wealthy, politically powerful neighbours had built fences around their substantial properties, impeding his ability to access his property and lead a traditional lifestyle. He believed he had a customary as well as a legal right to continue to access and gather natural products throughout the district (the *ahapua'a*), and with the help of a local, non-profit legal aid organization, he sued his neighbours.

Culturally, economically, and politically, William Kalipi was at a great disadvantage. He was a modest farmer working with pro bono lawyers challenging major landowners, a powerful financial entity, and the state government. When the case began, there were no books on Nation of Hawai'i Law, little scholarly research on Hawaiian history from a Native perspective, few interpreters of the Hawaiian language, and a lack of contemporary decisions or widespread knowledge related to Native Hawaiian traditional culture or land access rights. Among Native Hawaiians, community consensus is also highly valued, humility is prioritized, and peaceful coexistence, or *aloha*, strongly encouraged. William Kalipi felt so strongly about his rights and the cultural loss his children were being denied that he stepped forward individually to speak publicly. Additionally, the Native Hawaiian community was just beginning to rediscover its culture and traditions, and local Indigenous organizational structure to support his claims did not yet exist. What William Kalipi did have was orally transmitted knowledge of the land, a sense of obligation to his community and family, and a dedication to doing what was honourable and righteous.

William Kalipi was subjected to repeated, vicious attacks in court by the defence team for his statements concerning his rights, traditional culture, beliefs, identity, and practices. He was verbally provoked by defence attorneys who were ignorant about traditional cultural practices in Hawai'i, strongly opposed to Indigenous land control, and uninformed on the historic basis of the law. While at first he did not assert his identity as Hawaiian, after being subjected to repeated attacks, he began to state he was Indigenous and Native Hawaiian and to declare that regulations cannot extinguish Indigenous rights. William Kalipi further altered his arguments to support his assertions primarily according to Western forms of evidential proof, leading him to form more informed and directed responses. He authenticated past access through the presentation of his extensive knowledge of trails and natural resources throughout the district (*ahupua'a*), and argued his opposition was denying not only Native Hawaiian rights, but the historic foundations of current law and the traditions and culture of the state. William Kalipi, through his presentation, forced the state to reconsider the historical record and introduced an Indigenous historical perspective.

Politically, two important factors supported this case. First, occurring during the course of this case, in 1978 a Constitutional Convention was held in Hawai'i to redraft the original 1957 document. Given an opportunity for increased participatory government, Native Hawaiians became involved and became delegates. Once elected, these delegates drafted and the Convention passed fundamental changes in state law to acknowledge and protect Native Hawaiian culture and heritage, particularly traditional customary rights and practices (Meller and Kosaki 1980, 255-256). [9] To Native Hawaiians, these were groundbreaking legal developments in the law (MacKenzie 2012, 632). To William Kalipi, these new protections would add force to his argument, legal justification to his claims, and confirm the importance of Native Hawaiian heritage to the state.

The second important factor was that the Chief Justice of the Hawaiian Supreme Court was William S. Richardson, the first Native Hawaiian Chief Justice in the state, and a man who had been discriminated against in his youth in the Territory for being Hawaiian. He was very conscious of his heritage as a Hawaiian, as a member of a historically, politically active family, and a member of the political elite of Hawai'i. He worked to achieve a compromise between the economic interests of the state, the needs of the general population, and the rights of Native Hawaiians. Chief Justice Richardson demonstrated the value of education and was an example of an astute, politically savvy, Native Hawaiian leader, dedicated to the legal recognition and protection of Native Hawaiian rights and culture. He would go on to establish the law school at the

University of Hawai'i, and inspire, encourage, and mentor Native Hawaiian lawyers who were involved in the following cases.

Although William Kalipi would lose his case, the final case ruling was momentous for both Hawaiian law and Native Hawaiians: for the first time in contemporary history, the Hawaiian Supreme Court "recognized the *modern* legal bases of traditional and customary rights" in Hawai'i state law (Forman and Serrano 2012, 12, emphasis added). For Native Hawaiians, *kuleana* tenants would gain access rights, and Native Hawaiians would be inspired to pursue both opportunities for further heritage protections, as well as political, social, and economic capital. Significantly, the case demonstrated for Native Hawaiians the value of heritage as a legal tool in judicial processes in their quest for greater sovereignty. William Kalipi's involvement in the legal proceedings would reveal the potential for identity renewal and empowerment through Indigenous action in the courts. To bring the case to court, develop a narrative, and present, defend, and argue in court required him to set aside the traditional values of humility and acceptance, to disregard the cultural traditional of *aloha*, or getting along, to introduce Hawaiian words and concepts into the courtroom, and to endure rhetorical attacks on his identity and the history of the Native Hawaiian people. As he built a legal narrative from an Indigenous standpoint, he had to defend the importance of Native Hawaiians and their heritage to the modern state. No longer an individual fighting for land rights, William Kalipi became the lone court representative of a collective community with deep ancestral, spiritual, and political foundations in the Hawaiian Islands. By the end of the case, he had restored and introduced in-court cultural meanings, and presented to the state, the public, as well as to other Native Hawaiians, a newly empowered Native Hawaiian identity willing to engage the state for rights.

The second case: Pele Defense Fund v Paty (Pele)

The 1970s and 1980s were exceptional periods of awakening for Indigenous people worldwide and fostered new political actions for greater inclusion in democratic processes. These movements were known as "Indigenous politics" (Postero 2013, 109) and the "politics of recognition" (Coulthard 2007, 2014; Fraser 2000). Native peoples were rethinking the basis for power-based relationships and were discovering new ways to access power to improve their lives. 'Indigeneity' as an identity became the means for achieving greater rights and equal justice. Within the UN, in particular, Indigenous rights critically began to be linked with minority and ethnic rights (United Nations 2007, 2), and governments who signed treaties supporting human rights could now be pressured by other signatories to improve the lives of local Indigenous communities.[10] The Native Hawaiians involved in the Pele Defense Fund case would take this lesson seriously: a national Indigenous message well publicized based on human rights could put political pressure on local governments for Indigenous political recognition and bring about positive change.

In Pele Defense Fund v Paty, or *Pele,* Native Hawaiians formed an organization, the Pele Defense Fund (PDF), and successfully strategized to fight an enormous, public-private initiative to extract geothermal energy from the Island of Hawai'i. The proposed geothermal site is the sacred home of Pele, Hawaiian goddess of the volcano, and within a designated, environmentally sensitive conservation preserve that contained a *wahi pana,* or sacred site. The Native Hawaiians felt the project would desecrate Pele; destroy sacred lands; restrict religious worship; limit customary and traditional practices; inappropriately use conservation land placed in trust for Native Hawaiians; and threaten the relationship between Indigenous residents and their ancestral sites. In their legal battle, the Hawaiians fought the authority and power of the state and struggled against the economic and legal might of deep-pocketed private investors. Through their prolonged court battle, they encountered a lack of public knowledge about Pele and Native Hawaiian cultural practices.

Evidence of identity transformation was clear in this case. The Native Hawaiians, led by educated and informed Indigenous leaders, created a legal non-profit, organized public rallies, and filed a barrage of lawsuits in the courts, one of which (*Pele*) persisted for 13 years. In their professional actions and communal efforts, they forged tactical alliances with Native Americans, local citizens groups, and major national environmental organizations to develop a successful, comprehensive strategy of activism, including a dramatic national media campaign for attention and fundraising, thus building political, social and economic capital. They seized power in the court by assuming roles as judges, attorneys and expert witnesses, and they codified cultural knowledge and researched deeply into archives to find scientifically proven evidence of ancestral cultural practices, engaging Native Hawaiian academic experts to present evidence. Finally, they prepared the first official Cultural Impact Assessment in the state, documenting for public record the impact of development on the Hawaiian population. In doing so, they performed the assertive, educated, self-confident identity needed for sovereignty. Through their actions, they inspired widespread communal pride within the Native Hawaiian community and brought awareness to the fact that heritage was critical to survival and could successfully be used as a tool in the battle for recognition and rights. To the wider world, they demonstrated capability, education, fortitude, and an ability to fight for their rights successfully and professionally.

In this second lawsuit, it is evident from the narratives that Native Hawaiians began to explore the intersection between grassroots leadership and nascent organizational vision, as well as activate to build social, political, and economic capital. As a performative act, the use of a multi-faceted campaign to defeat geothermal development can be seen as an attempt to repair misrecognition by contesting the dominant culture's depiction of Native Hawaiian identity, and to re-establish control over representation in the 'politics of recognition'. Such actions, according to noted philosopher Nancy Fraser (2000, 110), are a performance of identity by "joining collectively to produce a new self-affirming culture of their own – [that when] publicly asserted, gain the respect and esteem of society at large. The result, because it was successful, was 'recognition'".

The third case: Public Access Hawai'i v Hawai'i County (PASH)

The final lawsuit took place during a time of expansive foreign development and investment in Hawai'i , fostered and encouraged by government initiatives to develop tourism to bolster the state economy. New real estate developments, especially along coastal areas, were impacting sensitive environmental coastlines and restricting Native Hawaiian access to traditional sites. Political from the start, this case pitted wealthy foreign investors and development advocates against a public recently made aware of the fragility of state environmental resources and the significance of Native Hawaiian customs and traditions. The collective group battling the project would experience widespread opposition both by the State and the public, since their efforts threatened the growth of tourism and development, major drivers within the state's economy.

In this lawsuit, an environmental organization, Public Access Shoreline Hawai'i, known as PASH, opposed a major developer's plan to build an expansive, multi-building hotel facility. In the interest of covering all of their bases, PASH involved a Native Hawaiian in their lawsuit so that if all of the environmental claims failed, a Native Hawaiian cultural rights claim could still be asserted over the loss of site access for traditional practices. The Native Hawaiian participation in the case proved critical, as the environmental claims did all fail and only the Indigenous rights claim remained. The collective effort between PASH and their Native Hawaiian supporters was effective, and the court ultimately allowed supplemental 'Friends of the Court Briefs' (*Amicus Curiae*) in support of the Native Hawaiian right to access traditional sites to be submitted by organizations in support of PASH's cause. Native Hawaiian groups and organizations responded, representing tens of thousands of members, presenting evidence through formal legal documents; demonstrating, for the first time, the presence of a multitude of organized Native Hawaiian groups with educated leaders, all dedicated to protecting and expanding Native Hawaiian rights, culture, and identity, and to achieving higher levels of sovereignty.

Evidence of Native Hawaiian identity transformation and empowerment was evident throughout this case. In the case narratives there was an evolution in mindset from victims to survivors, and from a defence of rights to a demand for political recognition. Additionally, the dramatic court presentations demonstrated a renewed and invigorated pride in ethnic identity and a determination for focused and effective change. The court participants also presented a distinctive reconsideration of Native Hawaiian collective narratives of the past, taking back the historical record and presenting it from an Indigenous perspective. Ultimately, they proposed the state further integrate cultural values into law to resolve future social and political differences.

The active, informed and widespread participation by a multitude of Native Hawaiians demonstrated a dramatic increase in ethnic affiliation and political engagement through participation in the hearings and the subsequent delivery of organizational narrative statements submitted to the court. Per Judith Butler (1990, 1993) and Nancy Fraser (1990, 1995, 2000), these communal acts can be seen as performative actions. Native Hawaiians had come together, informed through the previous legal actions, empowered by increased education, energized by demonstrations of capability and professionalism, and inspired by the growth of social and political capital. This profound increase in Indigenous court involvement contributed to a shift in authorized power, as well, and stimulated increased Indigenous ethnic identification and civic participation. Efforts taken to save the beach and access rights unified disparate Native Hawaiian groups in a show of ethnic pride, civic participation, and Indigenous nationalism. *PASH's* success in court also elevated the importance of Native Hawaiian traditional practices in Hawai'i, and demonstrated a new, valuable opportunity for Native Hawaiians in utilizing their heritage to control the development of traditional land. Importantly, *PASH* also demonstrated how dispersed and diverse groups can work together to transform their communities and ultimately empower themselves.

Conclusion

It is evident from following the archival evidence from these three significant Native Hawaiian lawsuits that Indigenous efforts to develop and support a legal narrative, including leadership in decision-making, archival research on culture and heritage, court performance, and public displays of support, can provide a new public voice, take back the historical record, inspire a renewed sense of belonging, and restore pride in an Indigenous identity. Furthermore, public acknowledgement of protected processes, practices, and sites may be used to build alliances with other special-interest groups using heritage to achieve common goals. Together these alliances may provide the social and political capital needed for increased political recognition and empowerment. Such actions by Indigenous peoples can advance upward social mobility, increase national sovereignty, encourage collective identification and civic involvement, regenerate cultural practices, and strengthen group identity.

There is a growing body of research in the field of heritage studies related to the formation of identity among Indigenous Pacific Island communities (Halualani 2002; Kana'iaupuni 2005; Linnekin and Poyer 1990; Smith and Akagawa 2009; Smith 2006; Trask 1999), and the politics of sovereignty and Indigeneity (Barker 2005; Fujikane and Okamura 2008; Smith 2004) in struggles for self-determination. This investigation adds to that body of knowledge by providing insight into the post-colonial, political value of Indigenous heritage by demonstrating how participation in the construction of legal narratives, including investigation into current practices, documentation of traditional knowledge, strategizing for effective presentation, and production of court performance, challenges current social norms, empowers communities and impacts perceptions of the past, identity, and relationships to land. This study, while based on research framed through Native Hawaiian land claims, is significant in that it may also be applicable to and useful for other groups in movements for achieving greater forms of empowerment and sovereignty.

Notes

[1] Native and Indigenous are used interchangeably throughout the paper.

[2] Native Hawaiian cultural practitioners are those individuals who are recognized within the Indigenous community as knowledgeable and experienced in traditional practices.

[3] Oxford Dictionaries, n.d., n*arrative.* https://en.oxforddictionaries.com/definition/narrative, Accessed 8 May 2017.

[4] Scholars disagree on the dates for the initial Polynesian colonization of Hawai'i. See Athens, Rieth and Thomas (2014) and Dye (2011) for discussions of recent scholarly investigations and methods utilized for the development of initial Polynesian settlement dates for the Hawaiian Islands.

[5] Pukui and Elbert, *Hawaiian Dictionary* (Honolulu: University of Hawai'i Press, 1986). [Hawaiian to English definitions are from this dictionary unless noted otherwise.]

[6] WebFinance, Inc., n.d., *legal rights*, http://www.businessdictionary.com/definition/legal-rights.html, Accessed 11 January, 2018.

[7] Article 12, Section (§) 7 of the Hawai'i State Constitution. [The terms "§" and "Statute" are used interchangeably.]

[8] See Native Hawaiian Rights Commission 1979; Pele Defense Fund v Paty III.B

[9] Hawai'i Constitutional Amendment XII §7 states:

> *The State reaffirms and shall protect all rights, customarily and traditionally exercised for subsistence, cultural and religious purposes and possessed by*

ahupua'a tenants who are descendants of native Hawaiians who inhabited the Hawaiian Islands prior to 1778, and subject to the right of the State to regulate such rights.

[10] The treaties include the UN Fund for Indigenous Populations (1985) and the ILO Convention No. 169 on Indigenous and Tribal Peoples in Independent Countries (1989), http://www.un.org/esa/socdev/unpfii/documents/SOWIP/en/SOWIP_web.pdf, Accessed 27 October 2017.

Bibliography

Andrade, Carlos. 2008. *Hä'ena: Through the eyes of ancestors.* Honolulu: University of Hawai'i Press.

Assmann, Aleida. 2008. "Transformations between History and Memory". *Social Research* 75 (1): 49-72.

Austin, John L. 1975. *How to Do Things with Words.* Oxford, UK: Oxford University Press.

Barker, Joanne, ed. 2005. *Sovereignty Matters: Locations of Contestation and Possibility in Indigenous Struggles for Self-Determination.* Lincoln: University of Nebraska Press.

Bederman, David. 2010. *Custom as a Source of Law.* Cambridge: Cambridge University Press.

Benson, Bruce L., 1988. "Legal Evolution in Primitive Societies". *Journal of Institutional and Theoretical Economics* 144 (5): 772-788.

Blaisdell, Richard Kekuni, John Keola Lake, and Healani Chang. 2005. "Cover Essay: Ka Ahupua'a". *EcoHealth* 2: 373-375.

Boyer, Pascal. 1994. *Tradition as Truth and Communication: A Cognitive Description of Traditional Discourse.* Cambridge: Cambridge University Press.

Bruner, Jerome. 1991. "The Narrative Construction of Reality". *Critical Inquiry* 18 (1): 1-21.

———. 2002. *Making Stories: Law, Literature, Life.* Cambridge: Harvard University Press.

Butler, Judith. 1990. *Gender Trouble: Feminism and the Subversion of Identity.* London: Routledge.

———. 1993. *Bodies That Matter: On the Discursive Limits of 'Sex'.* New York: Routledge.

———. 2012. "Your Behavior Creates Your Gender". *Patchwork Casopis.* Accessed 30 March, 2017. https://www.youtube.com/watch?v=WRw4H8YWoDA.

Butler, Judith, and Athena Athanasiou. 2013. *Dispossession: The Performative in the Political.* Cambridge: Polity Press.

Chen, Stephanie. 2012. *Where Blood Runs with the Land: Partition Actions and the Loss of Native Hawaiian Ancestral Land.* Honolulu: University of Hawai'i Ka Huli Ao Center for Excellence in Native Hawaiian Law.

Clark, Steve Headley. 2010. "Introduction: Paul Ricouer on Memory, Identity, Ethics". *Theory, Culture and Society* 27 (5): 2-17.

Cooper, George and Gavan Daws. 1985. *Land and Power in Hawai'i*. Honolulu: Benchmark Books.

Cover, Robert. 1983. "Forword: Nomos and Narrative". *Harvard Law Review* 97 (1): 4-68.

Coulthard, Glen S. 2007. "Subjects of Empire: Indigenous Peoples and the 'Politics of Recognition' in Canada". *Contemporary Political Theory* 6 (4): 437-460.

Daes, M. Erica-Irene. 2011. "Prevention of Discrimination and Protection of Indigenous Peoples and Minorities: Indigenous peoples and their relationship to land". *UN Commission on Human Rights, Subcommission on the Promotion and Protection of Human Rights*. Accessed 18 May, 2018. http://hrlibrary.umn.edu/demo/RelationshiptoLand_Daes.pdf.

Denoon, Donald. 1997. "Human Settlement". In *The Cambridge History of the Pacific Islanders*, edited by Donald Denoon, Stewart Firth, Jocelyn Linnekin, Malama Meleisa and Karen Nero, 37-77. Cambridge: Cambridge University Press.

Dershowitz, Alan. 1996. "Life is Not a Dramatic Narrative". In *Law's Stories*, edited by Peter Brooks and Paul Gewirtz, 99-105. New Haven: Yale University Press.

Foucault, Michel. 1977. *Language, Counter-Memory, Practice: Selected Essays and Interviews*, edited by Donald Bouchard and translated by Sherry Simon. Ithaca: Cornell University Press.

———. 1980. "Truth and Power". In *Power/Knowledge: Selected Interviews and other writings, 1972-1977*, edited by Colin Gordon and translated by Colin Gordon, Leo Marshal, John Mepham and Kate Sober, 109-133. New York: Pantheon.

Forman, David and Susan Serrano. 2012. *Ho'ohana Aku, a Ho'ōla Aku: A Legal Primer for Traditional and Customary Rights in Hawai'i*. Ka Huli Ao Center for Excellence in Native Hawaiian Law William S. Richardson School of Law, University of Hawai'i.

Fraser, Nancy. 2000. "Rethinking Recognition". *New Left Review* 3 (3): 107-120.

Fujikane, Candace, and Jonathan Okamura. 2008. *Asian Settler Colonialism: from Local Governance to the Habits of Everyday Life in Hawai'i*. Honolulu: University of Hawai'i Press.

Gearey, Adam. 2010. Law and Narrative. In *Routledge Encyclopedia of Narrative Theory*, edited by David Herman, Manfred Jahn, and Marie-Laure Ryan, 271-275. London: Routledge.

Geertz, Clifford. 1974. "'From the Native's Point of View': On the Nature of Anthropological Understanding". *Bulletin of the American Academy of Arts and Sciences* 28 (1): 26-45.

Goodyear-Ka'opua, Noelani, Ikaika Hussey, and Erin Kahunawika'ala Wright, eds. 2014. *A Nation Rising: Hawaiian Movements for Life, Land, and Sovereignty*. Durham: Duke University Press.

Halualani, Rona Tamiko. 2002. *In the Name of Hawaiians: Native Identities and Cultural Politics*. Minneapolis: University of Minnesota Press.

Halbwachs, Maurice. 1992. *On Collective Memory*. Translated by Lewis A. Coser. Chicago: Chicago University Press.

Handy, Edward, and Mary Pukui. 1950. "The Polynesian Family System in Ka-U, Hawai'i: II - The Physical Environment". *The Journal of the Polynesian Society* 59 (3): 232-240.

Ito, Karen. 1985. *Affective Bonds: Hawaiian Interrelationships of Self in Person, Self and Experience: Exploring Pacific Ethnopsychologies*. Berkeley: University of California Press.

Kanahele, George H. S. 1986. *Kü kanaka—Stand tall: A search for Hawaiian values*. Honolulu: University of Hawai'i Press.

Kana'iaupuni, Shawn Malia. 2005. "Ka'akalai Ku Kanaka: A Call for Strengths-Based Approaches from a Native Hawaiian Perspective". *Educational Researcher* 34 (5): 32-38.

Kovach, Margaret. 2009. *Indigenous Methodologies: Characteristics, Conversations, and Contexts*. Toronto: University of Toronto Press.

Linnekin, Jocelyn, and Lynn Poyer. 1990. *Cultural Identity and Ethnicity in the Pacific*. Honolulu: University of Hawai'i Press.

Lowenthal, David. 1990. "Conclusion: Archaeologists and Others". In *The Politics of the Past*, edited by David Lowenthal and Peter Gathercole, 302-314. London: Unwin Hyman.

———. 1996. *Possessed by the Past*. New York: Routledge.

Lowenthal, David, and Peter Gathercole. 1990. *The Politics of the Past*. London: Unwin Hyman.

MacKenzie, Melody. 2012. "Ke Ala Loa - The Long Road: Native Hawaiian Sovereignty and the State of Hawai'i". *Tulsa Law Review* 47 (3): 112-151.

MacKenzie, Melody, Susan Serrano, and Koalani Laura Kaulukukui. 2007. "Environmental Justice for Indigenous Hawaiians: Reclaiming Land and Resources". *American Bar Association* 21 (3): 37-42.

MacKenzie, Melody, Susan Serrano, and D. Kapua'ala Sproat, eds. 2015. *Native Hawaiian Law: A Treatise*. Honolulu: Kamehameha Publishing.

McGregor, Daviana P. 2007. *Nä kua'äina: Living Hawaiian culture*. Honolulu: University of Hawai'i Press.

McKubbin, Laurie, and Anthony Marsela. 2009. "Native Hawaiians and Psychology: The Cultural and Historical Context of Indigenous Ways of Knowing". *Cultural Diversity and Ethnic Minority Psychology* 15 (4): 374-387.

Niezen, Ronald. 2009. *The Rediscovered Self: Indigenous Identity and Cultural Justice*. Montreal: McGill-Queen's University Press.

Palmenfelt, Ulf. 2010. "Narrating Cultural History". *Journal of Ethnology and Folklorics* 4 (1): 63-73.

Perkins, Umi. 2013. "Kuleana: A Genealogy of Native Tenant Rights". University of Hawai'i, Department of Political Science, PhD Thesis.

Postero, Nancy. 2013. "Introduction: Introducing Indigeneity". *Latin American and Caribbean Ethnic Studies* 8 (2): 107-121.

Potter, Jonathan. 1996. *Representing Reality – Discourse, Rhetoric and Social Construction*. London: Sage Publications.

Pukui, Mary K., S. H. Elbert, and Esther T. Mo'okini. 1974. *Place names of Hawai'i*. Honolulu: University of Hawai'i Press.

Richland, Justin. 2013. Jurisdiction: Grounding Law in Language. *Annual Review of Anthropology* 42: 209-226.

Shenhav, Shaul. 2015. *Analysing Social Narratives*. London: Routledge.

Smith, Laurajane. 2004. *Archaeological Theory and the Politics of Cultural Heritage*. London: Routledge.

———. 2006. *Uses of Heritage*. London: Routledge.

Smith, Laurajane, and Natsuko Akagawa. 2009. *Intangible Heritage*. London: Routledge.

Smith, Laurajane, and Emma Waterton. 2009. *Heritage, Communities and Archaeology*. London: Duckworth.

Sørensen, Marie Louise Stig, and John Carman, eds. 2009. *Heritage Studies: Methods and Approaches*. New York: Taylor and Francis.

Sproat, D. Kapua'ala. 2008. "Avoiding Trouble in Paradise, Understanding Hawai'I's Law and Indigenous Culture". *Business Law Today* 18 (November/ December): 29-33.

Takagi, Dana. 1999. "Forget Post-Colonialism! Sovereignty and Self-Determination in Hawaii". *Colorlines* 2 (2): 5.

Tamanaha, Brian, Z. 2012. "The History and Elements of the Rule of Law". *Singapore Journal of Legal Studies* December: 232-247.

Trask, Haunani-Kay. 1999. *From a Native Daughter: Colonialism and Sovereignty in Hawai'i*. Honolulu: University of Hawai'i Press.

United Nations. 2007. *United Nations Declaration on the Rights of Indigenous Peoples*.

Van Dijk, Teun A. 2001. "Critical Discourse Analysis". In *The Handbook of Discourse Analysis*, edited by Deborah Schiffren, Deborah Tannen, and Heidi E. Hamilton, 352-371. Malden, MA: Blackwell Publishers.

Van Dyke, Jon M. 1998. "The Political Status of the Native Hawaiian People". *Yale Law and Policy Review* 17 (1): 95-147.

———. 2008. *Who Owns the Crown Lands of Hawai'i*. Honolulu: University of Hawai'i Press.

Walliman, Nicholas. 2006. *Social Research Methods*. London: SAGE Publications.

Youngblood Henderson, James. 2002. Postcolonial Indigenous Legal Consciousness. *Indigenous Law Journal* 1 (Spring).

Repurposing heritage

Chapter 6

The preservation of the *Uku* festival as cultural heritage in Umuchu, Anambra State, Nigeria

Ifeyinwa Emejulu

Nnamdi Azikiwe University, Awka, Nigeria

Abstract

Uku Festival is celebrated in *Umuchu* in Anambra State, Nigeria. It was previously celebrated to honour the *Uku* deity, emphasize the unity among the people and cleanse the land of illnesses and sacrileges. With the advent of Christianity, there was a decline in the celebration of the festival. However, presently, there has been a resurgence in the celebration with increased events and participation. Using primary and secondary sources, the study seeks to ascertain the reason for this metamorphosis and highlights the present cosmological, cultural and tourism relevance of the festival. The study is hinged on cultural Adaption Theory and also draws relevance from Hermeneutic Theory. The paper contends that the inculturation activities of some mainline churches and the quest for African identity have been responsible for the resuscitation of the celebration of *Uku* festival.

Keywords: resurgence, metamorphosis, inculturation, African Identity

***

Introduction

In African communities, festivals are used to commemorate important events. The importance of these festivals includes their role in preserving the cultures and traditions of the local people, and hence their heritage in the absence of written documentation. In Nigeria the federal government's cultural policy of 1988, while emphasizing the importance of festivals, views them as periods of celebration and also as avenues of "transmission of perceptions, ideals, aspirations and philosophies of the people for a meaningful living" (Federal government cultural policy 1988, 20). Rituals as mentioned by Opoku (1970) are an integral part of African festivals and this has led to a belief among scholars that festivals have always been a part of African religious belief systems. Achor (1998) classifies festivals into two types, namely general participation and limited participation festivals.

This study examines the preservation of *Uku,* a festival celebrated in Umuchu, southeastern Nigeria. The focus of the study is to account for the resurgence of the celebration after a decline occasioned by the emergence and inception of Christianity in 1926. Following Achor's (1998) classification, the traditional celebration had both aspects of general and limited participation. The cleansing ceremony performed by the traditional Chief Priest[1] and elders constituted the limited participation, while the Uku feast, masquerade, and betrothal ceremonies constituted the general. Post Christianity, some of the aspects of the festivals celebrated in the different African communities were seen as idolatrous and hence their celebration was stopped. With the resurgence of the Uku festival, some of the rituals (limited participation) associated with the festivals were removed while others (general participation) have been retained. This study seeks to explore reasons for the resurgence of the festival, to question the authenticity of the festival in view of the removal of these rituals, and also provide reasons for the resurgence of the festival. Importantly, the religious, social, and environmental relevance of the festival to the contemporary population is also highlighted.

Festivals like Uku remain a very important aspect of local cultural heritage. According to Green, Green, and Schuldenrein (2021, 3) heritage attaches:

> each human community to the History of its natural, physical, and social environments ... It combines community pride as the cultural – historical background upon which to build a sustainable future. It provides a vehicle for traditional knowledge to be brought forward within an understanding of how things have changed over time and how they must change in order to provide [the community] a successful future.

The paradox in the relevance of heritage can be seen in the theme of this volume—heritage in action—which highlights heritage as a wheel on which the society is propelled forward.

Heritage is the constant part of a community, frozen in the cultural values of the society yet also reflecting social and political change and thereby serving as the basis for community identity.

The Uku festival, celebrated from the pre-colonial period, has undergone changes by the people of Umuchu. The site of the festival has also experienced political, cultural, and social changes, becoming more tolerant of alternative celebratory transformations. This has resulted in an overall resilience for celebrating the Uku festival in a new way, thereby demonstrating and enhancing heritage as a social action, and encouraging the transmission of traditional cultural values from one generation to another.

The geography and people of Umuchu

Umuchu is a town located in Aguata Local Government Area of Anambra State, southeastern Nigeria. On the geography and population of Umuchu, Nnoli (1999) places Umuchu at a height of about 180 meters above sea level with a land mass of 48.6 square kilometres and a population of an estimated number of 98,698. The town consists of three major village groups: *Ihitenato, Amanasaa*, and *Okpu n'achalla*. The Uku festival is celebrated by the Amanasaa group. Umuchu shares borders with towns like Arondizuogu, Akokwa, Achina, Uga and Amesi. There are no discernible features separating the town from her neighbours. The people of Umuchu are ethnically of the Igbo tribe and live in different patterns of settlement in the community. The patterns of settlement include linear, nucleated, and dispersed forms of habitation. The choice of settlement pattern is informed by considerations of population, security, geographical formations, and landscape.

The Igbo values and worldview

Igbo people are acclaimed travellers and can be found in different parts of the globe. The appreciation of their adventurous nature is summarized by their proverb "A widely travelled man is wiser than the white-haired man". The Igbo man is reputed to be hard-working, enterprising, and resourceful and his world view consists of an admixture of beliefs, values, customs, and traditions. As Ekei (2016, 22) succinctly explains:

> The most basic vision of life (among the Igbo) is the belief in the existence of the order, harmony and interaction among all beings, insofar as they are in existence, the intricate connectivity is such that any attempt to disrupt it, causes a far-reaching calamity. The adverse effect of this disruption would not only affect the culprit but also the whole community. In fact, the danger associated with the disruption of the existing harmony is so drastic that the traditional Igbo dread it with all their soul.

This establishes a relatedness among all beings with the behaviour of each intrinsically affecting the other.

The Igbo world view in Madu's perception consists of a hierarchy of beings with the supreme being, *Chukwu,* at the apex, followed by the deities, spirit forces, and ancestors (Madu 2004, 5). While highlighting the place of man in this hierarchy, Madu asserts:

All interactive processes in the African world view are geared towards the welfare of man. In fact, gods exist for the sake of man, for man shops from god to god, in search of life and not necessarily to revere the gods.

In reference to Igbo world view, Udefi (2013, 100) explains, "… the observance of the *Omenani*—the totality of the customs and traditions and value orientation, is very important to the Igbo man".

In his definition of the world, Udefi believes the world is divided into two, the land of the living and that of the dead. Citing Uchendu (1965), he avers that there is constant interaction between the world of the living and dead, the visible and invisible forces. The Igbo man believes ardently in retributive justice, that if you sow evil, you reap evil and if you sow good, you reap good. Hence, his insistence on keeping his hands clean and holding on to *Ofo*, the god of justice who he believes will always fight for him, as long as his hands are clean.

The origin of the Uku festival

In presenting a traditional account of the origin of the Uku festival, Abarigwe (2015, 54) recounts that the festival was initially instituted to celebrate and commemorate the formation and subsequent unification of the core and initial settlers of the Amanasaa group. With time, it increased in size and intensity to include the payment of tribute to the Uku deity for a successful harvest, as well as for setting the calendar for the yearly events of the community. It went on to include entertainment by masquerades and betrothals. It is important to note that while the Amanasaa community celebrated its own festival, the other two groups of villages celebrated their own festivals as well. Importantly, while these other two festivals have almost gone extinct, only the Uku festival has survived until today. The impetus for the celebration of this Uku festival derives from the fact that it is celebrated at the end of the harvesting period, a period of leisure when there is no more work to be done on the farms.

The stages of the historic Uku festival

To explore the contemporary transformations that have taken place within the proceedings of the Uku festival, it is critical to clarify first the elements of the historic event. There were several stages to the traditional Uku festival. They were *Ina Uku, Ntunye Omu, Egba Ewe Uku, Igba Oziza*, and *Igba Mmanwu*.

Ina Uku—Festival date selection plus a time for the resolution of disputes

The celebration of the festival of a particular year started in the preceding year when the traditional priest of the Uku deity was presented with yams from the proceeds of the yearly harvest. The eating of the last tuber of yam by the chief priest coincided with his sighting of the moon. As soon as the moon was sighted, there would be the '*ina uku*' which is the proclamation and announcement of the commencement of the traditional preparatory period for the festival. With this announcement, the festival was expected to be celebrated in the next three market weeks, which is twelve days. The announcement of the festival also coincided with the shedding of the leaves by different trees, and this heralded the coming of the *harmattan* season, which usually took place around December and January. After the announcement, the shed leaves were collected and burnt. It was generally believed that the rising of the smoke from the burnt leaves ushered in the harmattan. The shedding of old leaves and the creation of a chance for the growth of new ones were both significant and symbolic. They were symbolic of an opportunity that was created among the people of the community to resolve old conflicts and create a new path for peace. To resolve conflicts, the elders of the community gathered at the grove of the deity for the cleansing, and a kind of judicial process was declared where all quarrels, disputes and misunderstanding were settled. It was taboo for people to celebrate the festival in enmity. After the adjudication and settlement of cases, the priest of the Uku deity offered sacrifices in supplication for a rewarding celebration. The priests of other deities were also invited to the sacrifice.

Figure 6.1 The Grove of the Uku Deity.

Photograph by the author 2021.

Ntunye Omu—Announcing the festival

The next important stage of the historic festival was the *Ntunye Omu*. In this stage, the masquerades appeared to the public, not to display and entertain, but to inform the people that the festival proper would take place in four days' time. Also, with this ceremony, the people of the neighbouring towns were notified that with the imminent celebration of the festival, there would be a prohibition of the sale of palm wine. This was to ensure the sufficiency of palm wine for the festival.

Egba Ewe Uku—The entertainment of guests

The *Egba Ewe Uku*, or entertainment of guests, took place on the eve of the festival. Visits which could not be accommodated on the festival day could be effectuated. Children usually visited their mothers' natal homes to familiarize and receive gifts from their maternal relatives. The nature and quality of these gifts conveyed the love and esteem in which the children were held. Apart from these gifts, the children were feted with sumptuous meals. Masquerades were not allowed to be performed on this day. On the festival day proper, visitors from long distances were entertained.

Igba Mmanwu—Masquerade performance

The fourth stage was *Igba Mmanwu*. It took place on the next day after *Egba Ewe Uku*, which was *Eke* market day. On Igba Mmanwu masquerades of different shades and colours paraded on the roads of Umuchu. The two hot spots of the masquerades' entertainment were the *Ama Oti* and *Mbareke* areas. There they performed and thrilled the audience. Women were strictly forbidden from these arenas where masquerades performed. It is significant to note that the continuation of the performances of these masquerades in these specific arenas constitutes one of the major reasons why the festival has not gone extinct despite the introduction and imposition of Christianity and Westernization.

Igba Oziza—The betrothal ceremony

The last stage of the traditional festival was *Igba Oziza*. It included two other important aspects of the Uku festival: the feasting and betrothal ceremonies for young girls who had come of age. In particular, the betrothal ceremony provided an opportunity for suitors to shower gifts on their prospective wives as well as on their mothers.[2]

Martin Mbamara is a retired teacher and the oldest man in his own kindred group in Amanasaa. He is 84 years old and an elder in the community. He has witnessed and participated in many Uku festivals. Commenting on the relevance of the betrothal ceremony, he explains that the fear of missing the gifts accruing from the ceremony kept a lot of girls of school age away from school, with the connivance of their mothers who anticipated the dividends of this ceremony (Mbamara, Personal Communication). The most noticeable consequence of this ceremony for the bride was that she started covering her midriff with a strand of cloth to distinguish her from her unmarried counterparts who wandered around naked. The brides also wore a particular kind of hairstyle known as *Isi Okpoko*.

Other important additions to their wardrobe were *nja* and *nkutowa* which are metal anklets. These were worn by brides, and they made noises as they moved around, announcing their presence wherever they were. Mbamara explained that the main aim of the *nja* and *nkutowa* was to discourage promiscuity as metal anklets reveal the whereabouts of the wearers anytime (Mbamara, Personal Communication). During the Igba Oziza ceremony, the brides visited the homes of friends where they were also showered with gifts. The ceremony culminated in the *Ahia Mbubu,* a celebration when these prospective wives visited the Nkwo market where they were hosted by their kith and kin. Abarigwe (2015, 68) reports this intriguing rite of passage, Igba Oziza, was held last in 1964.

Changes and continuity in the Uku festival

The coming of Christianity to Umuchu affected the celebration of this festival, which has continued to the present but in a different form. To make the Uku festival acceptable to a greater percentage of the people, most of whom are now acclaimed Christians, some activities considered contradictory to the tenets of Christianity have been removed. For example, sacrifices of food and meat are no longer presented openly to the deity as thanksgiving and appeasement. Additionally, presently, there is no traditional Chief Priest who attends to the Uku deity. However, there are insinuations that young men who seek favours from the deity still throng the deity's abode. This syncretic behaviour is rampant across Igboland. There is therefore clearly a need for more studies to be conducted on the prevailing cultural revivalism that pervades most Igbo communities and that has resulted in this clandestine patronage of local deities. The following are other features of the festival that have been impacted by the arrival of Christianity.

The fixing of the date for the festival is no longer based on the sighting of the moon. The fixing and planning of the festival presently falls under the responsibility of the Amanasaa Progressive Union, a body charged with the management of the social and political affairs of the group.[3]

There are no more initiation ceremonies for the boys of the town into the prestigious masquerade institution in preparation for the Uku festival. Additionally, there are no serious regulations of the activities of the masquerades. Infractions on the part of the masquerades are no longer addressed as seriously as in pre-colonial times. People can now hide under the masquerade to settle scores with perceived enemies. As a result, at times, the masquerades exhibit unruly and unacceptable behaviours like fighting between two masquerades or their attendants. This would not have been tolerated in the past for there was a code of conduct guiding the activities of the masquerade institution. Fighting occurs presently because the traditional framework that ensured absolute compliance of the dramatis personae has been dismantled. Another example is it was a grave offence for any part of the body to be seen, as this demystifies the masquerade.

The modern framework guiding the institution has been watered down. Consequently, even though masquerading has remained very vital in the lives of the people and remains an important component of the Uku festival, the rules are not as strictly adhered to as in pre-colonial times. For example, in the past there were rules guiding flogging by the masquerades.[4] They were not allowed to flog people on the shoulder and head, but only on the legs, and they were not allowed to flog somebody they did not know. To warn people of the arrival of the masquerades, each masquerade's attire had to include waist bells to indicate his approach. If the masquerades chanced on a woman, he was supposed to go away. For the womenfolk, the masquerades held a lot of fear and awe at the same time. The mere sound of a bell announcing the approach of a masquerade was enough to send any woman scurrying for safety. In spite of this, women enjoyed the eeriness of the masquerade since that which was supposed to frighten them, ended up attracting them. The chasing and running involved in masquerading also provided an opportunity for both groups to exercise themselves.

Today the masquerades flog people recklessly. There have been cases where boys whose love advances were turned down by girls take their pound of flesh while they are in their festival garb. The "offending" girls are chased and flogged. In this era of handsets/cell phones, masquerades have even been seen collecting phone numbers from girls (Okeke, Personal Communication). However, this anomaly has been addressed by the placement of a ban on the use of handsets/cell phones by masquerades.

In my previous published work, I asserted (2003, 63) that the masquerade myth in Igbo society has actually been sustained by the naivety of women who have chosen to believe some of the fallacies. Interestingly, the women, children and the uninitiated accepted all they were told about the masquerades even when they harboured doubts about the veracity of some of the stories. For instance, some of the myths associated with the masquerades included that participants emerge from ant holes. Surprisingly, most women today confess how diligently they tried this, in the secret confines of the compounds, without success in their childhood.

Figure 6.2 Masquerades performing during Uku Festival.

Reproduced with permission from In and around Umuchu Xmas and Tourism Magazine 2019.

There are also other positive aspects of the contemporary performances. First, masquerades now appear in more beautiful and elegant outfits. Second, in the present globalized world, it is interesting to see some masquerades performing the choreography of foreign musicians. Third, the traditional Igba Mmanwu—the masquerade dance and display—still takes place in the designated traditional arenas and continues to attract an increased number of visitors and spectators.[5] Last, like in the past, women are still not allowed at any of the Igba Mmanwu arenas. However, technology has come to the rescue of women by making all that happens in the display arenas available on tape, which women can now watch in the comfort of their homes.

An important heritage question can therefore be asked: with the retention and elimination of some activities of the Uku festival, how acceptable has it become to the associated population? Some Christians in Umuchu like Chidi Onuigbo, a retired university lecturer, believe there was nothing intrinsically evil about the traditional rituals of the Uku festival, so the retained cultural practices are acceptable. He feels that what the traditional deity chief priest did was harmonize available natural elements by gathering dry leaves shed by the trees and burning them. The resulting smoke from the burning leaves was believed to induce good weather in the West African season of harmattan (Onuigbo, Personal Communication). Consequently, in Umuchu as well as the larger Igbo society, the manipulation of weather elements either to induce or eliminate rainfall is still practised until today. Presently, there are also traditional rainmakers who are patronized by all (including Christians) during burials and other celebrations to ensure clement weather.

Other Christians assert that there is no evil associated with the contemporary cleansing aspect of the Uku festival because in the past all the traditional chief priest of the deity did during the cleansing was to pray for good fortune against the different calamities that manifest in the lives of the people. They suggest that this cleansing aspect can still be done in the different churches since the result borders on love, which is the cornerstone of Christianity.

Yet the authenticity of this new version of the Uku festival being celebrated in Umuchu has been questioned by a segment of the people. However, the majority reaction is to believe that if people derive fulfilment and draw identity relevance from the present celebration of the festival, it should be regarded as authentic. Some Christians believe that only the name—Uku—has a lot of fetish connotations and therefore it needs to be changed. In pursuance of this, the name of the festival was changed from Uku to *Ezumezu* in 2004. This was done to make it more acceptable to a greater percentage of the people. Nonetheless, it is difficult and rare to hear people refer to the festival as *Ezumezu.*

In regards the authenticity of Uku in its present form, it can be said that what is being celebrated is still Uku, but in a transformed form. Change implies continuity, and as Durkheim (1933) observes, both the individual and society which practice a particular culture keep influencing each other. As Nwankwo rightly notes, heritage is the only artefact that society can pretend to freeze over time. He says that even at that, "some maintenance can still be done on it, even if one strives not to alter the original pattern" (Nwankwo, Personal Communication). Festivals, he asserts, cannot be sealed in time. Changes over time to the festival are evident in numerous ways. Aspects of the Uku festival which are no longer in practice include the traditional regulation of the lunar cycle with its calendar of activities. With the introduction of the western means of calculating times and seasons, this aspect of the festival has become redundant. Additionally, the collection and burning of leaves which was believed to have induced the harmattan period is no longer done. While this has removed some of the nostalgia attached to the festival, it has brought the people of Umuchu to the reality of climate change. They may find it difficult to explain the reason behind the present irregular coming of the harmattan season, they know for certain that this particular climatic season is no longer as regular and intense as it used to be. Apart from the calendar and climatic aspects, other activities which have become redundant are the feasting, conviviality, betrothals, and subsequent marriages which can well be celebrated in other seasons without repercussion.

Figure 6.3 Spectators watching masquerades performance.

Reproduced with permission from In and around Umuchu Xmas and Tourism Magazine 2019.

Another aspect of the festival which has suffered a decline is the unfortunate neglect of the environment in which the Uku shrine is situated. In Africa, shrines of deities are sited in groves and valleys which are not chosen arbitrarily. The abodes of the deities and gods worshipped by a community are determined by the nature of these gods, hence as Umeji (2002, 55) points out:

> Coastal people worship the sea and waves, while inland people are beyond the area of jurisdiction of the sea. Similarly, the hills and valleys which are pathways to the cosmic world and the subterranean world of the dead respectably receive their due reverence. One sees the traditional religion of the Igbo as the result of their experience as they adapted to their physical and biological environment.

Sharing the same view, Okeke (1999) observes that in the traditional Igbo society, which is a polytheistic one, there was a belief in the existence of a Supreme God known as *Chineke* and other smaller gods and deities. While the supreme being, Chineke, lives in the sky, the smaller gods and deities reside in groves and are worshipped through dances, festivals, and sacrifices. These groves, he explains, are preserved and protected by customary laws and practices and apart from their cultural relevance, contain valuable plant species and herbs that protect the ecosystem as well as protect the soil from erosion, which is prevalent in the area.

Unfortunately, the groves have been altered over time. The reasons for the changes, as reiterated by Okeke (1999), include the advent of Christianity, which discouraged the worship of the deities, the civil war, which induced hunger and forced people to exploit the plants and animals in the groves for food, and incursions into the land for different forms of development, including the building of houses and churches. The effect of all these disruptions according to Okeke is the loss of resources for natural history, cultural institutions, instructional materials, and germplasm sources, and reduced attempts at forest conservation.

The theoretical framework for further analysis

This study examines the evolution of the festival and seeks to explain the reason for its evolution through several different stages. To do so, it adopts cultural adaptation theory and at the same time draws relevance from hermeneutic theory.

Cultural adaptation theory, formulated by Emile Durkheim between 1893 and 1933, upholds the notion that catalysts like urbanization and industrialization, as well as other social conditions, induce new patterns of behaviour and consequently, culture. These catalysts can be induced and affected by different conditions. Durkheim explains that those conditions that persist and that are theoretically relevant are those that are considered useful, meaningful, and indispensable to the community. These conditions are therefore sustained due to their applicability in society.

Furthermore, Durkheim raises the issues of rationality and individuality of cultural conditions and explains that rationality provides the ability to see these conditions from many perspectives, while individuality deals with the fact that even though prevalent cultural conditions may be generalized, they could be applied in different ways by different peoples (Parsons 1971). This leads to situations where an individual presents their beliefs and views as part of a group. The autonomy of the individual is of utmost importance to Durkheim. However, he points out that in assuming autonomy, the individual's membership of a society is emphasized so that both the society and the individual end up affecting each other (Durkheim 2013, 7). Other scholars, like Parsons, in adding their own perspectives to Durkheim's allusions, also highlight the importance of specific historical episodes as indexes and precursors of cultural adaptation.

Emile Durkheim's book, *Division of Labour*, focuses on industrialization, its division of labour and the resultant social changes. He periodizes the effects of the industrial revolution on human behaviour. Having dwelt specifically on industrialization, he consequently groups different and varied societies into the category of either industrialized or non-industrialized.

Within these two categories of societies, Durkheim also conceptualizes men as individuals and women as non-social beings. These postulations have generated a lot of controversy. This apparent relegation of women to the low end of the social ladder could be attributed to an inadequate appreciation of women's contributions at that time. Lehmann (1994, 3) acknowledges that Durkheim views women as being natural in a degrading manner and that women are "fundamentally, inherently intrinsically asocial and are part of nature rather than part of society". Durkheim also rejects feminism as an "unconscious movement [which] deceives itself when it formulates the details of its demands". Many scholars have argued against Durkheim's perception of women as not being part of the society. One wonders how he could have trivialized the contributions of women, especially during the industrial revolution when women needed to tend the home front while men or women went to work themselves. On the other hand, while not accepting and justifying Durkheim's views on women, it may be appreciated that during the industrial revolution, a greater percentage of the workforce were men who also formed unions and created the master/servant social relationship which provided part of the focus of Durkheim's study.

Again, his division of societies into industrialized and non-industrialized formations is contentious and an over-simplification of existing social structures, with Durkheim failing to acknowledge the unique features of the different societies. However, his classification of societies into industrialized and non-industrialized emanated from a need to focus on the problem at hand, the anomie in Western society that emerged as a result of industrialization (Durkheim 2013, 9). Since Western society has become industrialized, understanding the consequences and impact of this phenomenon on both the industrialized and non-industrialized has become imperative. Industrialization initiated a type of solidarity—organic solidarity as opposed to mechanical solidarity in non-industrialized society. Organic solidarity thrives on the division of labour in society in which the producers of tractors, for example, must be in affinity with the farmer that will purchase their machine. This kind of social dependence has inherent consequences for the relationship between individuals and this is what gives rise to the anomie in Western industrialized societies. One can argue that Durkheim's classification of societies is not entirely correct as he probably used the non-industrialized society as background to project his conceptualization of the Western society in view of his presumed remedy to their problem. His focus was not really the non-Western societies.

Despite the controversies and limitations inherent in Durkheim's book, *Division of Labour*, his cultural adaptation theory provides a pedestal on which the resurgence of the Uku festival in Umuchu can be studied. Durkheim explored cultural change that was witnessed in the metamorphosis of Western societies from non-industrialized to industrialized societies. Despite the limitations involved in using the West as an example, Durkheim's work offers insight into the dynamics of cultural change as witnessed in the resurgence and transformation of the Uku festival.

In consonance with Durkheim's and Parson's postulations that cultural changes are often induced by major historical events, the celebration of the Uku festival could be said to have been affected by the twin incidents of Christianity and colonialism. These two events introduced new beliefs and activities which led to the adoption of new values. While the people of Umuchu were affected by the social transformations, it also provided them opportunities to re-evaluate their perspectives relative to different aspects of their lives. This is possible in that people embody their culture, which is never static, and are continuously being affected by events around them. This leads to a new way of doing old things. If individuals adapt and change, ultimately their culture will adapt and change also, and they will draw and derive new meanings from what they had before, including from their heritage. This entails interpretation which takes cognition of the ability of the intellect to transform.

In cultural adaptation theory, Durkheim emphasizes that aspects of culture that are sustained are those that are considered relevant in the lives of community members. These aspects are an integral part of people's existence and manifest as common values and thus beliefs. They also serve as objects of identity. These aspects do not have alternatives and may be considered relevant, irrespective of the dynamics of change. However, some aspects of the culture that are dispensable are disposed of. Pertaining to the Uku festival, a cursory examination of historical documentation that is presently obtainable shows that some of the original activities are no longer practiced while the indispensable ones are practised until today, such as the masquerade display. In terms of periodization, the celebration of Uku can be seen to have occurred in three temporal stages. The first stage is the pre-colonial period when the festival was celebrated with the attendant rituals. The second stage witnessed the coming of Christianity and colonialization. In this period there was a kind of lull in the celebration of the festival because some of the activities were considered fetishes. In the third and present stage, there has been a resurgence in the celebration as the Umuchu Christian now exhibits a change in perception where he or she feels the need to retain a traditional identity and cultural values despite being a Christian. The basis for this need can be found through a discussion of Igbo heritage, which is to follow. In examining the resurgence of the festival, the importance and role of the masquerade, an important element of Igbo heritage, cannot be over-emphasized. For an effective examination of the concept of masquerades in Igbo cosmology, inferences may be also drawn from hermeneutic theory. Oguejiofor (2009, 80) defines hermeneutic theory as "bringing an inner meaning into the open. It entails making explicit, what is implicit".

Gadamer (as quoted by Clark [2008, 58]), in explaining the use of hermeneutics in human activities, refers to a 'horizon' as a pedestal on which meaning and understanding can be conceptualized. He further describes horizon as "the totality of all that can be realized or thought about a person at a given time in history and in a particular culture". This also applies to conditions. He affirms that in acquiring a horizon, one assumes the opportunity of having a holistic and better view of the issue at hand. Horizons, he explains, are affected by encounters, prejudices, language, imagination etc. In the process of gradual adoption, one aspect of the old can be used to interpret the whole. The masquerading aspect of the Uku festival has remained a driving force in the resurgence of the festival and can therefore be viewed as part of a horizon for this investigation. Despite Christianity and colonization, this aspect of the people's existence, the masquerade, has remained relevant both in the practice of their culture and revalidation of their identity.

The historical impact of Christianity and colonization on the Uku festival

An understanding of the history of the introduction of Christianity and colonization and their impact on the Uku festival is critical to this investigation. Christianity was introduced into Umuchu in 1916 through the Anglican Mission. The Roman Catholic Mission followed in 1918 (Nnoli 1999, 136). Presently there are many Pentecostal Churches in Umuchu which are not necessarily Anglican nor Catholic. The coming of these different missions and other religious groups affected the social, cultural, and economic lives of the people of the community. In encountering Christianity, they realized the immense benefits associated with it. These include improved health care and the building of new facilities like churches, hospitals, and schools. According to Baur (2009), the missionaries came with the twin aims of civilizing and evangelizing as well as introducing the new faith which was associated with reading and writing. Literacy provided an incentive for a new way of earning a living. With the promises of the new religion and improved economic opportunities, the people of Umuchu, goaded by the missionaries, embraced the new religion while relegating major aspects of their culture, including the celebration of certain festivals, to the background. Scholars, including Okere

(1975), Wambutda (1987) and Madu (2004), have written extensively on the harmful effects of introducing a European brand of Christianity into African communities. Considering that the birthplace of Christianity was in Judea, which was a province in the Roman Empire, Madu explains that for this singular reason, Christianity contains elements of Hellenism, syncretism, Platonism, and other belief systems. Having practised a form of Christianity for some time, Africans, including Igbo people, felt that there was a need to fill a cultural void that was glaringly present in their Christian religious practices. This explains why after embracing Christianity, Africans demanded an indigenized form of Christianity that would enable them to uphold their cultural values.

In different parts of Igboland there has been a resurgence in the practice of African traditional religion with the resultant syncretism. The foundation for this is based on further historical events. The missionaries who came to Africa did not take out time to differentiate between African traditional religion and African culture. Both were lumped together and subsequently suppressed to enable the growth of the new blended Christian religion. The missionaries further failed to heed Shanahan's[6] admonition that what African traditional religion needed was transformation and not destruction. He believed there were areas of convergence for the two religions, Christian and traditional African, and these included belief in an afterlife and the veneration of saints and ancestors. The predicament of the missionaries and their inability to place African culture and religion on their rightful pedestal should be appreciated. At the point the missionaries came to Africa and particularly Igboland in the early twentieth century, not much was known about Africa. Citing some of their comments, Obiefuna (2018, 291) said even Homer referred to Africa as a "remote place at the extreme of the universe where people worshipped and sacrificed to the gods". For Hobbes, Africa was "a timeless place where there is no art, letters or social organization but instead only fear and violent death" (In Obiefuna 2018, 291). While subsequent studies have proven these assertions to be untrue, such comments influenced to a large extent the mindset with which the early missionaries initiated the evangelization of Africans who were portrayed as individuals without worldview and in need of a complete overhaul of their belief and value system. The missionaries believed as Baur (2009) notes, that there was a need not just to evangelize the African but also to civilize him.

Judging from the current number of Christian faithful, as well as Indigenous Christian priests and religious in Umuchu, it can easily be deduced that the Christian enterprise in Igboland has been a success.[7] However, the extent of this success is yet to be ascertained as Obiefuna cautions that despite this obvious achievement "there is an evident lack of depth in the faith and commitment of converts and an increasing proliferation of Afro-Christian Churches" (Obiefuna 2018, 287). These churches according to Gbenda (2012,

492) included the Apostolic Church, the Cherubim and Seraphim and the Celestial Church of Christ. They have incorporated some of the cultural practices of Africans, like spirit possession and the functions of magicians, medicine men and diviners into their worship. While the establishment of the Indigenous churches has given the African Christian a sense of belonging, it has also encouraged a lot of syncretic practices. This has led scholars like Nwankwo (2012) to question the level of spirituality of African Christians that is the "transformative innerconnectedness with the divine" (363). In revisiting the activities of the missionaries, it is important to highlight once again that one of the institutions in Igboland, including in Umuchu, that has been severely and negatively affected by the coming of the missionaries and Christianity is the masquerade institution and the subsequent celebration of festivals like the Uku festival.

The erosion of the masquerade in Igbo society and in the Uku festival

In a bid to Christianize and civilize the African, a lot of traditional and cultural values were eroded. This can easily be seen in the relegation of the masquerade institution from what it used to be in the life of the people to what it is now. However, the fact that the masquerading, in particular, has remained a strong reason for the resurgence of the Uku festival shows that it continues to be relevant in the lives of Umuchu people. This brings to the fore, per Durkheim's and Parson's assertions, the idea that the aspects of people's lives which are indispensable will always be retained.

For a proper understanding of the place of the masquerade in both the people's lives as well as in the Uku festival, the further relevance of hermeneutic theory must be highlighted. As was discussed previously, hermeneutic theory entails interpreting and understanding from someone's perspective and through the creation of a horizon, different perspectives which can be assigned to an entity or condition. Being part of a particular horizon informs a person's view or perception.

In Igbo cosmology, masquerades are corporeal representations of ancestors. It is strictly a male-exclusive institution and is open only to the initiated. Women and the uninitiated are strictly forbidden from learning or participating in the mystery and myth of the Igbo masquerade. Nnoli (1999) classifies Umuchu masquerades into day and night masquerades. The day masquerades include *Mmonwu-ija, Mgbadike, Isi-okpo*, and *Ooji-onu*. They perform during the day and are mainly for entertainment. The night masquerades include *Achikwu* and *Okuekwe*.

Madu (2004, 57), in surmising the place of masquerades in Igbo cosmology, asserts that although masquerades are the development of human intelligence, the institution goes beyond this mundane perspective into the realm of the Supra mundane. In it, the human-spirit encounter is expected. Igbo people express their cosmological beliefs in the ancestor whose decrees to man are not questionable. Thus by the exalted status of the ancestors in the Igbo ontological hierarchy, they can influence the affairs of the living. Since they are impartial and morally upright according to Igbo worldview, they act as agents of social control and adjustments in the lives of the people.

To fully appreciate the place of the ancestors in Igbo cosmology, Madu (2004, 12) recounts an encounter that took place during the nascent period of evangelization in Igboland between Igbo elders and missionaries. The missionaries were preaching to the elders on the need to be good Christians and the importance of aspiring to live in heaven where God resides. One of the elders then asked if their dead ancestors could be found in that heaven. The missionaries replied that since the ancestors were not baptized, it was most unlikely they would be there. The elder then exclaimed that there was therefore no need to aspire to go to heaven if his ancestors were not there!

The name of the masquerade was also impacted by the arrival of the missionaries. Traditionally, the masquerade is known as *Mmanwu* though there are dialectical variations to that title. The missionaries, who had the powers of written language, provided the appellation of 'masquerades' to the Mmanwu concept. This in no way encapsulates the totality of the concept. Asigbo (2012) prefers the use of 'spirit manifests' which better captures the essence of the masquerade myth. The visiting missionaries obviously and understandably were not able to appreciate and understand Igbo culture and world views. As with most aspects of the people's culture, the masquerade (Mmanwu) institution was consigned to the 'fetish' bin (Obiefuna 2018). Metuh (1987) condemns the missionaries' intolerance of the desire of the African converts to introduce elements of their culture into Christianity. This led to the clash of world views and the inability of the missionaries to come to terms with traditional African cosmology.

This clash of world views has left a lacuna in the psyche of the African Igbo, who, while accepting Christianity, still desires to retain his identity. This problem has resulted in the deep-rooted desire to uphold and sustain the masquerade institution in Umuchu. The veracity in Madu's assertion that man relates to life with gods and deities, not just to revere them but to find meaning, is substantiated by the masquerade myth in Igbo society. In search of the meaning of life, the Igbo believe that life does not end here on earth but stretches beyond, and the masquerades remain an important link between the living and the dead. The missionaries did not fully appreciate this role and the importance of the masquerade in Igbo culture. Onyeneke (1984, 52) accuses Christianity, especially Roman Catholicism, and urbanization of constituting strong challenges to the mask institution by undermining the values on which the system is founded.

As has been mentioned, the entertaining aspects of the masquerade as well as the relevance of the masquerade in the life of the people are the main reasons for the resurgence of the Uku festival. However, at present Christians in Umuchu are divided on the retention of masquerade activities in the town. Abarigwe (2015, 85) reports that while the clergy in the mainstream Christian sects—the Roman Catholic and Anglican churches—believe that the Uku festival can be adapted to become a Christian festival that depicts the people's culture, the pastors of the Pentecostal churches, Assemblies of God, Mountain of Fire, and Salvation Army dismiss the idea of finding any Christian relevance in the festival, affirming never to have anything to do with it.

The answers provided by the pastors and priests reflect the horizons referred to by Gadamer (as quoted by Parsons 1971) as a product of the interaction and experiences of those religious leaders. The stance of the mainstream Christian churches probably is an attempt to correct the previous mistakes made by their missionaries in not appreciating the culture of converts in these communities. The stance of the Roman Catholic church in particular can be appreciated in view of the inculturation policy of that religious institution. In referring to the origin of this inculturation policy, Obiefuna (2018) explains that while the use of the concept might be relatively new, the old problem of clashes between Christianity and African culture which the church seeks to address has always been a reoccurring issue. Citing Metuh, he said it was used in a theological sense by Joseph Masson, a Professor at Pontifical Gregorian University Roma, in reference to "an urgent need for a Catholicism that is enculturated in a variety of forms" (2018, 28-29). Pope Benedict XVI, while highlighting the importance of inculturation, emphasized the need for the church to undertake a thorough discernment to enable it to identify aspects of culture which present obstacles to evangelism, as well as those which promote it. The essence of these efforts is to produce an African church that is intensively Christianized and would witness the transformation of the different levels of life, laws, customs, moral values, and a worldview in light of the gospel message. Nwankwo (2012, 361), in emphasizing the relevance of inculturation, presents it as the articulation of an African cultural system and milieu which will lead to the church in Africa being "an African Church without at the same time being less the church of Christ and in communion with the churches of Europe, Asia or America".

The Catholic Church in Igboland has built bridges between traditional culture and Christianity. The decision to permit the Catholic faithful to take the prestigious *Ozo*[8] title previously regarded as a pagan title is a major milestone. Some parishes also encourage their faithful to engage in masquerade activities seeing it purely as entertainment. In the meantime, while the controversy on the suitability of the Uku festival for the Umuchu Christian rages on among the mainstream and Pentecostal churches, the celebration of the festival continues to intensify to a large extent in Umuchu.

The Uku festival and tourism

Presently, people converge from far and near to celebrate the Uku festival, thereby increasing the tourism relevance. Mrs. Igwe, a trader at Nkwo market, revealed that Umuchu shop owners record increased sales and patronage during the festival (Personal Communication). Increasingly Umuchu people in the diaspora have also become quite influential in the sustenance of the festival. They encourage the production and sale of videotapes of the festival and stay back after the Christmas celebration to be part of the Uku festival celebration.

Figure 6.4 Large crowd of spectators at the festival.

Reproduced with permission from In and around Umuchu Xmas and Tourism Magazine 2019.

The resurgence of the Uku festival in Umuchu can never be fully explained and appreciated without mentioning the contributions of Chief Odi Oti, a business mogul and a major stakeholder in the Uku festival, whose antecedents had the opportunity of hosting the Igba Mmanwu or masquerade dance right from pre-colonial times.[9] He felt that as a successful entrepreneur, he could contribute towards improving the hospitality aspect of the festival by providing drinks and different beverages for the people's entertainment and toward their relaxation during the festival. This has encouraged others to join this act of philanthropy and offer additional incentives to the people for attendance at the Uku festival.

On his views about the Uku festival, Chief Odi Oti said that there is nothing wrong or syncretic with the Umuchu Christian participating in a festival which could be likened to Halloween. He feels that it is just an entertainment festival with no fetish ritual and has been adapted to suit the convictions of a Christian population. Some Umuchu Christians in turn, have changed their perceptions of the festival to re-establish and maintain a sense of continuity with the culture and traditions of the people. Chief Odi Oti further maintains that the activities of the masquerades are now regulated through supervision. Participants have to abide by a general code of conduct and are made to face penalizing panels for infractions. There is also a requirement for registration, and all masquerades desiring to participate in the festival have to acquire identifying numbers.

In emphasizing the tourism potential of the Uku festival an analogy could be drawn from Bruner and Kirshenblatt-Gimblett's (2015) article "Massai on the lawn: Tourist realism in East Africa". The article portrays how the twin concepts of tribalism and colonialism have been used in entertaining visitors in Kenya. This entertainment, like the Uku festival, has been turned into a tourist event. The highlighted and interesting aspects of the article are that activities that happen in Massai, a hinterland in Kenya, are acted out on a lawn while serving tea.

Conclusion

Presently, there has been a resurgence in the celebration of the festival. This resurgence stems from an increased appreciation of traditional values by the people of Umuchu, both at home and in the diaspora. In their practice of Christianity, the people of Umuchu desire to be differentiated and identified as African Christians. It is important to them that this unique blended identity be established for a meaningful and fruitful acceptance of Christianity which for the African should not and can never be practised in a cultural vacuum. Theirs must be an identity which should be established from their values, traditions, and culture, containing those elements which set them apart as a unique and distinctive group. In assuming the toga of Christianity, there is no need for an identity crisis since Christianity should be practised from a cultural perspective without compromising its dogmas and tenets.

In this study, cultural adaptation theory has been used to explore and explain the evolution of the Uku festival. The evolution of the festival was examined through phases of change over time. In the first phase, the historic festival was celebrated to cleanse the land of different forms of calamities and was also a celebration of conviviality and the betrothal of maidens. It also unified the people and was a major form of entertainment by masquerades. The second phase witnessed the effect of the arrival of the missionaries and Christianity on the Uku festival, which led to a subsequent decline in the celebration of the festival since some of the activities associated with the festival were considered fetishes. During this second phase, there were also concerted efforts by the different Christian missions to establish their presence in Umuchu, by winning converts and producing Indigenous Christian priests and other religious personnel for their congregations. Furthermore, there was a tendency for the Indigenous people to disassociate themselves from some of the traditional activities considered inimical to their Christian beliefs. They sought a new identity with Christianity.

In the third and contemporary phase, the people of Umuchu, having accepted Christianity, have felt the need to uphold their traditional cultural values and assert their local identity. Encouraged by changing church policies, for example within the Roman Catholic Church and their inculturation programme, the Christian faithful have, over time, come to appreciate the fact that there can and should be a nexus between Christianity and some aspects of the people's culture. There have also been attempts by the church to encourage the adoption and practice of some traditional local cultural activities that do not conflict with Christian beliefs. As a result, the Uku festival has been adapted to respond to modern realities and cultural needs. At the same time too, the Igbo communities, based on their experiences and historical events, have also changed their perception of issues happening around them. The festival is now celebrated not just as a form of recreation with high tourism value but also as an avenue to retain and preserve their local Igbo culture and identity.

Using hermeneutic theory, this study reviewed the activities and relevance of the masquerades' institution, its role in Igbo cosmology, and the reason behind its continued relevance in Igbo society as a whole. The study acknowledges that the word, 'masquerade' given to it by the Western missionaries does not convey the full and actual meaning of the 'Mmanwu' concept. It also examined the contemporary and varied reactions of the Igbo communities to masquerading and the authenticity of the Uku festival, as is presently celebrated in Umuchu. From all indications, the Uku festival will be celebrated in Umuchu for many years to come because of its social value and the cultural lacunae it fills in the lives of the people, affirming the views of Gbenga (2012) that in spite of the contact with Westernization, some aspects of African culture have remained unchanged and that culture is fundamental to societal development, and of Ozoigbo (1999), that the more the Igbo change, the more they appear to be the same.

Finally, Asigbo's (2012, 1) view that "masquerades as representations of the ancestors must adapt and change and be in the image of a twentieth century ancestor" becomes particularly salient in rationalizing the continued importance and relevance of the masquerade and the Uku festival in Umuchu.

Notes

[1] A Chief Priest is a person in African traditional religion who has the authority to serve or tend a deity. He serves as a mediator between the people and the deity. He also serves as a spokesman for the deity.

[2] A betrothal ceremony is for girls who have reached puberty in the Umuchu Community. In this ceremony, the girl who is also engaged to be married is showered with gifts from both her prospective husband and friends.

[3] A socio-political body of elected members, chosen by the people to oversee the smooth running of the affairs of the Amanasaa group of villages.

[4] Flogging remains an integral and approved aspect of masquerading in Igboland. However, there are established rules guiding the flogging to avoid abuse.

[5] This is the masquerade dance done mostly during the Uku festival. It admits only male and initiated members of the community.

[6] Joseph Shanahan, a Holy Ghost Priest, was born on June 6, 1871, in Ireland. After his ordination in April 1900, he became the Prefect Apostolic of Southern Nigeria. As a Missionary Priest, he worked extensively in Southern Nigeria where he trekked long distances, converting and educating the indigenes. He emphasized the importance of appreciation of indigenous culture and traditions for effective conversion of the people. Hence, he ate indigenous foods and spoke the local language of the people which endeared him to them.

[7] Christian priests are ordained ministers of the mainstream Christian Churches – the Anglican and the Catholic Church. They serve as a link between the faithful and God.

[8] This is the highest title in most Igbo communities to which people can aspire. For a long time, there was an intense debate on whether it is proper to allow Christians to take this all-important title. In line with the inculturation policy of the Roman Catholic Church, the Catholic faithful are now permitted to take the title since the fetish aspect of the ceremony has been removed. See Obiefuna 2018:. 250; Madu 2004.

[9] A major stakeholder in the resurgence and celebration of the Uku festival. He added to the mirth associated with the celebration of the festival by providing a conducive environment and refreshments for the festival.

Bibliography

Abarigwe, Anayo. 2015. *History of Uku/Ezumezu Festival in Amansaa, Umuchu, 1916-2004.* Nnamdi Azikiwe University, Awka, Nigeria, M. A. Thesis.

Achor, Lilian. 1998. *The role of festivals in Tourism Development in Anambra State*. University of Nigeria, Nsukka, Nigeria, M. A. Thesis.

Asigbo, Alexander C. 2012. "Transmutations in Masquerade Costumes and Performances". *Unizak Journal of Arts and Humanities* 13 (1). Accessed 11 August, 2022. https://www.ajol.info/index.php/ujah/article/view/83227.

Baur, John. 2009. *2000 Years of Christianity in Africa. An African Church History*. Kenya: Pauline Publications Africa.

Bruner, Edward, and Barbara Kirshenblatt-Gimblett. 2015. "Maasai on the lawn: Tourism realism in East Africa". *Cultural Anthropology* 9 (4): 435-470.

Clark, Jeff. 2008. "Philosophy, Understanding and the Consultation: A Fusion of Horizon". *British Journal of General Practice* 58 (546): 58-60.

Durkheim, Émile. 1933. *The Division of Labour in Society*. New York: Free Press.

———. 2013. *The Division of Labour in Society*. 2nd Edition, edited by Steven Lukes. London: Palgrave Macmillan.

Ekei, John C. 2016. *Philosophy of Igbo Traditional Government and Authority*. Awka, Nigeria: Fab Education Books.

Emejulu, Ifeyinwa. 2003. "Women and Masquerades in Igbo Society". In *Readings in Humanities*, edited by A.O. Obiajulu. Enugu, Nigeria: John Jacob's Classic Pub. Ltd.

Federal government cultural policy. 1988. *Cultural Policy for Nigeria*. Nigeria.

Gbenda, Joseph. 2012. "The Impact of Colonialism on African Indigenous Religion". In *Colonialism and the Transition to Modernity in Africa*, edited by Joseph Mangut and Terhemba Wuam. Lapai, Niger State, Nigeria: Ibrahim Badamasi Babangida University.

Green, Stanton, Claudia Green, and Joesph Schuldenrein. 2021. "Archaeology as Public Good". *Archaeologies – Journal of the World Archaeological Congress* 17 (1): 1-18.

Lehmann, Jennifer. 1994. *Durkheim and Women*. Lincoln: University of Nebraska Press.

Madu, Jude. 2003. "Symbolism in African Cosmology. The Igbo Perspective". In *Readings in Humanities*, edited by A.O. Obiajulu, 66-68. Enugu, Nigeria: John Jacob's Classic Pub. Ltd.

———. 2004. *Honest to African Cultural Heritage*. Onitsha, Nigeria: Coskan Associates.

Metuh, Emefie Ikenga. 1987. *Traditional Religions*. Onitsha, Nigeria: Imico Publishers.

Nnoli, Leonard. 1999. *The Culture – History of Umuchu from the Earliest Times to 1999*. Enugu, Nigeria: Nolix Education Publications.

Nwankwo, Lawrence. 2012. "Religion, culture and Social Regeneration". In *Bountiful Harvest*, edited by Anthony B.C. Chiegboka, 354-364. Nimo, Nigeria: Rex Charles and Patrick.

Obiefuna, Boniface Anthony Chijioke. 2018. *Issues in Religion and Society*. Awka, Nigeria: Fides Communication.

Oguejiofor, Josephat. 2009. "Negritude as Hermeneutics: A re-interpretation of Leopard Sedar Senghor's philosophy". *American Catholic Quarterly* 83 (1): 80.

Okeke, S. 1999. "The Vanishing Sacred Groves in Igboland: A case for immediate Action". *Nigerian Heritage Journal of the National Commission for Museums and Monuments* 8: 136.

Okere, Theophulius. 1975. "African Philosophy: Some Distinguishing Criteria". Paper presented at the Department of Philosophy, University of Nigeria, Nsukka.

Onyeneke, Augustine. 1984. "Christianity and the Masquerade Society in Igbo Land". *Ikoro Bulletin.* Hansberry Institute of African Studies, University of Nigeria Vols. (1 & 2).

Opoku, A. A. 1970. *Festivals in Ghana.* Accra: Ghana Publication Corporation.

Ozoigbo, Ikenga. 1999. *A History of Igboland in the Twentieth Century.* Nsukka, Nigeria: I.R.A. Ozigbo.

Parsons, Talcott. 1971. *Societies: Evolutionary and Comparative Perspectives.* Englewood Cliffs N.J.: Prentice-Hall.

Uchendu, V. C. 1965. *The Igbo of south-eastern Nigeria.* Chicago: Holt Reinhart and Winston.

Udefi, Amaechi. 2013. "Philosophy and Igbo Cultural Practices". *Odu: A Journal of West African Studies* 44: 97-112.

Umeji, Obianuju. 2002. "Geological aspects of Igbo Religion". *Nigerian Heritage Journal of the National Commission for Museums and Movements* 11: 53-57.

Wambutda, Daniel. 1987. "The interplay between Cosmology and Theology: A matrix for African Theology". *The State of Christian Theology in Nigeria 1980-81.* Mercy Oduyoye ed. Ibadan, Nigeria: Daystar Press.

Glossary

Amansaa	A village that comprises seven clans.
Chineke	A variant of the titles of Chukwu—the Supreme God. Chineke literally means God the creator.
Chukwu	The Creator-God pantheon. It was who created the lesser gods, man, and beasts. He is so great that the Igbo could not approach him directly but through user gods and deities.
Ezumezu	General Assembly.
Igboland	Found in southeast Nigeria. The people's language is Igbo and one of the oldest Indigenous peoples of West Africa.
Isi Okpoko	A hairstyle in which three or four strands are lied vertically up and adorned with ornaments.
Ofo	The Igbo symbol of justice and uprightness. This was possessed by most men in pre-colonial times.
Omenani	The entirety of Igbo customs and tradition.

Chapter 7

Heritage, ritual, and power—the making of a sacred space in an east Indian village

Bishnupriya Basak

University of Calcutta, India

Abstract

The chapter makes a modest plea to unhinge heritage from its prevailing archaeological and anthropological understanding in South Asia. It challenges any static, inert view of an object, arguing instead that heritage is a contingent process in the present. I show how an archaeological artefact accrues meanings and values through discursive processes involving the practices of two ritual ceremonies through the lens of ethnographic fieldwork. These bear on annual festivals revolving around a 'folk' deity and a medieval saint of Bengal in a village settled by low caste groups located in the deep recesses of Sundarbans in West Bengal, eastern India. In anthropological studies, ritual has been upheld as a crucial site of power relations. Taking this as my basic premise I argue that the nature of struggles, resistance, and conflicts tends to differ as rituals are 'products of historically distinctive forces' and no two contexts are homologous.

Keywords: heritage, ritual, power, folk, non-folk, contingent, medieval, discourse, Sundarbans, performance, collectivity, archaeology, cultural memory, arena

***

Heritage, ritual, and power

Heritage has increasingly emerged as a discursive field over the past two decades, and its everyday consumption and production cannot be segregated from political and social developments at multiple scales. However, the prevailing majority vision that privileges old, grand, expert-approved archaeological sites, buildings, and objects and an unbroken continuity of ways of life still continues to impact and influence what is preserved and what is transformed in spaces, artefacts, and Indigenous traditions. In this chapter, I aim to unhinge the concept of heritage from such a stereotypical understanding and project it as a complex and ongoing social and cultural process in the present in which materiality is important but does not form the core of it. I aim to do this by focusing on two case studies of ritual worship—the first centring a folk-deity, and the second, a medieval seer. Informed by Critical Heritage Studies (Smith 2012), I move beyond materiality to probe cultural complexities that the idea of heritage helps to mediate. In this conception, heritage, which emerges from the past and is essential in communal memory-making, is impacted when an archaeological object becomes embedded in the process. The discovery, claim, and use of the object has the potential to be transformative, as senses of belonging, which are often challenged, become centred on the object(s), empowering the participants. This is problematic, for invoking any memory of the archaeological past in the present is usually considered to be an isolated and unrelated exercise toward comprehending the fixed inert meanings associated with communities within the archaeological past. Even this phrase is problematic as the usage of the terms past and archaeological are often conflated. The past is lived in the present, which interrogates any notion of archaeology that restricts itself to a study of objects that are held as diagnostic to particular cultures in a temporal frame.[1] That the 'past' is not transparent or unproblematic is rarely considered as important as archaeological studies of materiality. I argue that the past is ceaselessly extant, which I propose to engage with in this chapter.

South Asia offers an immense field to probe these processes of memory making. However, archaeologists and anthropologists have only pursued isolated and disconnected ventures toward interpreting past materiality or contemporary ways of life. While archaeologists have tended to seek direct analogical relationships between the past and contemporary modes of living,[2] anthropologists have concentrated on isolated studies of Indigenous communities and caste groups.[3] The idea of heritage that has emanated from these specialized perspectives rests on fixed meanings of tangibility and intangibility, the two often seen as sundered entities.

In her recent book *Indian Cultures as Heritage* historian Romila Thapar (2018) has addressed some of these issues from a perspective that perceives heritage as a component of culture. Objects, ideas, or practices that are inherited from the past are classified as heritage. The politics of maintaining or rejecting the contents of heritage, it is argued, yield to a construction of culture in the present. Thapar explicates these processes by citing many instances from early India. While the historian's perspective such as this is closer to the perception of heritage that I am upholding, there is a significant difference. To historians like Thapar, heritage still forms a component of culture as an ensemble of ideas, objects, and practices that are being selected or rejected by forces external to it, as seen in a political dynasty or a cohort class seizing upon certain items to authenticate or legitimize their privilege of dominance. She cites many instances of those that are abandoned and fall outside the dominant discourse, like the hero stones and the cult of the Ayyanar linked to certain low-status groups. Hero stones are memorial or commemorative stones raised in memory of the deceased warrior or chieftain that are found scattered in different parts of the Indian subcontinent, their chronology ranging anywhere between the sixth century BCE to the eighteenth century CE. A good instance of the cultural connotations of hero stones may be seen in their supposed association with the local worship of Ayyanar, a village deity, in many villages of Tamil Nadu, another state in southern India.

The site of ethnography

The idea of heritage that is being argued for here is novel: tangible, historical material, found by a contemporary community who recognized its importance from a sacred site and cast it in an entirely original use, which has provided the item new significance, value, and cultural meaning. The item has now taken on a new communal significance, and the knowledge and values associated with it, when passed down through generations—though not in an unchanging manner—will become heritage. Here heritage material is being created without an associated past.

This is contrary to the way in which Romila Thapar (2018) conceives heritage. To her heritage means inert archaeological objects and intangible practices/ traditions that are inherited from the past and become components of culture. The dynamics of heritage as a contingent process in the present are not considered as significant in her definition. The theory proposed here is also contrary to the ways in which heritage is understood in Critical Heritage Studies.

To investigate and secure this topic, I have chosen ethnography as a methodology. The chapter results from an ethnographic survey, based on field interviews, of two religious festivals that I undertook in February 2019 in Damdama-Keorakhali in the South 24 Parganas district in West Bengal. The district incorporates the Indian portion of the Sundarbans[4] region. A reconnaissance survey was done in February 2018.

Damdama-Keorakhali is a small hamlet settled by low-caste groups of Bagdis, Sardars, Paiks, and Rajbangsh. It is located in the border zones of two *thanas*, or administrative divisions, of Kultali and Joynagar in the district of South 24 Parganas in the state of West Bengal, India. Keorakhali is a *para* or locality that has grown as an offshoot of the main settlement at Damdama. The oral accounts of these groups trace the settlement to their moments of arrival more than three hundred years ago. Essentially migrant communities, nothing else seems to be preserved in orality other than the names of places from where their forefathers arrived.

The worship of a folk-deity—the Batsorik puja

Figure 7.1 The quern worshipped as the deity.

Photograph taken by the author.

Every year in February, or the Bengali month *Magh*, four days prior to the full moon or *Maghee Purnima*, a four-legged archaeological quern, locally known as the *gareya*, becomes the pivot of a day-long ritual at Damdama.[5] Recovered from the near vicinity—the act of recovery is claimed by the elderly interviewees to have been made more than three hundred years ago—the quern, which was possibly used in crushing grains, is associated with the archaeological context of the early historical period.[6] Such artefacts are not uncommon from early historic sites in Bengal and northern India. Accidental unearthing of material remains in the course of ploughing the land or digging a pond is also quite commonplace in the subcontinental landscape. The villagers, however, remain unaware of any such knowledge. Instead, the quern has transformed into a shrine of a local deity *Harijhi Chandi* whose *Batsorik puja*, or annual worship, forms the core of the ceremony. In the absence of any scriptures or textual tradition, the story is anchored in an oral narrative prevailing in the community of devotees, reflective of a process of formation of cultural memory. This aligns with Maurice Halbwach's (Coser 1992, 22) definition of collective memory as "a socially constructed notion". It has also been posited that cultural memory may be seen as a form of collective memory only so far as it evokes a group identity. However, in a Deleuzean sense, identity is not Sameness (Deleuze 1984). Such was evident in the course of my ethnographic study of the ritual when I saw that one of the elderly interviewees emerged as the main spokesperson relating the oral accounts. All others directed me to record his version. Yet there were accounts challenging his version, albeit not overtly. These instances may not evoke group identity(ies); instead, positing the image of group cohesion to an outsider was considered crucial. Thus, although I am considering cultural memory to be a part of collective memory, I remain doubtful whether it ever coincides with group identity.

The quern, also regarded as *sinhasan,* or the throne of the deity, was earlier placed on a raised ground where the rites of worship were made, before being transferred to a modest mud enclosure. A new dedicated shrine to *Harijhi Chandi* and *Bonbibi*—one of the most revered folk deities of the region—was established in 2012, when the 'throne' was transferred to its new ritual space from the open-air ground where it was earlier worshipped. I have used the term 'folk' to mean a rather loosely knit category of deities who continue to exist outside the Brahmanical fold. However, I remain fully cognizant of the long-drawn-out processes of acculturation and assimilation that challenge any neat demarcation of the Brahmanical and non-Brahmanical tradition. *Bon bibi,* whose clay image is encountered in the nooks and crevices of the region, is the more famous among the representative deities of the folk-family in the Sundarbans.

The shrine now houses all the folk deities of the Sundarbans who are worshipped simultaneously on the same day. Over the years the shrine has become a nodal point of congregation on the particular day for devotees, not only of this village, but also of neighbouring ones.

The worship of a medieval seer—the Mahotsab

Next to the *than,* or the seat of worship, is another shrine housing an idol of *Chaitanya,* the sixteenth-century Vasihnava seer of Bengal who is believed to have passed through the forested route on the way to Neelachal,[7] now in modern Orissa, another east Indian state. At the end of the day-long worship of the deity, a *Mahotsab,* or mega-festivity, commences the next day at the second shrine and includes an entangled web of rituals, oral accounts, and performances invoking Hindu gods and goddesses, including the pastoral god Krishna. Extending over a period of two to three days, this transforms into an arena of performance with enactment of *Ras leela*[8] and a two-day long session of sacred chants or *naam-gaan.* The groups involved with the *Batsorik puja*—the name by which the worship of the folk deity is popularly known—also join, but there is a distinct change of guard as the cohort group of personnel who are in charge of this *puja* is replaced. The high- and middle-caste groups also participate in this festival, thronging from other localities.

Figure 7.2 The idol of Chaitanya and the shrine of the Mahotsab.

Photograph taken by the author.

The *Mahotsab* constitutes a dominant discourse of the Bengali *Vaishnava*[9] tradition. The dominant discourse was represented—as I gathered from initial conversations in my first visit to the village before the ceremony—as a weaker force unable to bear down on the local, lesser-known discourse functioning at the subaltern level, and tending to get subsumed within the latter. In my second season of fieldwork in 2019, I realized that the processes and ways in which these forces operated were far more complex than what appeared initially. There are gaps and inevitable ruptures which frustrate any ethnographer. But it is the challenge that lies in capturing the moments of 'absence' and making sense of them that makes the effort worthwhile. Throughout the chapter, I will be talking as much about what was experienced as that which was not.

Ritual and power

The festivals are instances of local, sacred places gaining in significance over the years, drawing in pilgrims from other localities, and commemorating beliefs born and strengthened in the environment. The cultural memory accruing around the folk and the non-folk traditions is thus annually reinforced. Its custodians, the local patrons, are invested in the maintenance and propagation of the narrative that escaped the literati. The formation of a cultural memory is far from a simplified, linear, and peaceful process and is rarely emphasized in studies on cultural memory, but is constitutive of many-layered tales of contestation, struggle, and power asymmetries, with significant ruptures and disruptions. Recent anthropological studies uphold ritual as a crucial site of struggle. In a stimulating study of the festival of Aiyanar in the Tamil country, Nicholas Dirks (1994) argues that while rituals mark defining moments of collectivities and provide articulations of power and hierarchy, they are most potent in highlighting conflict. He uses the village festival as a trope to show how the ordinary lies entwined with the "extraordinary" and struggle or resistance occurs precisely "where it is least expected" (Dirks 1994, 488). One of the several illustrations he gives to validate this is a ritual seizure by an untouchable of the higher-caste headman's spear, signifying subversion. The ritual process, he claims, has a disorderly character, and hence ritual becomes the primary arena where politics is located. He prefers to see power as "an endless series of relations" (Dirks 1994, 502), characterized by struggle.

It is in this mode of viewing ritual as a site of politics that I choose to analyse these festivities. But I also seek to go further, to argue that the possibility of exploring these relations varies contextually. The nature of struggles, resistance, and conflicts tends to differ as rituals are indeed the "products of historically distinctive forces" (Asad 1993, 54), never 'transhistorical', and the ways in which power relations are inscribed in two separate contexts may not be homologous. To an ethnographer some of the relations emerge as amplified; others tend to lie as subterranean forces, not always pronounced. The challenge lies in teasing out the moments of struggle.

While a demarcated shrine/cult spot becomes the pivot, an outer public space is transformed into a repertoire of performative acts. The term 'public' and what it entails has been the focus of animated debates and discussions among social scientists, political theorists, and historians. Concerning primarily the urban context, we rarely come across any non-urban/rural connotations of the term. While this demands a deeper epistemological pursuit, I am using 'public' loosely to mean the heterogeneous village community/groups participating in the festivities. In an urban context, collective activities exploring the genres of public performances, collective ceremonies, and collective protests have been explored to examine the "political economy" of the north Indian city of Banaras (Freitag 1989). Public arenas where these processes pan out emerge as shared worlds of cultural values and assumptions expressed in metaphors, symbols, and actions participated in by elite and lower castes alike.[10] The cultural implications of a public arena in a rural setting of ritual spots will tend to be different yet crucial. Before I seek to explicate these processes, I turn to the wider universe of Sundarbans with its tales of wilderness.

The Sundarbans—tales of wilderness

Figure 7.3 Map of the Sundarban biopsphere region.

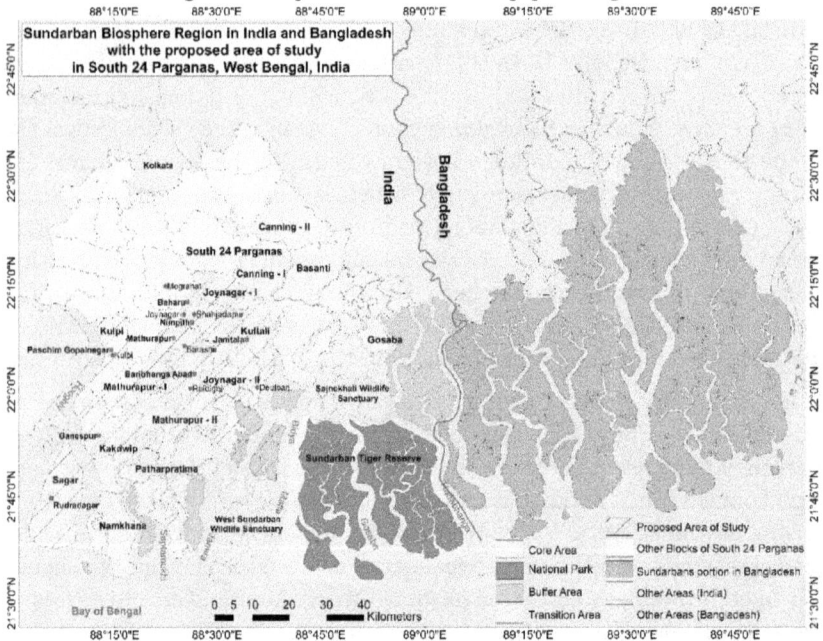

Image by Priyank Patel, printed with permission.

Sundarbans is now a congested landscape of villages and small towns in its northern part and forested tracts with unique biodiversity (that secured its recognition as the UNESCO's World Network of International Biosphere Reserves in 2001) in the south. It has a cultural aura around it, fanned mostly by grassroots scholarship expressed in prolific writings in Bengali on local history and 'folk culture', and published in abundance from the local district towns. This tradition has persisted over the years, largely overlooked and marginalized by mainstream history-writing. It was believed for a long time, mainly following Beveridge, a colonial scholar-official writing in the nineteenth century in the pre-independent context, that Sundarbans—a tiger-infested land—never possessed an early history of human settlement. Paradoxically, it was the colonial policy of land clearance in the late eighteenth century for settling populations that made inroads in the hitherto unexplored terrain, exposing many vestiges harking back to antiquity. Pioneering initiatives of an unknown local scholar, Kalidas Datta, wrested Sundarbans from archaeological and historical oblivion (Basak 2011). It was Datta's untiring journeys into the nooks and crevices, traversing dense forests and unfamiliar stretches to recover numerous objects of art and structural remains from excavations of ponds, canals, and ditches, that retrieved the history of the Sundarbans. The region can now claim an archaeological time frame of at least two millennia.

In Sundarbans, an archaeological 'past' is more often than not enmeshed in a 'folk culture'. I am using 'folk culture' as a direct translation of the more commonplace usage of *lokasansanskriti,* which the grassroots practitioners of ethnography use in documenting the numerous rites, practices, and religious festivals that are widely prevalent among the indigenous communities of the Sundarbans. A more incisive analysis of the phrase as to what it entails or leaves out may be an interesting study of the politics of knowledge formation.

Numerous practices of 'folk religion' prevail in the representation of many cults of local gods and goddesses. The most famous of these are the syncretic cults of *Dakshin Ray, Barakhan Ghazi* and *Bon Bibi.* Constituting part of a local discourse, they continue to exist outside the haloed precincts of the Brahmanical pantheon and mainstream Islam, featuring largely in *punthis*—a body of textual tradition that thrived in the lower deltaic Bengal between the seventeenth and nineteenth centuries in paeans dedicated to the deities composed in Bengali verse. The narratives primarily catered to professional groups intimately entwined with forest livelihood, like the woodcutters, honey gatherers, beeswax gatherers, so on and so forth. Among others, the *Raimangal, Ghazi-Kalu-Champavati Kanyarpunthi* and the *Banabibi Jahuranama* are the more prominent. Disseminated widely among the marginalized sections, these texts, like many others current in the contemporary milieu, did not depict reality, but held out promises and favours at the end of propitiatory rites to the worshippers. These promises and favours lay embedded in metaphors and imageries, and emerged as particularly meaningful for groups embarking on their daily forays into a treacherous land.

Ritual ceremonies like the *Batsorik* and the *Mahotsab* are instances of many other practices that do not find mention in the *punthis* and hence go largely unnoticed. But they may not be entirely divorced from the chief deities, as evinced in parallel worship that is meted out to them, often at the same spots. These parallel practices, unlike Brahmanical/Hindu rituals, are not governed by authoritative texts or scriptures, but follow norms drawn from a prevailing body of oral tradition passed down through generations.

Harijhi Chandi, the 'folk' deity, and its emergence as the most crucial village ritual

Gopendrakrishna Bose (1966, 87-92) considered *Harijhi* as a 'minor' folk deity in his monograph, *The Folk deities of Bengal (Banglar Lok debata)*, whose worship, he observed, was mostly confined to the district of South 24 Parganas. Interestingly, in this brief account, among the two sacred places associated with the deity, the sacred place at Damdama-Keorakhali finds mention prior to its transformation into the modern shrine. Following his description of the 'folk' aspects of the deity, it would appear that her worship was always prevalent among the low-caste groups including communities of shamans or exorcists (*ojhas, gunins*) who are generally drawn from the impoverished Muslim classes. It is claimed that the latter reposed beliefs in the snake-healing power of the goddess, as disclosed by a close study of their utterances. However, unlike other folk deities like *Sitala* and *Manasa* who are ascribed specific qualities of healing from particular diseases (*Sitala*—from smallpox; *Manasa*—from snake bite), *Harijhi* is hailed as an overall protector from all evils and perils, one who eradicated all diseases. On the occasions of floods which Bose recorded more than five decades ago, the quern, or the seat of the goddess, was carried to the riverbank, as it was believed that its inherent power would stall the deluge. The image of the goddess as the guardian deity of the village has percolated to its current inhabitants.

For historians of early India, it may be an essential historical exercise to explore the space of "non-Brahmanic, non-Sanskritic reservoir of ritual practices" (Chattopadhyay 2017, 138) among communities who were not governed by "the hegemonic Sastric[11] ritual tradition". However, reflections on tales of supersession, subordination, dissonance, and struggles involving rival/contesting cults that may exist in an oral tradition or a written narrative— *Banabibi Jahuranama* is an important instance for the Sundarbans—tend to remain unattended in this domain. The possible invention or construction of the tales of struggle and the interpolations by groups who worshipped them remains elusive. Forming challenging areas for a social historian or a cultural anthropologist, these practices are most relevant when situated in the present. Narrowing my focus to the *Batsorik,* I seek to show how the ritual of a 'minor' deity has emerged as the most crucial village ritual, subordinating all others that occur in the calendrical and cosmological agenda of the village, and the knowledge of which lay dispersed in different groups laying claims to the deity as their own. The religious process that unfolded in the course of its emergence could have seen an infusion of *tantric[12] Nathapanthi[13]* elements in the construction of this deity, who may have been a goddess worshipped initially by the *Sabars* or an indigenous ethnic group (Bose 1966). These groups no longer form part of the clientele involved in the ceremony. Is the 'absence' indicative of forces of conflict?

Interestingly, the interviewees often identified *Harijhi Chandi* with *Chandi*, an important goddess of the pantheon whose idol is found next to the seat of *Harijhi*. When asked, they were unable to furnish any information as to how these came to be identified in their worldview. This forms another instance of 'absence' that confronts an ethnographer.

Concerns in anthropology have long moved away from viewing ritual as a centre-stage practice, extricated from everyday life.[14] While such concerns continue to provoke us, the observance of a religious ceremony also arrests our attention to how certain activities are privileged and upheld as distinctively different from routine ones. Viewing ritual as a site of politics, I have reoriented some of the devices that Bell suggests in her study of ritualization, which she advocates as first and foremost a strategy "for the construction of certain types of power relationships effective within a particular social organization" (Bell 1992, 197). The ceremony projects a scene of equanimity, participated in by marginalized communities. However, I will show how power relations are played out, not only in a repressive external way, but also in a parallel resistance; how the control of the rite in the hands of a few apparently empowered actors, is actually constrained by other forces; and how an ambience of 'negotiated participation' is fostered by forces of domination and resistance.

Migration and occupation

The village is not a flourishing one, the occupants being chiefly engaged in agricultural labour or other professional occupations elsewhere. Conversations with the village elders of the Paiks/Sardars, Rajbangshi, and the Bagdi communities[15] revealed that their forefathers had arrived from Nalgarh, Joynagar/Mograhat (all located in South 24 parganas) and Uluberia (in Howrah district, to the north) respectively, more than three hundred years ago. While there is no way to ascertain whether they arrived prior to the colonial land reclamation of late eighteenth/early nineteenth centuries, it is obvious that these remote areas were populated by many such instances of migration of low caste groups from other areas. The reasons could have ranged from localized tensions erupting from proprietary rights over fishing (as retold by Bhim Bagh, a Rajbangshi I interviewed) to any other. Seizing upon the quern and suffusing it with a value of sacrality may be seen as an empowering strategy of validating their occupation of an unknown, unfamiliar landscape. The efficacy of worshipping *Harijhi* as the guardian deity not confined to any specific healing power but signifying an all-encompassing protection against all evils, may be explained by this. The interviewees proclaimed *Chandi* to be the universe, the *jagat-sansar,* again not distinguishing her from *Harijhi Chandi.*

The shrine: playing out of power relations

The sacred space that becomes the shrine is sanctified and marked off with restricted access. Yet it is in this space that collections of sweetmeats and edible items, to be offered to the deity and be distributed later to the community as *Prasad*[16], accumulate; the community's incursion in the space happens surreptitiously. I was allowed to enter with my photographer for a video recording, perhaps on account of being a special guest, but which also implied that the barriers constructed could be occasionally violated. Two Brahman priests in red shirts and *dhotis* (the traditional bottoms worn from waist down by Indian men) coming from a nearby village officiated the rites of worship, assisted by three devotees from the village. They claimed that their family had provided the officiating priests for three generations. On the contrary, Bose had observed more than fifty years ago, a member of the residing lower caste groups of the village served as the priest. I remain unaware of any contestations over rights of control that may have happened.[17]

Figure 7.4 The shrine of the Batsorik with the entire pantheon.

Photograph taken by the author.

If a control of the rites of folk deity worship invests the Hindu Brahman priests with any power to dominate the social order of low-caste groups, this is counterbalanced on the one hand by a consent of the participants and on the other, by constraining forces perceived first and foremost in having to preside over a non-Sastric, non-Brahmanical tradition of worship of a fetishized object. All the idols in the sacred space representing the local deities of the Sundarbans represent this tradition—*Narayani, Jarasur, Shitala, Basanta Ray, Panchanan,* with his two aides *Pencho-Khencho, Ateswar, Sashti, Harihar, Manasa* and *Chandi.* The *mantra*(s) or utterances invoking the deities broadcast over the loudspeaker were not recited from any text, indicative of a silent acquiescence by the local lower caste population to a tradition that was not their own.

The invocation of the folk deity by Hindu rites, on the other hand, signifies distinctive ways of appropriation. *Harijhi Chandi* is invoked first with *ghats* (earthen vessels) filled with milk, fruits, and sweetmeat; *dali,* or a cane tray with flowers; and *arati,* the lighting of earthen lamps. Only after the invocation of the goddess are other deities invoked through *chakshudan,* a rite of invocation by touching the idol's eyes and placing the *ghat* before it with a plant stem. The functioning of this rite is held behind a white transparent veil, signifying an artificial demarcation from the devotees waiting outside, emphasizing a more restricted access.

Figure 7.5 The deities of Islamic influence.

Photograph taken by the author.

In the adjoining space that is separated by a half-raised wall, idols of Islamic influence were propitiated by a *sebait* (one who serves) woman of the Paik community who was entrusted with the worship. Locally called *Bibi ma-er than,* or the Sacred Space of *Bon Bibi, Bon Bibi* and the seven associated *bibis,* or deities, occupy the space with *Manik Pir* and *Barkha Gazi.* Syncretic processes, which possibly emerged as part of a social strategy in an uncertain existence, form a unique feature in the Sundarbans. This enforced a certain fluidity, indicated in shared metaphors and symbolism, although existing tales of coercion and conflict between rival groups dominate the *punthis*. On the day of the ceremony, no elaborate rituals were observed, as the *sebait* Rupali Paik continued with the daily offering of flowers, sweetmeat, and fruits. The idols were freshly garlanded and decorated. The role of the priests was conspicuous by their non-functionality in this space.

Oral accounts and the stakes in the ritual

"Ritual", as Dirks shows, "was a discursive and practical field in which a great deal was at stake and a great deal was up for grabs" (1994, 494). On my first visit to the village Bhutiram Sarada, or Sardar, an elderly member of the Sardar community presented himself as the bearer of the oral account of the worship of the deity.[18] Bhutiram spoke of a divine boat full of booty that had appeared in the pond adjacent to the shrine, following which *Harijhi Chandi*'s seat of worship was sanctified. During the ceremony, he was pushed forward by a coterie of persons as one who 'knew' the story well. This was also an empowering act that sustained him when he was denied access to the ceremonial space.

Appropriations alternate with struggle in a ritual, and at times it is difficult to identify and differentiate between the two, as I experienced in my recording of the oral accounts. Bhutiram's oral account represented the narrative of the Sardar caste group, and there were other tales struggling to be heard. Rajbangshi Nabakumar Bagh seized the opportunity to recount another version in his interview on the day of the ceremony. He claimed that the *sinhasan,* or the quern, had floated to the riverbank one night when the goddess appeared in the dream of his forefather, and impressed upon him to initiate her worship in the village. The Rajbangshi's stake to power over custodianship of the *sinhasan* lay interspersed with conflict. In this version, Muslim invaders were blamed for usurping the throne, but were forced to return it by the power inherent in the sacred seat. Which of the tales plays an appropriating role viz a viz a struggling one? Each of these discourses was related in an animated setting with many prompting the speaker, egging him on to 'disclose' the entire story. Sections of these could have been invented anew.

Relations of domination and subordination were orchestrated by cohort groups at the helm of the *puja* committee. Only after seeking permission from them could I conduct my interviews, which too were coordinated by the nominated members of two caste groups, the Rajbangshis and the Bagdis: Rajbangshi's Nabakumar Bagh, Madhai Mondal and Bhim Bagh, and Bagdi's

Nirmalkanti Mondal. These communal negotiations led to interesting questions: Were opposing voices muted? Were situations of conflict deliberately suppressed? What determined a person's involvement in the ritual practices?

The productive forces of power, vow-making and the body

If cohort groups sought to enforce their specially ordained positions, the productive forces of power could be seen to traverse through the social body of the village in a unique mode of participation that made the ceremony possible. As Foucault (1972, 110) has stated:

> What makes power hold good, what makes it accepted, is simply the fact that it does not only weigh on us as a force that says no, but that it traverses and produces things, it induces pleasure, forms knowledge, produces discourse. It needs to be considered as a productive network which runs through the whole social body, much more than as a negative instance whose function is repression.

On the eve of the *puja,* residents engaged in ritual begging in the name of *Bonbibi* and *Chandi,* going from house to house and soliciting offerings in cash or kind. No hearth was lit in any home, nor was food cooked. The entitlement of each individual to the puja was reinforced through this ritual that resisted any repression and may be viewed as foundational to the holding of the ceremony. This enhanced the collective spirit that I elaborate below.

Holding a vow to propitiate the goddess and seek her boon by making offerings is a common feature of Hindu rituals. Individual vows involving forms of self-mutilation like hook-swinging (in which iron hooks are pierced through the devotee's body), existing in many ritual ceremonies of South Asia, have occasioned debates among anthropologists and social historians, particularly on the role of the colonial state. (Dirks 1997). Issues of victimization, moral culpability on the part of the social order, and native public opinion, were emphasized by the colonial state, as opposed to agency and voluntary action. The bearing that such debates may have on prevailing practices is of absolute relevance, however, the subject goes beyond the scope of this chapter.

Previously I noted two strategies of vow-making which were at variance with one another in their modes of functioning. The first was a nonviolent, low-key procession, in which the devotees carried *cchhalan murtis* or votive offerings of clay images displaying a fusion of folk and non-folk forms on their heads, perambulating around the shrine accompanied by drum-beating, percussion, and dance. But it was the second act of vow-making that directly engaged with the body where power relations were found to be most expressive, issues of agency and voluntarism tantalizingly placed alongside coercion. This is significant in that the place of body in anthropology is an acutely discursive field.[19] Foucault reminds us that it is political: "Power relations have an immediate hold upon it; they invest it, mark it, train it, torture it, force it to carry out tasks, to perform ceremonies, to emit signs"(Foucault cited in Bell 1992, 202). While the *puja* continued in the sanctum, large groups of women who had kept *manat* (or a solemn vow) to carry out a form of self-penance to win the goddess's favour for the granting of a boon, took a dip in the adjoining tank and threw themselves on the earth, lying prostrate and making moves forward by dragging their entire bodies along the ground. Each prostrating move was followed by standing up with bowed heads and folded hands in acquiescence in the direction of the shrine, and then repeating the entire act. This continued until three circles around the shrine were completed. In these acts of self-penance carried out through regular, sustained, and repetitive actions, each wet, clay-laden body inflicted with pain and suffering became the seat of empowerment. These acts of disciplining or punishing the body induced prestige and a sense of gratification. Each woman was transported into a trance-like state, and through this she was bestowed with a special status in the community. Known as *dandi kata*, it was a spectacle that drew the milling crowd.

The committee members endorsed and ratified the act wholeheartedly— each woman was doing it for her family's prosperity and for a cumulative good involving the whole village. Invisible forces of a coercive order lay enmeshed with individual agency and redemption. If "power traverses and produces things" (Foucault 1972, 119), we need to look for it in these mutually opposed forces that pull at each other, compromising on occasions, superseding on others, remaining in perpetual tension. The penultimate part of *dandi kata* took place when the women in their mud-laden saris were made to sit in rows outside the shrine with earthen vessels placed on their heads. Groups of men threw camphor in the vessels, igniting fire; very soon rising flames engulfed the space.

The ceremony ended in a bodily act of the ritual animal sacrifice[20] for propitiating the goddess. A local agent from the village was entrusted with the task. His body was trained and marked to carry out violence under order in the space outside the shrine. In a transformed ambience, the regimented agent, soaked with blood spewing from the sacrificed goat, appeared to become the source of ultimate agency in the heightened moment of sacrifice. In the haze of incense penetrated by a beating of drums and percussions reaching a crescendo, the crowds swelled around the sacrificing arena, gripped with an unmatched exhilaration. The entranced state of the agent with bloodshot eyes, the swerving gesture of his arm that landed the sanctified axe on the neck of the beast fixed to the altar, the swift disembodying of the head from the torso, may perhaps be seized as the ultimate moment of agency and not simply as a mere executing act instituted by the social order. Foucault (1972, 98) reminds us:

> In other words, individuals are the vehicles of power, not its points of application … it is already one of the prime effects of power that certain bodies, certain gestures, certain discourses, certain desires, come to be identified and constituted as individuals … the individual which power has constituted is at the same time its vehicle.

Two bananas in an earthen dish, dripping with the sacrificial blood, were handed over to the priest, who placed them before the seat of the goddess. Decoding the meaning of symbols in societies that lack any "authoritative exegesis", Asad (1993, 61) points out, is a difficult task. There is a greater degree of uncertainty associated with their interpretation, and often the ethnographer relies on the help of 'Indigenous exegetes' to interpret them. In many situations such as this particular one, no explanation was furnished other than a commitment to a routine practice that was inherited.

The dominant discourse of the *Mahatsab*—an appropriation?

Chaitanya Mahaprabhu, the medieval seer of Bengal who lived between 1486 and 1533, was the proponent of the school of Bengali devotional Vaishnavism that enthralled and enraptured sections of elite and non-elite Bengalis over generations. The cultural memory of Chaitanya and the Bengali Vaishnava devotional tradition were strategically used by the *bhadralok*[21] (gentlefolk) of the late nineteenth century in the context of anti-colonial nationalism in Bengal, as a recent work has shown (Bhatia 2017). Interestingly, Bhatia draws our attention to a popular piece published in a Bengali daily sometime in 2013 by Nrisingha Prasad Bhaduri, an exponent of Vaishnavism and Hindu scriptures, who urged his readership to renew their engagement with Chaitanya and Bengali Vaishnavism (Bhatia 2017, 1). Furthermore, it was Chaitanya, the article claimed, who was instrumental in forging the 'middle way' in Bengali cultural life, a way that lay between the eclectic scholasticism of Vedanta and folk traditions of the Bengali *mangalkabyas*, a medieval textual tradition written in Bengali. Six years later, in August 2019, the Chief Minister of West Bengal Mamata Banerjee inaugurated a three-story museum in Kolkata, the first of its kind, dedicated to the life and teachings of Chaitanya Mahaprabhu. The Chief Minister's opening address at the event was significant as she focused on the urgency of spreading messages of peace and prosperity as propagated by the Saint to counter all divisiveness.[22]

This may be taken as our point of entree. A political strategy was seemingly constructed through articles and by building the museum to rally many among the *Namasudras* (traditionally treated as untouchables in the *jati-varna* social order) like the *Matuas*, whose faith relied on *Vasihnava* devotionalism, to build a wider base for the ruling party. This may hint at a cultural amnesia existing among the urban literati towards the tradition that Bhaduri was bemoaning. The continuity of the tradition in the deep recesses of the Sundarbans thus calls for deeper reflection. The patronage of the *Mahotsab* (the day-long ritual ceremony) resided with the same low caste groups who organized the 'folk' ritual, although high and middle caste groups joined from neighbouring villages. Texts like *Chaitanya Bhagavat* describe Chaitanya's pilgrimage through the wildlife-infested land to reach Neelachal, or Puri, in Orissa, spreading messages of his faith on the way. If we surmise that remote spots such as this may have come under the spell of his fervour, it is also noteworthy that a Chaitanya shrine is not a familiar sight in the Sundarbans.

Strangely, no oral account exists among the resident groups of the village concurring with this. The only surviving account revolves around the tale of goddess *Tulsi* (the name of a holy plant worshipped in many Hindu rituals) and her relations with *Narayana*, one of the five *Vyuhas* of Lord Visnu, all of which are cosmic emanations of him. Narayana's worship in Hindu shrines is aniconic, as evidenced in the form of a black stone commonly called *Narayan shila*. During my fieldwork in the village, I encountered a similar worship in the shrine of the *Mahotsab*, although that stone was not stationary at the shrine, but a prevailing custom ensured its transport from the home of the officiating Brahman priest who carried it forth and back at the end of the ceremony. The presence of the *Narayana shila* may be associated with a larger Vaishnava worldview of which Chaitanya's creed was a later manifestation.

The cultural memory of the resident groups has thus crystallized around only a segment of the *Mahotsab* ceremony. Such practices are reflective of how a heritage narrative is construed and replicated, and may be openly imaginary. More importantly, the narrative relayed to me during interviews appeared to be an appropriation of a dominant discourse by a subaltern variant that was anchored in Bhutiram Sardar, by the same individual who narrated the account of the *Batsorik*. However, my study demonstrates that appropriation is not unproblematic, and we must be attentive to contests over authority and power that continue to take place and are expressed through ritual practices and idioms.

A subaltern voice recounting a 'dominant' narrative

Bhutiram recounted a long, winding tale of deceit, deception, and conspiracies involving gods, goddesses, and demons, surrounded by fellow caste members from whom he continued to draw succour, and who prodded him, occasionally giving him cues if he missed any detail. The account revolved around fixed gods and goddesses who find mention in different Puranic traditions, but this clearly was an extrapolation that may have been renewed from time to time. For example, the Goddess Tulsi had expressed a desire to marry Narayana who refused and cursed that her husband would be the demon *Shankhachur.* Shankhachur, on receiving a boon from Brahma, the Supreme God, had become extremely powerful in heaven, causing havoc to all the divinities. Harassed, under the leadership of Brahma, they conspired with Narayana to kill the demon. A consensus was reached that the demon—who was also a worshipper of Krishna—could only be exterminated if his wife was robbed of her chastity. Narayana in the guise of Shankhachur entered into a sexual union with Tulsi. As the goddess, caught unaware, lost her virginity, the demon who was then embroiled in a battle with the divinities died and his body was floated in the river. The conch shell (*shankh*) used in the *puja* is believed to have originated from the dismembered body of the demon. When Narayana was on the verge of escaping having accomplished his task, the Goddess Tulsi realized that she was deceived. So she cursed Narayana to be reduced to stone. Among the several associative threads in the tale, the worship of the *Narayana shila* and Tulsi emerge as an entwined one. Bhutiram concluded that no worship of Narayana is complete without the bestowing of leaves from the Tulsi plant. A Tulsi plant draped in a *sari* was likewise placed outside the shrine as an object of worship. Inherent in these accounts, therefore, were struggles of contesting traditions vying for supremacy, ending in an accommodative mode.

This oral account makes no mention of Chaitanya, the chief cause of the *Mahotsab.* When asked, Bhutiram readily responded that only the *adhibas,* or invocation of the gods, happened in this festival, while the actual *puja* was over the day before, alluding to the *Batsorik.* Interestingly, Bhutiram began his narrative by invoking the names of Chaitanya *Mahaprabhu* (the Great Lord) and his associates, *Nityananda, Advaita, Srivasa* and *Gadadhara,* who are incarnates of *Panchatattva.* In the Vaishnava tradition of Bengal, this constitutes five aspects of God or Absolute Truth, manifest in Chaitanya and his associates. My repeated queries to Bhutiram on how the legend concerning Narayana and Tulsi got entwined with the sixteenth-century seer were met with impatience; clearly, he felt no urgency to interrogate a tradition that he had inherited from his forefathers.

It is obvious that this narrative segment has prevailed and continues to be circulated at least among the low caste groups. That their claim that the ritual spot for the *Mahotsav* was incepted only after *Harijhi Chandi's* worship took firm roots in the locality may signal competing strategies and the struggle of one group to project the 'folk' deity as a more rarefied entity. The present shrine has been constructed in recent times, as previously the seat of worship was a modest mud enclosure with no idol. Only the *Narayan shila* used to be brought by forefathers of the Brahman priest. Thus, seeking the 'origin' of a ritual may be futile in a linear narrative of historicity. Rather we may need to construct its genealogy, the twists and turns, the sudden ruptures and the connections which shape it.

The ceremony of the Mahotsab

The actual ceremony can be seen as an establishment of dominant practices pertaining to a Hindu religious worship, as evidenced by the rites idolizing the medieval saint. The preparation begins in the shrine on the day following the *Batsorik*. The five-armed Chaitanya idol occupying the central locus is an integrated imagery of *Krishna* with a flute in one hand and *Rama* holding a bow in one and an arrow in another hand. The merger of Rama in a conspicuous indigo blue is significant as it is unusual for Chaitanya, considered to be an incarnation of Krishna, to be associated with Ramathe, an epic hero with a warrior stance. The preeminent rite observed was the adhibas, a ritual associated with the ceremonial awakening of the gods. It was initiated with the placing of six *ghats* or earthen vessels within the shrine. The *Panchapallab* (or leaves of five designated plants) were kept in the *Devi ghat* (the earthen vessel in which the goddess was invoked) and the *Shanti ghat* (the earthen vessel filled with holy water). Chaitanya and his associates embodying the *Panchatattva* were invoked. The *Devi ghat* was the principal vessel, draped with red strips of cloth and smeared with vermillion, placed in front of the idol with a green coconut covering its mouth. Bounded by threads this constituted the main sacred space for the *puja*. The *Shanti ghat* was placed in one corner. The other four earthen vessels contained *amrapallab* or leaves of mango trees, and all other necessary ingredients crucial to worship like *pancha phal* (five types of fruits), *panchashashya* (five types of food grains), *shiddhi* (a particular kind of libation), and certain herbs that were also placed in the *ghats*. A mirror was kept in one of the vessels meant for the reflection of the idol as part of the ritual. Tulsi was worshipped in the garb of a banana plant draped in a sari that was placed outside the shrine in one corner of an enclosed space.

"Ritual discourse" and "ritual practice", Dirks (1994, 495) argues, are open to many contesting and resisting forces. The appropriation of a dominant discourse by a subversive oral account was resisted by the practice of the *puja* officiated by the Brahman priest who retained the custodianship of the Narayan *shila*. In this predicament the appropriation was incomplete, as patronage was retained in the village community, while the participation of upper/middle caste groups remained peripheral to ceremony. The transformative power of ritual lay in these compelling forces of struggle and tension, which were always kept in abeyance.

The making of a 'public' arena

The fissures of power are uncovered in the public arena that also contains them. It is in the public arena that the ordinary lies entangled with the extraordinary, where the most dramatic shares space with the least visible. Chaos is intended to subvert order. This is evident in how these processes have unfolded over the course of the two ceremonies inside versus outside the shrine.

In the *Batsorik,* the wider arena outside the shrine—iridescent in kaleidoscopic canopies, drapes and blaring music—acts to congeal and reinforce ties between the committee members, the participants of the procession, and the *dandi,* the local agent executing the sacrifice, as well with the residents of the village who may not be direct participants yet throng to the arena. Performances of the acts, gestures, movement, and "orality" are constitutive of a "repertoire"—all actions that are usually thought of as "ephemeral, non-reproducible knowledge'"—as opposed to the "supposedly stable objects in archive" (Taylor 2003, 18). The space of performance is transmuted into an electric ambience of contests, struggles, and resistance that are writ large in ritual acts and annual socializing, present even when a local fair with ramshackle structures put up hastily as stalls is held. Here, collective activity is not restrained by the physical limits of the space. The entire village becomes an extended arena and a metaphor for the collective spirit. The arterial path of the village becomes denser with enthusiasm and an excited clamour of voices as the day wears on and the ceremony progresses, the crowds spilling over into the path from houses crammed with visitors who had been arriving from distant parts. The collective act is reinforced by the ritual begging held prior to the beginnings of the ceremony. The animated spirit of the multitudes caused the organizers to feel that their god has been honoured and their management has been successful. The final act that reinstates the collective is the occasion when fistfuls of sweetmeats or *batasha* are thrown over a frenzied crowd, who scramble to retrieve them from an intensely packed space enveloped in a thick air of incense, sounds, and shades. Such acts of subversion of the normal social order are inscribed within the ritual.

If the ceremony of the *Batsorik* registered movement only among lower caste groups in ways in which they could stake out cultural and social power in a world discreetly their own, the *Mahotsab* was constituted by a mixed clientele. The most remarkable part of the *Mahotsab* ceremony lies in the nature of its collective performances of shared values and cultural aesthetics perpetuated by both the upper caste and the lower caste groups. Interestingly, the area immediately outside the second shrine transmutes into an animated space of *Hare-Krishna naam, kirtan* and *Ras Leela.* The first constitutes chants and prayers for Visnu and Krishna, the revered divinities in the Vaisnava creed; the second relates to devotional songs; and the third is a performative style in songs and dance celebrating the celestial love of Krishna and Radha. The performances, each genre displaying a certain degree of fluidity and improvisation, last for three days and nights, and the entire village takes part. The subversive act of the *Ras Leela*, with a performing actress from the village in centre stage, was one of gay abundance, explicit in lusciousness, improvised gestures, and seductive moves. The transcendental love was transmuted to earthy sensual desires that collapsed barriers and dissolved cultural norms. Such ritual acts of subversion have been widely analysed in anthropology in a Bakhtinian mode of examining periodic subversion of order and containment (Bakhtin 1984). Significantly, the *Ras of the Mahotsab* formed a part of this spectacle in a limited way: the forms managed to mobilize in a public arena congeries of people of different professions, castes and communities, thus reinforcing the power inherent in the ritual.

Conclusion

The two ritual contexts emerge as far from homologous, containing power relations which are not explicable in a straightforward interpretation of domination or accommodation. Moments and instances of tension and conflict, eruption and suspension, define these relations. Heritage is thereby shaped and transformed by these exigencies and contingencies that defy any homogenized, unproblematic understanding of intangible ritual tradition or tangible materiality. Heritage, as can be seen here, is always in the process of becoming. The quern becomes the locus of the synergies which eventually overpower it, running through the liminal social space. The sense of belonging of the different groups seen through the lens of power asymmetries thus appears as fraught, but nonetheless enduring.

Neither of the ceremonies could be tracked down to a clear beginning, temporally. This did not cause any hindrance to the sense of pronounced importance of the ceremonies that inheres within the communities. This helps to reinforce the idea of heritage as a process which cannot be constructed by means of an unchanging linear narrative. Nor is heritage an inert entity lacking inertia. As this chapter has demonstrated, heritage continues to evolve through unexpected turns and bends, impacted by the power imbalances that I have sought to tease out through an elaboration of the ritual practices in each case. The fissures and cracks that are inscribed in heritage are rarely dwelt upon in any study of its practices in the sub-continent, calling forth a need for more sustaining and critical studies.

There also prevails an urgency that demands to be tackled. It is crucial to document these ritual sites and practices and all that they entail. The marginalized, subaltern communities are facing challenges of slow, imperceptible erosion of values as younger generations are migrating to urban nodes, lured by livelihood opportunities. The social fabric embedding these practices is fast crumbling.

The chapter, through its attempt to project the nuances of community participation that embeds any ritual site, emphasizes the important manner in which heritage practices have emerged and serve to mitigate differences between different social groups. In a rapidly changing world, there is a sustained need for more such intergroup dynamic engagements.

Acknowledgements

I am deeply indebted to Sri Sanjay Ghosh, local ethnographer of Joynagar-Majilpur for bringing the ritual to my knowledge and for helping me in organizing my ethnography in Damdama-Keorakhali. I remain especially grateful to Dayal da of Monirtat and his wife for putting us up in his house. The warm hospitality still resonates. I thank all the committee members of the festivals mentioned in the text, the people of Damdama, Sanjukta, Dr. Rajat Sanyal and Dipankar Basak. My gratitude to Samir Das, as ever, for drawing my attention to crucial texts.

Notes

[1] I have discussed this at length in my Presidential Address of the Archaeology Section at the Indian History Congress, 81st session, Chennai (Basak 2022).

[2] Scholars like D.D. Kosambi and Nirmal Kumar Bose followed uncharted ways in their times—the early second half of the last century—in reconstructing and drawing meaningful relations without staying confined to their respective disciplinary fields (see Basak 2018). Their works rarely find mention in Indian Ethnoarchaeological studies in which ethnographic analogies are sought in constructing unbroken continuities with the past. For a critique see Basak (2006) and Varma (2006).

[3] Caste is a form of social organization that is considered as fundamental to an understanding of Indian society. The roots of this social organization may be seen in a *varna-jati*system, the functioning of which may be traced to early India. The evolution of the concept of *Varna*, which is now translated into ritual status, may be seen originating from the Vedic Sanskrit corpus, and it is the *varna* system dividing society into four hierarchical groups—the brahman (priest), *kshatriya* (warrior king), *vaishya* (cultivator and trader) and *shudra* (who labours for others), with the fifth, the untouchable, existing outside the society—that gave the frame for a hierarchical social order. However, the concept of *jati*, literally meaning 'birth' explains the social order more. The number of *jatis* are mentioned in different textual sources, and these groups are too numerous to be counted. Both the concepts of *jati* and *varna* overlap in part but are also distinct. There is no unanimous position on how exactly the caste society evolved and which preceded—the *varna* or the *jati*. The caste society as we find now is a hierarchical social order, in which birth, occupation

and religion play overlapping roles. It is marked by regional differences, e.g. the dominant caste groups outside the Brahman category vary between Bengal and North India. A substantial number of marginalized groups—many of whom are still regarded as untouchables—are clubbed under Scheduled castes.

[4] Sundarbans perhaps derived its name from *Sundari*or mangrove vegetation, the largest such area in the world, forming a part of the lowest section of the vast Ganga-Jamuna-Brahmaputra-Meghna Delta. Its geographical space and vast tracts of forested land infested by wild animals fostered an imagination of a dark and mystic land, recounted in a literary tradition and folklore.

[5] The knowledge of the festival was unknown to me till it was drawn to my attention by Sri Sanjay Ghosh, a local grassroots scholar of Joynagar-Majilpur.

[6] In Indian archaeology that may be placed between 500BCE-300 CE.

[7] A few hagiographic texts like *Chaitanya Bhagavata* written by Vrindaban Das describe the saint's travels to Neelachal or Puri in modern Orissa, regarded as a sacred site for those belonging to the *Vaisnava* faith.

[8] *Ras leela* or *Ras* dance forms part of a mythology surrounding Lord Krishna described in scriptural texts like the Bhagavata Purana and ancient literary texts like the Gita Govinda as his act of dancing and merry-making with his beloved Radha and a bevy of ladies.

[9] Vaishnavism is one of the major Hindu creeds along with Shaivism and Shaktism, which considers Lord Visnu as the Supreme Lord. The Bengal tradition was moulded under Sri Chaitanya in the sixteenth century.

[10] Freitag shows very eloquently how a consistency of the symbols emphasize 'process-ual' elements 'inherent in the world' that project a historical change.

[11] Sastra is a Sanskrit word meaning precepts, rules, texts or treaties and is used as a suffix for non-religious texts or religious scriptures in ancient India literary tradition.

[12] Tantras refer to Hindu or Buddhist mystical texts dating to 7th century CE or earlier constituting mantras, meditations, yoga and ritual Tantric refers to an adherence to these principles.

[13] Nath is a surname common among the scheduled or reserved castes of Bengal. Nathapanthis are persons bearing this surname who are engaged in certain tantric practices.

[14] See Dirks (1994) for his brief incisive review in the introductory part of this chapter.

[15] Interviewed on February 16, 2019.

[16] This is a devotional offering made to a deity, typically consisting of edible items, which is shared with the devotees at the end of the worship.

[17] There is no surviving knowledge on how the Brahman family came to be invested with the worshipping rights. As such the priests remain an external force who are accepted by the low caste groups and it is possible that this could be indicative of the latter's desire for upward social mobility.

[18] Interviewed on February 8, 2018.

[19] See Bell (1992) for a critical review.

[20] There are of course many anthropological studies of the sacrifice. For an incisive analysis see Bell (1992).

[21] Literally meaning gentlefolk the term was used to define the *nouveau riche* of nineteenth-century Bengal. The current usage denotes the upper caste elites of Bengal.

[22] https://www.newindianexpress.com/cities/kolkata/2019/aug/08/kolkata-to-get-worlds-first-museum-on-chaitanya-mahaprabhu-2015979.html.

Bibliography

Asad, Talal. 1993. *Genealogies of Religion: Discipline and Reasons of Power in Christianity and Islam.* Baltimore and London: The John Hopkins University Press.

Bakhtin, Mikhail. 1984. *Rabelais and his world.* Bloomington: Indiana University Press.

Basak, Bishnupriya. 2002. "Relocating Archaeology and Local History—The Cultural Historiography of the Sundarbans". Presidential Address, Section V: Archaeology, Indian History Congress, 81st Session, Chennai.

———. 2006. "Ethnoarchaeological Research in India: Issues and Perspectives". In *Past and Present: Ethnoarchaeology in India*, edited by Gautam Sengupta, Suchira Roychoudhury and Sujit Som, 3-26. New Delhi: Pragati Publications in collaboration with centre for Archaeological Studies and Training Eastern India.

———. 2011. "The Journey of Kalidas Datta and the Construction of Regional History in Pre-and Post-Independent Bengal". *Public Archaeology* 10 (3)(August): 132-58.

———. 2018. "Kosambi's Combined Method and its Relevance to the Study of Past Material Culture". In *Early Indian History and Beyond: Essays in honour of B.D. Chattopadhyay*, edited by Osmund Bopearachchi and Suchandra Ghosh, 409-422. Delhi: Primus Books.

Bell, Catherine. 1992. *Ritual Theory, Ritual Practice.* New York: Oxford University Press.

Bhatia, Varuni. 2017. "Introduction". In *Unforgetting Chaitanya: Vaishnavism and Cultures of Devotion in Colonial Bengal.* New York: Oxford University Press.

Bose, Gopendrakrishna. 1966. *BanglarLoukik Devata* (in Bengali). Kolkata: Dey's Publishing.

Chattopadhyay, B. D. 2017. "Festivals as Ritual: An Exploration into the Convergence of Rituals and the State in Early India". In *The Concept of*

Bharatavarsha and Other Essays, edited by B.D. Chattopadhyay, 138-162. Ranikhet: Permanent Black in association with Ashoka University.

Coser, Lewis A. 1992. "Introduction". In *On Collective Memory,* edited by Maurice Halbwachs. Translated by Lewis A. Coser. Chicago and London: The University of Chicago Press.

Deleuze, Gilles. 1984. "Introduction" and "Difference in itself". In *Difference and Repetition.* Translated by Paul Patton. New York: Columbia University Press.

Dirks, Nicholas B. 1994. "Ritual and Resistance: Subversion as a Social Fact". In *Culture/Power/History: A Reader in Contemporary Theory,* edited by Nicholas B. Dirks, Geoff Eley, and Sherry B. Ortner, 483-503. Princeton, New Jersey: Princeton University Press.

———. 1997. "The Policing of Tradition: Colonialism and Anthropology in Southern India". *Comparative Studies in Society and History* 39 (1 January): 182-212.

Foucault, Michel. 1972. *Power Knowledge: Selected Interviews & other writings 1972-1977,* edited by Colin Gordon. Translated by Colin Gordon, Leo Marshall, John Mepham, Kate Soper. New York: Pantheon Books.

Freitag, Sandra B. 1989. *Culture and Power in Banaras: Community, Performance and Environment 1800—1980.* Delhi: Oxford University Press.

Smith, Laurajane. 2012. "Editorial". *International Journal of Heritage Studies* 18 (6): 533-540. DOI: 10.1080/13527258.2012.720794.

Taylor, Diana. 2003. *The Archive and the Repertoire: Performing Cultural Memory in the Americas.* Durham and London: Duke University Press.

Thapar, Romila. 2018. *Indian Cultures as Heritage: Contemporary Pasts.* New Delhi: Aleph.

Varma, Supriya. 2006. "Ethnography as Ethnoarchaeology: A Review of Studies in the Ethnoarchaeology of South Asia". In *Past and Present: Ethnoarchaeology in India,* edited by Gautam Sengupta, Suchira Roychoudhury and Sujit Som, 27-42. New Delhi: Pragati Publications in collaboration with centre for Archaeological Studies and Training Eastern India.

Glossary

Adhibas	A ritual associated with the ceremonial awakening of the god/goddess in a Hindu puja.
Arati	A Hindu religious ritualistic act in which light in earthen lamps/holders or brass holders is offered to the deity as part of the *puja* or worship.
Batasha	A sweetmeat made of sugar or jaggery.
Batsorik	Annual.
Cchhlan murti	Clay images which are given as votive offerings in a 'folk' ritualistic setting in the Sundarbans. Thus, the phrase has a localized usage.
Chakshudan	A rite of invocation of the deity performed by the priest by touching the idol's eyes, occasionally with a plant twig.

Dali	A wicker tray or basket.
Dandi	A ritualistic act of hardship performed by the devotees in a Hindu religious festival commonly seen in Bengal. The devotees wriggle on their bellies for a long distance to reach the temple shrine, believing that their prayers will be heard through this self-penance.
Dhoti	The traditional clothing bottoms worn from the waist down by Indian men.
Ghat	Earthen vessels.
Jagat-sansar	Colloquial phrase meaning the universe in Bengali.
Kirtan	Devotional songs.
Manat	A solemn vow made to the god/goddess to make an offering in lieu of fulfilment of a wish or grant of a boon.
Naamgaan/ Hare Krishna naam	Sacred chants. These could be specifically invoked for Gods Visnu and Krishna.
Namasudras	Namasudras were traditionally known as *chandalas* and were treated as untouchables for generations. Historically residing in the eastern and central parts of pre-independent Bengal, they began mobilizing against the Brahmanical caste hierarchy in the nineteenth century, under a socio-religious sect called the Matuas.
Ojha/gunin	Shamans/exorcists.
Pancha pallab	Leaves of five designated plants held as auspicious in a Hindu *puja.*
Pancha phal	Five designated fruits considered as auspicious in Hindu worship.
Pancha shasya	Five types of food grains held as auspicious in the *puja.*
Panchatattva	In the Vaishnava tradition of Bengal, this constitutes five aspects of God or Absolute Truth, manifest in Chaitanya and his associates, Nityananda, Advaita, Srivasa and Gadadhara.
Para	Locality/Neighbourhood.
Prasad	A devotional offering made to a deity, typically consisting of edible items, which is shared with devotees at the end of the worship.
Puja	Worship.
Punthi	Hand-written ancient texts which form a rich body of textual tradition in rural Bengal, belonging to the eighteenth-nineteenth century.
Raas leela	Performances/dances that evoke Lord Krishna's act of dancing and merry-making with his beloved Radha and a bevy of ladies, forming part of a mythology surrounding him in

scriptural texts like the Bhagavata Purana and ancient literary texts like the Gita Govinda.

Shiddhi   A form of libation made from the leaves and shoots of hemp and pulped in milk/coconut milk. It is occasionally partaken by the devotees after a *puja*.

Than   Sacred seat of worship which could be a make-shift structure raised for the deity under a tree or on the roadside. The Indian landscape is strewn with many such structures.

Conclusion: The future of heritage

Susan Shay

Heritage Research Centre, University of Cambridge, United Kingdom

Kelly M. Britt

Brooklyn College and The Graduate Center,
City University of New York, United States

Abstract

The concluding chapter provides a brief review of the section themes and a summary of the chapters. It then explores how heritage was employed in the development and implementation of the projects, highlights the interdisciplinary nature of the case studies, and examines the impacts the findings had, and continue to have, on the social, economic and/or political well-being of the associated communities. It examines the interconnected nature of heritage, social stability, and resilience, and highlights how heritage can be successfully employed to support community needs in a changing world.

The chapter discusses how the findings demonstrate how heritage is not static, but by necessity changes, morphs, and transforms to stay relevant, useful, valid, and meaningful to individuals, communal groups, societies, and nations. The chapter concludes by suggesting ways in which the case studies demonstrate useful and valuable applications for a wide range of communities, stakeholders, and policymakers.

***

Heritage, the use of the past for present purposes, is an essential part of the social fabric that knits families, communities, and nations together. At its foundation, it is based on communal memory (Halbwachs 1992) and composed of shared narratives that are reinforced through tangible and intangible culture (Smith 2006; Smith and Akagawa 2009). Rather than being fixed, frozen, and documented for local or state protection, the true nature of heritage is that it is dynamic, and it evolves and responds to changing times and needs. Importantly and critically, in order to stay relevant to contemporary populations, heritage must organically change in response to challenges in a changing environment. This volume presents a wide spectrum of examples in which different communities are actively engaged with interpreting the past to address current challenges and thereby build a more supportive and sustainable future for themselves.

Holtorf and Högberg (2021, 2) in their volume *Cultural Heritage and the Future* confront the role heritage has in our future-making endeavours, stating that heritage should be "future thinking ... anticipating what lies several years or even decades ahead, informing how they [people] act today". They critique how much of the current heritage discourse is presentist, despite their visions for the future, for that discourse is grounded more in a static view of heritage—how it exists and is used and interpreted now, not how society may view, use, and need it in the future. As they point out in their introduction, heritage itself is not static, yet in so many instances, it is treated so. They advocate that rather than building time capsules that capture specific memories (whether individual or collective in the linear trajectory), we think of and plan for the future of heritage in ways that allow for it to morph and transform in response to communal memories, as they evolve, change, and at times, even disappear.

We feel this volume begins to grapple with this call to envision heritage with a "future thinking lens" (Holtorf and Högberg 2021, 2). As the chapters and case studies presented show, to envision the future means to actively change the present, whether that is through community action, policy, law, or collective or individual praxis. All the chapters presented in this volume demonstrate how responsive and dynamic heritage is, both in tangible and intangible forms, and how, with that dynamism, individuals and communities are actively reshaping their views of heritage in the present, with their hopes and visions for the sustainable, resilient, equitable, inclusive, and secure future in mind. Some of these visions are more complete, with specific, actionable methods for employing heritage in the present for a better future, such as the chapters working at the nexus of heritage law and Indigenous sovereignty or response to climate change. Others propose ways forward to rethink heritage through different lenses, such as urban planning policies or exhibits on peace, decentring the traditional focus on what *has* happened, to what *could* potentially happen through a refocus in perspective. For many sites, their practical, present context directly informs how their associated community members can imagine their future. This is due to the fact that until recently, the communities have had little to no voice in how or if their heritage should be maintained, preserved, or interpreted. The lack of participatory inclusion may be due to racial, ethnic, political, or economic discrimination; power struggles within administrations, management boards, and/or community stakeholders; financial constraints; a lack of political, economic, or social capital or will; or simply a lack of physical people with the time and vision to do the labour of future thinking. What is critical is that action in the present is needed first to create future possibilities. All the chapters in this volume demonstrate and confirm the importance of this process: reshaping the present, particularly with its direct relationship to current social needs, can directly influence a more nuanced, future-thinking form of heritage.

What is heritage?

The innovative research and case studies presented in this volume demonstrate that heritage has great significance for addressing social concerns and finding solutions to contemporary social, political, and environmental challenges. Through a wide variety of cultural lenses and case studies from around the world, the chapters have highlighted and illustrated valuable ways in which heritage is intentionally employed to better the lives of contemporary communities and societies. These investigations call for a reconsideration and re-evaluation of the field of heritage studies and stress the potential for researchers to discover innovative solutions to current environmental, social, and political challenges that may be rooted in traditional or historic knowledge, or tangible or intangible culture. As discussed in these chapters, the investigation of 'heritage' is a relatively new study area, and there are many areas of interest yet to be explored. This volume has investigated one of those areas, communal memory, the basis for heritage, and offers new and innovative ways that the past can be employed to support individuals and societies.

Importantly, this volume has provided insights from scholars around the world, offering global perceptions and interpretations from a wide array of cultural, intellectual, and epistemological perspectives. This inclusive approach was created to provide new insights and emphasize to heritage researchers the multiplicity of ways in which we view the world and interact, within and outside the community, and within and outside the natural world. Critically, it furthers our understanding of how heritage has continued to provide insight and knowledge about who people are and how they make meaning in relation to the world. Furthermore, this research suggests that heritage, rather than being viewed as fixed to a particular time period and emerging from a particular location, documented and state protected, or commodified, should be viewed as emerging through continuous social interaction over time, influenced by a multitude of stimuli, and transforming organically to provide meaning making, a sense of belonging, and identity.

As illustrated through these chapters, there is no one fixed academic or legal definition of heritage. However, heritage can be further determined to have certain characteristics. First, heritage is based on shared, communal memory. This memory is supported and encouraged through tangible and intangible culture. Second, heritage is not history, which is documented and proven through archival, scientifically proven means of research. It is instead generationally transmitted and based on narrative stories. Last, in order to stay relevant and valuable to people, heritage has to be living and dynamic, allowed to change in response to stimuli, according to need, or to challenges in a changing environment. It is not static and does not situate itself in one time and place. Significantly, as has been demonstrated in the chapters in this book, heritage is the application of memory to respond to a current need by a contemporary individual or community. Among these needs are:

- The need for a sense of security
- The need for a sense of identity
- The need for a sense of belonging
- The need for empowerment
- The need for unification

All of these needs must be met to develop individual and communal resilience and security, and to support identity and well-being.

The interdisciplinary nature of heritage research

Heritage studies is a relatively new academic discipline that encompasses many different areas of study. As is evident in all of the investigations and case studies in this volume, heritage investigations are multi-faceted and interdisciplinary. For example, Ionesov's theoretical analysis of the purpose and effectiveness of peace museums focuses on both the intangible narratives and practices presented in museums, as well as the tangible cultural remains displayed in cases and exhibits, and how they presented, informed, and inspired actions. His study is highly political and cultural, involving issues of psychology, political science, cultural studies, archaeology, anthropology, architecture, and museum display. Emejulu's study in Nigeria of the rebirth of a traditional festival includes analysis of historic change of intangible African heritage practices through colonization and religious proselytizing, the sociological examination of postcolonial community transformation, and anthropological interviews to investigate the modern motivations for change and communal response. Basak examined a southeast Asian archaeological site in India through an anthropological, cultural, and sociological lens, considering how political and economic forces have driven community members toward greater interaction, and how the resulting communications have altered their perceptions and practices. Importantly, she notes how tangible remains of the past can be repurposed and thus become heritage material for the future.

In the centre of the ocean and on the other side of the Pacific, the chapters on Indigenous empowerment in Hawaii and Canada involve a wide range of other academic disciplines, including Indigenous studies, post-colonial studies, law, political science, anthropology, environmental science, and archaeology. These disciplines are incorporated into investigations of the historic, political, economic, and social impacts of historic injustice, and the legal marginalization of Indigenous people. Hoffman et al. investigate how these disciplines are used as the basis the creation of a program for political, legal, and restorative justice, increased Indigenous sovereignty and land control, sustainable environmental management, and cultural site protection, while Shay looks at empowerment through legal narrative construction and court presentation and explores how such actions strengthen identity and positively impact processes of empowerment.

Turning toward an entirely new direction in heritage valuation for future building, Britt looks at the ways experiencing heritage through sensual experiences combines with historic preservation and urban planning policy to empower a community fighting back the erasure of their history in the urban landscape. Her research acknowledges that heritage is dynamic and asks heritage professionals to be enterprising in how heritage sites are assessed, documented, and determined 'significant'. Much of US preservation policy prioritizes the tangible qualities to heritage sites, yet Britt illustrates that the intangible is not only just as important in assessment, but it can be accessed through the built environment, used successfully to empower people and communities, and used strategically toward future building. While her project is one still in development, it shows the power of sensing a place as an organizing tool for communities.

And finally, Baram, through his discussions of a range of archaeologically significant coastal sites adversely affected by climate change, demonstrates the vast number and variety of interdisciplinary topics with which heritage researchers are concerned in their investigations. His case studies cover such topics as Indigenous studies, colonization, African American racial injustice, environmental science, climate change, community engagement, educational presentation, and cultural site maintenance. His case studies significantly contribute to the broad nature of topics in this volume. Collectively, these investigations from around the world just begin to illustrate the vast interdisciplinary nature of heritage, and the very wide impact it has, and can have, on lives throughout the world.

The impact of the use of heritage on the social, economic, or political well-being of community members

The influence of these projects on the associated local communities has been meaningful. Substantial, positive changes have been observed and documented in this volume about, in particular, the role of community inclusion and participation in project implementation and management.

- In Nigeria, Ifeyinwa Emejulu notes the Umuchu community has revived and updated a traditional celebration lost during transition to Christianity, and in doing so, rebuilt social connections, and strengthened communal identity.

- Kelly M. Britt's work in Brooklyn, New York, offers a look into sites of heritage through the heuristic use of the senses and how an experiential framework has mobilized the community to preserve tangible and intangible heritage places.

- Uzi Baram in Florida discusses the substantial social and political capital gained by marginalized communities, the bridges built of understanding and mutual respect between different groups, and the pride that has accrued from local community inclusion in site excavation and interpretation.

- The cooperative program of Indigenous land management presented by the Canadian researchers introduces an ongoing platform for the restoration of Native heritage practices for environmental sustainability and cultural renewal, and the creation of a foundation for ongoing government cooperation with new levels of respectful interaction and understanding.

- In Hawai'i, Susan Shay has determined that through a series of lawsuits over time, the Native Hawaiian community was strengthened, encouraged, and invigorated toward greater involvement in legal and political processes necessary for sovereignty. In the process, traditional knowledge and practices lost over time were uncovered and revealed, inspiring greater communal identification, increased cultural practices, and fostering a new, modern Native Hawaiian identity.

- The dynamic nature of heritage is the focus of Bishnupriya Basak's research in India, and her study demonstrates the ongoing, long-term impact that personal interaction between different groups with varying degrees of social and economic power can have on heritage identity, social cohesion, and understanding.

- Finally, Vladimir Ionesov's in-depth theoretical analysis of the complex nature of the promotion of peace through museum spaces provides food for thought on what peace actually means, and how through the presentation of different elements of material culture from multiple perspectives in an interactive environment, museums can positively impact society. Importantly, through such new and innovative presentations, museums of peace could have the potential to inspire peaceful cooperation between disparate groups in the future.

Heritage is dynamic

In all the chapters in this volume, heritage is witnessed continuously changing in response to present challenges. As Barbara Kirshenblatt-Gimblett (1998, 149-150) states, "heritage is a mode of cultural production in the present that has recourse to the past". It is precisely with this dynamism that heritage has and can hold its power. As people and communities shift in demographics, philosophies, politics, etc., their heritage or relationship to that heritage shifts as well. This can be witnessed most profoundly through the recent social and cultural dynamic shift as a result of the Black Lives Matter movement, and its intense and dramatic impact in the US on Confederate monuments, which commemorated the nineteenth-century US Civil War. The shift led to the ultimate devaluing and the subsequent global removal of memorial shrines and markers connected to those that were proponents of slavery. Importantly, the chapters in this volume highlight other valuable shifts, focusing on how heritage is remembered, memorialized, consumed, and presenting how it is, and can be, used for addressing present day issues.

Each of the authors in this volume in their own way demonstrates the dynamic nature of heritage and how it can be used in future thinking. Shay's findings demonstrate how Native Hawaiian archival research required for narrative construction and defence inadvertently revealed missing, forgotten, or outlawed information about Indigenous traditional practices and beliefs—important heritage material lost through colonization, marginalization, or authorized discrimination. This information was then utilized it to challenge current understandings of the past, highlighting previous community strengths and resilience, and thus contributing toward restoring Indigenous communal pride. Significantly, this knowledge is also being used to build greater and more effective claims in court over control of land. Similarly, Britt explores how a mutual aid group, once a pillar of the community in New York, began to regain its legacy through public outreach and education, thus attracting and gaining new members and working toward a planned preservation of its headquarters. While this once-secret society continues to protect and hold secret sacred aspects and rituals of the organization, their history, stories, and home are no longer isolated and remote, but now are and will continue to be shared with the community. And finally, Emejulu investigates how an annual, traditional festival in Nigeria was revived, with old elements restored or reinterpreted and new elements and practices established, all in response to current needs and demands to rebuild and reinforce a unique, communal identity.

The authors additionally demonstrate how tangible and intangible heritage are closely interwoven, and thus should both be considered to inform future efforts. They note how through careful and thoughtful investigations and interpretations of the past new meanings and applications of heritage, both tangible and intangible, can be used to build and restore communal bonds for future initiatives. For example, Ionesov investigates museums and discusses how although they are filled with tangible objects that are considered important, the presentation and interpretation of their value is the responsibility of the curators. Yet he also interrogates this notion of curatorial direction and control, for in his view, an object is only valuable if the community finds it worthy of that designation. To be worthy, it must have intrinsic value, i.e. be associated with a story, memory, or message that is meaningful and relevant to the viewers. His research findings suggest that community participation in museum presentation and interpretation is vital for creating long-lasting and meaningful impacts toward peace.

Furthering the case for communal participation and discovery, Baram's case studies illustrate how tangible heritage, in this case archaeological findings, can reveal for communities their ancestral programs for addressing climate change, demonstrating a historic resilience, identifying new techniques for recovery, and providing a new source of pride. In this case, as with the Native Hawaiian case study, it is the revelation and adoption of new information that can foster communal belonging and strengthen identity. In other words, where once knowledge of the existence of ancestors at a site without tangible proof was important, the discovery of evidence can engender great pride and foster communal action. In Baram's case study, increased knowledge in multiple case studies was subsequently used and interpreted by each community for greater outreach and engagement. Additional evidence of the concept of transformation through evidence discovery and interpretation can be found in Basak's investigation of how and why specific practices evolved, and how they transformed over time with the arrival of new cultural and ethnic groups. Her research highlights the inherent flexibility of heritage, and how it can and does transform in response to external forces to best serve the needs of community members. And finally, the Canadian group of scholars and traditional knowledge holders clearly and significantly demonstrates how heritage can purposefully, sensitively, and meaningfully protect traditional resources and aid in reinstating Indigenous control over land management, and in doing so, build and strengthen community to better understand and mitigate climate change and its impacts on the environment.

Heritage, social stability, and resilience: enabling positive change in response to a changing world

The use of heritage to solve social and environmental issues is a new and emerging field, and the number of academic titles available is therefore extremely limited but evolving (Shepard 2023; Holtorf and Högberg 2021; Harrison et al. 2020; Bryne 2008; Fairclough et al. 2008; Smith 2006). The existing titles focus primarily on what heritage is, rather than how it can be applied strategically in new ways to tackle emerging issues (Harrison 2013; Fairclough et al. 2008; Carmon 2002; Lowenthal 1985). Research on how heritage can be used to solve social issues has been undertaken primarily by international organizations in the last few years, such as The World Bank and UNESCO, and has focused on disaster recovery and economic development. This edited collection has investigated current issues worldwide and has proposed new solutions and provided new perspectives on how our past can inform our present to build a safer, more sustainable, and resilient future. In doing so, it has provided a new way of thinking about the uses of heritage and has begun to expand our understanding of the broad scope and possibilities within the field of heritage studies.

Potential application for communities, stakeholders, and policy makers

We hope the findings in this volume will provide guidance and inspiration for other communities in their future building efforts. Indigenous involvement in land claim cases can have a dramatic impact on and within Indigenous communities. It can restore pride, engage community members, and build an identity of strength with support that can more effectively advocate for future sovereignty and land control. The sensual experiences of being in a site stimulate the mind and body to grapple with important collective memories that can be harnessed for social justice action. By moving beyond the usual forms of engaging with historic sites, such as taxonomic classifications of architecture or objects and start with the experiential component of sites, communities can share experiences as narratives and harness their power for organizational action. The reconstruction and revival of traditional festivals and practices can reengage community members and begin to reinstate social behaviours that developed over time but were abandoned with the advent of colonialization. The restoration of those traditional values and behaviours re-establishes aspects of culture that are unique, thus reinforcing social bonds and rebuilding disrupted communities. Additionally, such events also attract the attention of and inspire a source of pride among diasporic communities in host nations, encouraging social and ethnic connections of support that may have been severed due to distance. Museum presentations, displays, and human interactions within museums of peace can and should be useful, not as deterrents of conflict, but of and for the promotion of greater levels of understanding, respect, and peaceful interactions. And associated descendent community participation has been found to be critical in archaeological programs for strengthening existing relationships, building local pride, bridging social divides, and for engaging with the wider world in building and maintaining political and economic capital for community unification and well-being.

Our global collection of case studies provides just a glimpse of the wide variety of ways forward. Our hope is that this collection illuminates the potentiality of heritage, and that this volume will stimulate additional discussions and inspire further investigations into the uses of heritage to improve communities and to build a better tomorrow for us all.

Bibliography

Byrne, Denis. 2008. "Heritage as social action". *The Heritage Reader,* edited by Graham Fairclough, Rodney Harrison, John H. Jameson Jr., and John Schofield, 149-73. Abingdon and New York: Routledge.

Carman, John. 2002. *Archaeology and Heritage: An Introduction.* London and New York: Continuum.

Fairclough, Graham, Rodney Harrison, John H. Jameson, Jr., and John Schofield, eds. 2008. *The Heritage Reader.* Abingdon and New York: Routledge.

Halbwachs, Maurice. 1992. *On Collective Memory.* Chicago: The University of Chicago Press.

Harrison, Rodney. 2013. *Heritage: Critical Approaches.* Milton Park Abingdon: Routledge.

Harrison, Rodney, Caitlin DeSilvey, Cornelius Holtorf, Sharon Macdonald, Nadia Bartolini, Esther Breithoff, Harald Fredheim, Antony Lyons, Sarah May, Jennie Morgan, and Sefryn Penrose. 2020. *Heritage Futures: Comparative Approaches to Natural and Cultural Heritage Practices.* London: UCL Press.

Holtorf, Cornelius, and Anders Högberg. 2021. "Introduction: Cultural Heritage as a Futuristic Field". In *Cultural Heritage and the Future*, edited by Cornelius Holtorf and Anders Högberg, 1-28. London: Routledge.

———. eds. 2021. *Cultural Heritage and the Future.* London: Routledge.

Kirshenblatt-Gimblett, Barbara. 1998. *Destination Culture: Tourism, Museums, and Heritage.* Berkeley: University of California Press.

Lowenthal, David. 1985. *The Past is a foreign Country.* Cambridge: Cambridge University Press.

Shepard, Nick, ed. 2023. *Rethinking Heritage in Precarious Times.* Routledge: London.

Smith, Laurajane. 2006. *Uses of Heritage.* London: Routledge.

Smith, Laurajane, and Natsuko Akagawa, eds. 2009. *Intangible Heritage.* London: Routledge.

Contributors

Co-Editors

Susan Shay, PhD, AIA, is an Affiliated Scholar of the Heritage Research Centre at the University of Cambridge and a US Registered Architect. Her research investigates how participation in legal processes both impacts Indigenous heritage and is a meaningful tool for Indigenous empowerment. She has advised communities and non-profits on the development of preservation and empowerment programs, including technical and cultural exchange and disaster response and recovery initiatives. Prior to pursuing academic research, Susan had an extensive career in private and public practice as a Registered Architect, specializing in historic preservation, adaptive reuse, and disaster recovery, mitigation, and redevelopment. She holds a Doctorate in Heritage Studies from the University of Cambridge, a master's degree in Historic Preservation from Columbia University, and attended Cambridge University's Judge Business School for mentorship in the development of new business initiatives.

Kelly M. Britt, PhD, RPA, is an Assistant Professor of Anthropology (Brooklyn College and The Graduate Center, CUNY) as well as the Director of the Center for Brooklyn and Chair of the Museum and Cultural Organizational Studies minor (Brooklyn College). Her collaborative projects are located in urban settings and focus on gentrification, climate change, and trauma. These include community-based work with the United Order of Tents Eastern District #3, the oldest Black women's benevolent society in the United States, and the Flatbush African Burial Ground Coalition. She also works in a collective of anthropologists exploring COVID-19 materiality as a response to trauma, and with the Van Cortlandt Park archaeological legacy/orphaned collection from the NYC's LPC's Archaeological Repository: The Nan Rothschild Research Center. These research themes are highlighted in her writing, including her latest co-edited volume on *Archaeology and Advocacy: Urban Intersections* that was published in the spring of 2023.

Contributors

Uzi Baram, PhD. As Professor of Anthropology at New College of Florida, Uzi Baram taught archaeology, cultural anthropology, and heritage courses for 25 years. As founding director of the New College Public Archaeology Lab, Uzi experimented with "radical openness" for community collaborations, undergraduate research opportunities, and representations of the ancient and recent past of Gulf Coast Florida. Dr. Baram is currently Director of Public Archaeology for Marie Selby Botanical Gardens, in Sarasota, Florida.

Bishnupriya Basak, PhD, is Associate Professor in the Department of Archaeology, University of Calcutta. She has been a recipient of many grants and awards, including a post-doctoral Visiting Fellowship in the UK in 2001 and others in 2009 and 2015; and two short-term grants in 2001 and 2009 to pursue archival research in Paris and Lyon. She was also nominated by the Indian Council of Cultural Relations as a member of the Indian delegation that visited Vietnam in 2005. Among other honours, she was an Honorary Lecturer of University College London, 2010-14. Her specialization is in Bengal prehistory but she also researches extensively on Archaeological Theory, history of Indian archaeology, and Heritage Studies. She has more than thirty published papers to her credit in peer-reviewed journals and as book chapters, as well as a monograph and two (co) edited volumes. She is on the editorial board of peer-reviewed journals like *Public Archaeology*.

Ifeyinwa Emejulu, PhD, holds a Doctorate in Archaeology specializing in Tourism from University of Nigeria, Nsukka, Nigeria. Presently she teaches in the Department of History and International Studies, Nnamdi Azikiwe University, Awka, Nigeria. She was the Head of Department from 2010-2014. Her research area is Heritage Management with an emphasis on Gender studies, particularly focused on the Igbo of South Eastern Nigeria. She is currently working on a biography of an exceptional Igbo woman who defied widowhood to impact tremendously on her family and society.

Tanja Hoffmann, **PhD**, is a Leverhulme Research Fellow at the University of York's Heritage for Global Challenges Research Centre. Dr. Hoffmann is engaged in community-based research in the United Kingdom where she is exploring the intersections between agroecology and inter-generational farming heritages. Additionally, Dr. Hoffmann has worked with and for the Katzie First Nation of British Columbia, Canada, for over 25 years to co-produce solutions-oriented research outcomes that address Katzie priorities. Her work has examined how intangible heritages are mobilised and attended to within the context of Indigenous/non-Indigenous economic development partnerships in Canada. Previously she was a postdoctoral fellow with the Johnson Shoyama Graduate School of Public Policy at the University of Saskatchewan. She is also an Affiliated Scholar with the Cambridge Heritage Research Centre at the University of Cambridge.

Vladimir I. Ionesov, PhD, has 30 years of experience studying the symbolic and ritual practices in transitional culture. He is a Professor and Chairman of the Department of Theory and History of Culture, the Samara State

Institute of Culture, and Director of the International School for Advanced Research in Cultural Studies. He participated (1984-1994) in archaeological excavations of Bronze Age sites in Uzbekistan. Author of over 350 scientific works, five monographs and over 30 edited books, his articles have been published in *Current Anthropology, Peace Review, Minerva, Journal of Kyoto Museum for World Peace* and others. Dr. Ionesov is a member of the European Academy of Sciences and Arts, Chairman of the Regional Center on Urgent Anthropological Research in Samara, and Founder and Chairperson of the Samara Society for Cultural Studies.

Roma Leon is a mother, grandmother, wife, and Katzie traditional knowledge holder. Roma works tirelessly to ensure that the knowledge gifted to her from Katzie knowledge holders is passed on to future generations. She does this by taking an active role in revitalizing traditional resource management and harvesting practices, and by sharing her findings with her community, and with western scientists.

Natasha Lyons, PhD, is a founding partner of Ursus Heritage Consulting and Adjunct Faculty in the Department of Archaeology at Simon Fraser University. Natasha has over two decades of professional experience as a community-based archaeologist and practising archaeobotanist. She enjoys longstanding research partnerships with Sq'ewlets, Katzie, and Sts'ailes Nations of the Pacific Northwest and the Inuvialuit of the Canadian Western Arctic. Natasha publishes widely on ethical research practice, community heritage, human-plant relationships, and the digital humanities: https://www.ursus-heritage.ca/team/natasha-lyons.

Index

www.ingramcontent.com/pod-product-compliance
Lightning Source LLC
Chambersburg PA
CBHW072103020426
42334CB00017B/1619